EMPTY FIELDS, EMPTY PROMISES

RURAL STUDIES • Conner Bailey and Jennifer Sherman, editors

Rural Studies publishes books on a wide range of social issues with the goal of advancing the scholarly, political, and public discourse on rural spaces and the people in them. The titles in this series seek to foreground important experiences and processes concerning rural life, communities, and the environment in an effort to improve the lives of rural people at the local and global levels.

A complete list of books published in Rural Studies is available at https://uncpress.org/series/rural-studies/.

EMPTY FIELDS, EMPTY PROMISES

A State-by-State Guide to Understanding and Transforming the Right to Farm

LOKA ASHWOOD • AIMEE IMLAY
LINDSAY KUEHN • ALLEN FRANCO
AND DANIELLE DIAMOND

The University of North Carolina Press
CHAPEL HILL

© 2023 Loka Ashwood, Aimee Imlay, Lindsay Kuehn, Allen Franco, and Danielle Diamond

All rights reserved
Set in Utopia and DIN by Rebecca Evans
Manufactured in the United States of America

Cover: *top*, photograph by Angela Lumsy / Stocksy via Adobe Stock; *bottom*, photograph by somrerk via Adobe Stock.

Complete Library of Congress Cataloging-in-Publication Data is available at https://lccn.loc.gov/2023008526.
ISBN 978-1-4696-7458-2 (cloth: alk. paper)
ISBN 978-1-4696-7459-9 (paper: alk. paper)
ISBN 978-1-4696-7460-5 (ebook)

FOR THE FARMERS WHO THOUGHT IT WAS THEIR FAULT
AND THE NEIGHBORS WHO BORE IT
RESTORATIVE TRUTH
AND THE HATE THAT FALLS AWAY BEFORE IT

CONTENTS

List of Illustrations ix

The National Impact of Right-to-Farm Laws 1

State Summaries of Right-to-Farm Laws 37

Alabama 39

Alaska 42

Arizona 45

Arkansas 49

California 53

Colorado 58

Connecticut 61

Delaware 65

Florida 70

Georgia 76

Hawaii 81

Idaho 85

Illinois 90

Indiana 94

Iowa 99

Kansas 106

Kentucky 109

Louisiana 113

Maine 118

Maryland 122

Massachusetts 126

Michigan 130

Minnesota 135

Mississippi 138

Missouri 143

Montana 148

Nebraska 152

Nevada 154

New Hampshire 157

New Jersey 162

New Mexico 167

New York 171

North Carolina 176

North Dakota 184

Ohio 187

Oklahoma 191

Oregon 195

Pennsylvania 201

Rhode Island 207

South Carolina 212

South Dakota 217

Tennessee 221

Texas 225

Utah 230

Vermont 234

Virginia 238

Washington 242

West Virginia 248

Wisconsin 254

Wyoming 257

Cultivating Democracy in Agriculture 261

Acknowledgments 279

Appendix 281

ILLUSTRATIONS

Figures

1.1 Timeline of RTF Case Law 15

1.2 Regional Shares of Case Law by Party Type Wins 17

1.3 Comparison of Outcomes by Party Type According to State Levels of Poverty 24

1.4 Comparison of Outcomes by Party Type According to Rural Racial Minority Levels 25

Tables

1.1 Party Types for All RTF Cases 9

1.2 Party Wins by Type 9

1.3 Large CAFO Sizes by Animal Sector 10

1.4 Change in Number of Farm Operations by Sector, 1978–2017 13

1.5 State-Specific Number of Case Wins by CAFOs and/or Firms and Governmental Bodies 18

1.6 States with Top Five Animal and Timber Inventories 19

1.7 Case Wins by Party Type, Based on Animal or Timber Sector 21

1.8 Prevalence of Party Types per Court Level 27

1.9 Percentage of RTF Cases Won by Each Party Type by Court Level 27

2.1 Alabama's Key RTF Provisions and National Comparison 40

2.2 Alaska's Key RTF Provisions and National Comparison 43

2.3 Arizona's Key RTF Provisions and National Comparison 47

2.4 Arkansas's Key RTF Provisions and National Comparison 51

2.5 California's Key RTF Provisions and National Comparison 55

2.6 Colorado's Key RTF Provisions and National Comparison 59

2.7 Connecticut's Key RTF Provisions and National Comparison 63

2.8 Delaware's Key RTF Provisions and National Comparison 67

2.9 Florida's Key RTF Provisions and National Comparison 73

2.10 Georgia's Key RTF Provisions and National Comparison 79

2.11 Hawaii's Key RTF Provisions and National Comparison 83

2.12 Idaho's Key RTF Provisions and National Comparison 87

2.13 Illinois's Key RTF Provisions and National Comparison 92

2.14 Indiana's Key RTF Provisions and National Comparison 96

2.15 Iowa's Key RTF Provisions and National Comparison 103

2.16 Kansas's Key RTF Provisions and National Comparison 107

2.17 Kentucky's Key RTF Provisions and National Comparison 111

2.18 Louisiana's Key RTF Provisions and National Comparison 115

2.19 Maine's Key RTF Provisions and National Comparison 120

2.20 Maryland's Key RTF Provisions and National Comparison 124

2.21 Massachusetts's Key RTF Provisions and National Comparison 128

2.22 Michigan's Key RTF Provisions and National Comparison 133

2.23 Minnesota's Key RTF Provisions and National Comparison 136

2.24 Mississippi's Key RTF Provisions and National Comparison 141

2.25 Missouri's Key RTF Provisions and National Comparison 145

2.26 Montana's Key RTF Provisions and National Comparison 150

2.27 Nebraska's Key RTF Provisions and National Comparison 153

2.28 Nevada's Key RTF Provisions and National Comparison 155

2.29 New Hampshire's Key RTF Provisions and National Comparison 160

2.30 New Jersey's Key RTF Provisions and National Comparison 165

2.31 New Mexico's Key RTF Provisions and National Comparison 169

2.32 New York's Key RTF Provisions and National Comparison 174

2.33 North Carolina's Key RTF Provisions and National Comparison 181

2.34 North Dakota's Key RTF Provisions and National Comparison 185

2.35 Ohio's Key RTF Provisions and National Comparison 189

2.36 Oklahoma's Key RTF Provisions and National Comparison 193

2.37 Oregon's Key RTF Provisions and National Comparison 199

2.38 Pennsylvania's Key RTF Provisions and National Comparison 205

2.39 Rhode Island's Key RTF Provisions and National Comparison 210

2.40 South Carolina's Key RTF Provisions and National Comparison 215

2.41 South Dakota's Key RTF Provisions and National Comparison 218

2.42 Tennessee's Key RTF Provisions and National Comparison 223

2.43 Texas's Key RTF Provisions and National Comparison 228

2.44 Utah's Key RTF Provisions and National Comparison 232

2.45 Vermont's Key RTF Provisions and National Comparison 236

2.46 Virginia's Key RTF Provisions and National Comparison 240

2.47 Washington's Key RTF Provisions and National Comparison 246

2.48 West Virginia's Key RTF Provisions and National Comparison 251

2.49 Wisconsin's Key RTF Provisions and National Comparison 255

2.50 Wyoming's Key RTF Provisions and National Comparison 258

3.1 Existing and Potential Rights-Based Constitutional Amendments 274

EMPTY FIELDS, EMPTY PROMISES

The National Impact of Right-to-Farm Laws

For two generations, Paul A. Lewis and his family made White Oak, North Carolina, their home. Mr. Lewis's mother took her first breath on their 106-acre farm, born on an expanse of land that they—unlike many Black families before them—could proudly call their own. They treasured rural living, outdoor cookouts, hanging clothes on the line, and drawing water from their own well.

Mr. Lewis called it "quiet and peaceful" until 1995, when a concentrated animal feeding operation (CAFO) started fattening 14,700 hogs some 600 yards from his home. The stench rushed through the half-mile of timber between his homestead and the hog confinements. The odor and dust particles started clinging to clothes on the line. The cookouts came to a stop. Swarms of flies and other insects gathered around the porch and made their way inside the windows. Dead hogs fell off trucks running in the night. Manure mist and fumes from the lagoon and spray field system made it difficult for Mr. Lewis to breathe. In unfolding years, he was diagnosed with asthma, chronic skin disorders, sinus problems, depression, and a suite of other health issues.[1]

It appeared that Mr. Lewis might finally have his day in court when he filed a complaint against the hog operator, Murphy-Brown Limited Liability Company (LLC) in 2020. He did so in defense of his property rights, alleging the pollution was a nuisance that took away the enjoyment of his home and the use of his land. He also sued for negligence, stating that the company knew the harmful effects of its operation but continued anyway.[2] Murphy-Brown's ultimate beneficiaries traced back to WH Group Ltd., one of the world's most powerful financial holding companies involved in food production.[3]

Midway across the country, amid the row cropland of Fort Branch, Indiana, Glenn and Phyllis Parker similarly looked to the courts for justice.

Like Mr. Lewis, Mr. Parker's mother had passed the farmland down to him. Together, the Parkers built their lifelong home on the land in 1972, without a second thought to the neighboring 100-head dairy that had been there as long as they could remember. Mr. Parker farmed the land part-time until he retired in 2005 and decided to rent it to a local grain farmer. Five years later, the once-familiar dairy farm added on a 900-head dairy CAFO and incorporated it a stone's throw away from his home. Less than a year after it became operational, the elderly Parkers filed a nuisance suit, alleging noxious odors and property devaluation.[4]

"The odor lingers in our garage and in our clothes . . . when we open the backdoor, it reefs into the kitchen," Mr. Parker said in his deposition. "We often have people who come to visit us and say, 'How do you stand this?'"

Phyllis, whom Mr. Parker had been married to for fifty-four years, had long suffered from depression, but after the building of the CAFO, it became severe. She could no longer garden and observe the birds, her favorite pastimes that brought her joy.

"You go from a family farm that doesn't bother anybody to one who makes your life almost unbearable," Mr. Parker said.[5]

ACROSS DIFFERENCES OF GEOGRAPHY AND RACE, and similarities of rural living and multigenerational farms, Mr. Lewis's and the Parkers' cases shared the same fate. They lost in court, in large part due to what are called right-to-farm (RTF) laws, statutes active in every U.S. state that were often passed with the purported intent of protecting family farms.

But these laws did not protect the Parkers' and Mr. Lewis's family farms. Rather, they made them acutely vulnerable, especially in Indiana and North Carolina, two states where CAFOs and business firms like corporations use RTF laws the most to their advantage. What, in fact, are RTF laws? How do they differ across the country? What has their impact been, and whom have they benefited? And, perhaps most importantly, if they are not serving agricultural, rural, and environmental justice interests, how can they be reformed for the better?

Through the first nationally comprehensive analysis of RTF laws and their associated cases, our book answers these questions. We collected the original and 2021 RTF statutes in every state, as well as the preambles that justified them, to study national changes in statutes over time. We studied publicly available cases going back fifty years that utilized RTF laws in court since their inception. Our team of sociologists and practicing lawyers coded and analyzed court cases, state-level socioeconomic and agricultural census data, and statutes for trends and patterns. Interested readers can learn more about our methodology in the appendix. In this first section of the book, we identify key elements of the law, geopolitical structures, and litigation outcomes to help make sense of RTF laws nationally. In the next section, we provide summaries of how the RTF laws operate in each state. We also provide a table for each state that identifies key RTF provisions and how they compare to others nationally. In the book's final section, we use our research to consider how to change RTF laws as part of a broader movement to democratize agriculture.

The History of RTF Laws

RTF laws hit legislative floors during one of the most severe agricultural crises in the history of the United States. In the early 1980s, farmers went out of business in droves and farmer suicides hit record highs as debt soared, land prices collapsed, and commodity prices bottomed out as part of the U.S. grain embargo against the Soviet Union. Just as interest rates on farm debts rose in the late 1970s, the first, more explicit RTF laws were enacted in Alabama in 1978, followed by Florida, North Carolina, and Washington the next year. By the end of the 1980s, another forty-two states would pass RTF statutes enabled by rhetoric that promised support to family farms. By the mid-1990s, the four remaining states would enact them.[6]

The legislators who introduced RTF laws offered them as a saving grace for agriculture and the farmer. Early advocates of RTF laws caricatured the threatening, sue-happy urbanite moving out to the country as unfamiliar with the sights and sounds of agriculture. Likewise, they warned of the litigious lawyer, evoking long-simmering resentment by rural dwellers toward extractive urban centers.[7]

"Hopefully, this will send a message to the public that if they move next to a farmer, they have to accept how he operates," said Owen Mohler, then president of the Indiana Farm Bureau in 1987, praising the state's RTF law.[8]

Under such premises, RTF statutes began to fundamentally change the meaning of private property rights in the United States. Property holders' constitutional right to the enjoyment and use of their land became subject to RTF laws' protections of agriculture—as it was defined by each state. Property rights matters formerly subject to the fact-finding authority of the judge in court instead became subject to RTF laws passed by state legislators and the lobbying efforts behind them.[9]

Transnational corporations have advocated for and heralded RTF laws, inflaming urban-rural animosity, but without mentioning their dangerous implications for property rights. Keira Lombardo, Smithfield Foods' vice president of corporate affairs, claimed in 2019 that the laws served the best interests of family farms. Like Murphy-Brown LLC, Smithfield Foods Inc. also is a subsidiary of WH Group Ltd., a company mostly owned and operated by investors in China. After her company lost RTF-related cases in North Carolina, Lombardo wrote in an email to a reporter that "the negative verdicts have scared family farmers and lawmakers whose states' livelihoods and fundamental characters depend on agriculture." She went on to welcome amendments to make it more certain that Smithfield Foods Inc. would win in the future: "Legislation seems like a commonsense reaction to what many understandably perceive to be a threat to their ability to earn a living and cherished way of life."[10]

Yet only one state in the country, Minnesota, even from the very inception of RTF laws, included family farms anywhere in the statutory provisions passed supposedly in their defense. In its 1982 statutes, Minnesota defined a "family farm" as an "unincorporated farm unit owned by one or more persons or spouses of persons related to each other within the third degree of kindred according to the rules of the civil law at least one of whom is residing or actively engaged in farming on the farm unit, or a 'family farm corporation.'"[11] Since then, Minnesota has stricken this provision. Like most other states, it now protects agricultural operations, defined as "facilit[ies] and [their] appurtenances for the production of crops, livestock, poultry, dairy products or poultry products." Some states also insulate the labor and employment practices used by such operations from nuisance suits, demonstrating just how far RTF laws have moved away from the family farms they often purport to protect. While only four states initially insulated agricultural operations' labor and employment practices from nuisance suits, today over a quarter of all states do so.[12] Further, twenty-four states explicitly include processing as part of the agricultural activities and operations protected by RTF laws. This makes doing the work of farming or processing even more vulnerable. During the height of the COVID-19 pandemic, workers at large meatpacking plants—often people of color and immigrants—were subject to dangerous and deadly working conditions.[13] Where RTF laws protect processing alongside labor and employment practices, such workers may face more barriers if they try to seek compensation for hazardous working conditions.

Terms such as "residence" or "home" are conspicuously absent in the protective provisions provided to farmers in RTF laws today. In effect, RTF

4 THE NATIONAL IMPACT OF RIGHT-TO-FARM LAWS

laws enable outside capital investment, consolidation, and the encroachment of absentee production over that which is place-based. When the
Indiana appellate court ruled against the Parkers, the court even viewed
a home as oppositional to a farm. The court called their residence "non-
farming" and noted that the residence now "extend[s] into agricultural
areas," even though the house had been there since 1974 and the CAFO
was built in 2010.[14]

Originally, the most common statutory provision in twenty-nine states
was the extension of immunity from nuisance lawsuits to agricultural operations in the event the locality around them changed. On a surface level, such
language appeared to ensure that what was there first, like Mr. Parker's farming homestead, where a family had lived for generations, could be protected
in the face of something like suburban sprawl that came later. Yet no state in
the nation explicitly bars industrial or residential development of agricultural land through RTF statutes.[15] However, since the inception of RTF laws,
twenty-four states have included a provision that once an operation is up
and running for a year, it is immune from nuisance suits. Because the term
"operation" is broadly defined, industrial agriculture operations receive
protection even if they were developed after a residential family farm. For
example, in 1980, the Supreme Court of Alabama ruled that Faye Ward Born
could not sue the Exxon Corporation's oil-treating facility for light and odor
trespass because her suit was "barred by the one-year statute of limitations."
The court cited Alabama's RTF law, that "no agricultural, manufacturing or
other industrial plant or establishment, or any farming operation facility,
any of its appurtenances or the operation thereof shall be or become a
nuisance, private or public," when it "has been in operation for more than
one year."[16] Provisions similar to the Alabama one, combined with a suite
of other protections that have been tacked onto RTF laws through ongoing
amendments, are used by CAFOs and absentee business firms across the
nation to win in court.

These immunity provisions have dramatically increased the power of
industrial operators over residential farmers and neighbors. States have
moved swiftly to extend additional RTF protections through statutory
amendments. For example, only Pennsylvania originally provided agricultural operations immunity from nuisance suits if they used a new technology. Today, another fourteen states have adopted similar provisions. In a
2015 case heard by the Supreme Court of Pennsylvania, thirty-four property
owners—many of them longtime residents—sued farm owners and Synagro
Central LLC, and Synagro Mid-Atlantic, described in the ruling as "corporate

entities engaged in the business of recycling biosolids."[17] For three years, the company applied 11,635 wet tons of biosolids to 220 acres scattered across fourteen fields proximate to the plaintiffs' homes. The smell of rotting fish was constant. Their eyes burned and their throats were sore. They coughed and had headaches and nausea. Parents tried to protect their children by confining them indoors. The court ruled, however, that such activities were farming activities consistent with "technological development within the agricultural industry" and were therefore entitled to protection.[18] That included a corporation spreading biosolid waste from the city.

Originally, no state statutes provided explicit protection to operations if the product or activities changed—for example, if a veggie farm turned into a CAFO. Now, thirteen states do. South Dakota and West Virginia were originally the only states to protect operations if they stopped operating for a period of time or were interrupted. Now another eleven states have adopted similar provisions. These amendments dramatically extend and transform the protections afforded to so-defined operations, regardless of the long-standing fabric of the communities around them.

Other significant amendments to RTF laws have enabled the concentration and corporatization of agriculture and extended special protections to ostensibly nonfarm industries. The most common amendment to RTF laws since their inception is the provision of RTF protections from nuisance lawsuits to forestry, trees, or silvicultural products. Initially, nine states had such a provision. Now, thirty-two states extend RTF protections to the timber industry. In 1995, a paper mill in Mississippi successfully utilized the RTF defense to avoid culpability for the alleged discharge of dioxin sludge when the court ruled that the timber-derived products produced by a paper mill are a crop.[19] Another eighteen states also amended their laws to shield the use of chemicals, like pesticides, and nutrient application from lawsuits. Dorothy and Joshua Collett of Louisiana tried to sue neighboring timberland companies for damages from chemical exposure to formaldehyde at their home, which they argued gave rise to their severe immunological and autoimmune disorders. The court ruled that the timber companies could use the state's RTF law in their defense.[20]

Most RTF laws also now have provisions that remove democratic oversight by communities, effectively ensuring that the most dangerous, unfamiliar, and often unwanted operations are allowed despite local objections. RTF laws thus impose a form of takings not only on family or individual property rights but also on more collective residential and community self-determination. From the start, eighteen states removed to various extents local governments' power over protected agricultural operations, with provisions like that in Alaska, which since 1986 has allowed RTF laws to "supersede a municipal ordinance, resolution, or regulation to the contrary."[21] Since their initial inception, another thirteen states have likewise followed suit. Thus, ordinances passed by communities that prohibit trucks running at certain hours of the night or that try to limit the size or expansion of operations often become null and void. Today, thirty-one states have statutory provisions that restrict local governmental decision-making or regulatory authority over agricultural operations, and separately New York removes local government's power only in agricultural zones.

Taken together, 62 percent of states use RTF laws to weaken democratic control over land use and siting decisions with sometimes severe consequences.[22] For example, in Missouri, Lincoln Township attempted to exert oversight over an enormous hog operation through setback requirements for sewage lagoons and finishing buildings.[23] Premium Standard Farms, now another subsidiary of Smithfield Foods Inc., had sited ninety-six hog confinements and twelve waste lagoons on its 3,084-acre location. "After approval by the vote of the people," the county sought to exert oversight designed "for the purpose of promoting health, safety, morals, comfort or the general welfare of the unincorporated portion of the township, to conserve and protect property and building values, to secure the most economical use of the land, and to facilitate the adequate provision of public improvements."[24]

The county's zoning regulations in agricultural areas permitted feedlots and sewage systems but required lagoons to be at least a mile from residences or dwellings. The county also required that lagoons be bonded for at least $750,000 in case there was a spill or the company went bankrupt (which Premium Standard eventually did). For Premium Standard Farms' lagoons, that meant $9 million in bonds to ensure each of the fifty-eight-acre lagoons holding millions of gallons of hog waste could be accountable in the event local people needed to claim compensation.

Premium Standard Farms refused to comply, and the township responded by suing it for public nuisance. The court concluded in 1997 that the township and the county had no authority to govern as such, because the RTF law protected Premium Standard Farms. The court designated the livestock sewage lagoons and finishing buildings as "farm structures" protected by Missouri's RTF law. It concluded, then, that the setback and bonding requirements were "impermissible," as zoning could not impose regulations or require permits for farm buildings and structures.[25] The court added that more generally the township did not have the right to prosecute a public nuisance, removing a crucial form of local governance.

The Beneficiaries of RTF Laws

Who are the typical parties in RTF lawsuits nationally? They fall into two camps: plaintiffs—those filing the lawsuits—and defendants—those defending themselves against the lawsuits. Whether defendant or plaintiff, landowners like the Parkers and Mr. Lewis are by far the most common party type, populating 117 of 197 cases brought throughout the United States from 1971 to 2021 (see the appendix and table 1.1). The next most common party types are governmental bodies (97 cases) and business firms (92 cases), which include companies like Premium Standard. Parties can be more than one type; for example, a sole proprietor farmer can also be a landowner. The category of government encompasses different scales of governing bodies, ranging from townships and villages to regulatory agencies or attorney generals. The term "business firms" refers to legal entities formed to limit liability or shield investor status, such as limited partnerships, limited liability companies, and corporations.

What parties, then, are most likely to win when they go to court? Overall, most of the time plaintiffs lose and defendants win in RTF cases. This generally signals that those suffering from a nuisance—like the Parkers and Mr. Lewis—lose in court. However, based on the level of the court case, sometimes residents, for example, can be defendants, and sometimes they can be plaintiffs. An examination of party types—regardless of plaintiff or defendant status—gives further insight into who benefits the most from RTF laws. Residents (those who live in the places they seek to defend), homeowners (those who own the home they live in), and landowners are less likely to win than CAFOs and business firms (see table 1.2).[26] Sole proprietor farmers—farmers who operate by their own name and personhood—are the least likely of any party type to win in RTF cases. Yet the strongest supporters purported that such farmers would benefit the most from the passage of RTF laws. The USDA reports that "the vast majority of family farms (eighty-nine percent) are operated as sole proprietorships owned by a single individual or family, and they account for fifty-nine percent of the value of production."[27] The vast majority of those benefiting from RTF laws, however, are not sole proprietors.

Rather, large CAFOs, those with over 1,000 animal units (see table 1.3), are the party type most likely to win when they go to court. The implications

8 THE NATIONAL IMPACT OF RIGHT-TO-FARM LAWS

Table 1.1 Party Types for All RTF Cases

	% of total case law	Total cases
Landowner	59%	117
Governmental body	49%	97
Business firm	47%	92
Resident	30%	59
Homeowner	24%	48
Sole proprietor farmer	21%	41
CAFO	18%	36

Note: The percentage column includes all RTF cases where a party type appears. There are more party types than cases, as any single party can fit various typologies. For example, a landowner can also be a homeowner, or a CAFO can also be a business firm.

Table 1.2 Party Wins by Type

Winning party	% of cases won	Total cases won	Win as defendant	Win as plaintiff	Split ruling
CAFO	69%	25	17	4	4
Business firm	67%	62	44	8	10
Governmental body	65%	63	43	13	7
Resident	54%	32	3	21	8
Landowner	47%	55	22	26	7
Homeowner	42%	20	1	15	4
Sole proprietor farmer	41%	17	15	0	2

Note: The winning party could be a defendant or plaintiff or in split ruling. The first column, percentage of cases won, is the total number of cases with winning party type—defendant, plaintiff, and split ruling—divided by the total number of cases with that party type (see table 1.1). Split rulings are where the party type won some merits of the case but not all. In some cases, party types are both defendant and plaintiff, which counts separately in those columns but counts as only one case overall in determining the final percentage won.

of living next to facilities of such magnitude are significant. Epidemiologists in North Carolina found that most of those in their study who lived within one and a half miles of an industrial swine operation reported odor more than half of the time.[28] Those living proximate to CAFOs often became depressed and isolated, socializing less.[29] Risks of zoonotic diseases that cross humans and animals are greatly intensified. Drugs like antibiotics and antimicrobials are used broadly in CAFOs, because animals often become sick without access to space, fresh air, and foraging. The use of antimicrobial additives in animal food and antimicrobial drugs compromises how well

Table 1.3 Large CAFO Sizes by Animal Sector

Animal sector	Number of animals
Cattle or cow/calf pairs	1,000 or more
Mature dairy cattle	700 or more
Veal calves	1,000 or more
Swine (weighing over 55 pounds)	2,500 or more
Swine (weighing less than 55 pounds)	10,000 or more
Horses	500 or more
Sheep or lambs	10,000 or more
Turkeys	55,000 or more
Laying hens or broilers (liquid manure handling systems)	30,000 or more
Chickens other than laying hens (other than liquid manure handling systems)	125,000 or more
Laying hens (other than liquid manure handling systems)	82,000 or more
Ducks (other than liquid manure handling systems)	30,000 or more
Ducks (liquid manure handling systems)	5,000 or more

Note: Under the Clean Water Act, the EPA sets these size-based categories for large CAFOs. However, these are not binding thresholds, as states sometimes use different numbers.

Source: "Regulatory Definitions of Large CAFOs, Medium CAFOs, and Small CAFOs," U.S. Environmental Protection Agency, accessed October 21, 2002, https://www3.epa.gov /npdes/pubs/sector_table.pdf.

new antimicrobial drugs can fight infectious diseases in humans while also making existing ones less effective.[30] More drug-resistant enterococci aerobic bacteria work their way into the air and onto surfaces from cars driving behind poultry trucks carrying farm animals.[31] Rural kids going to school next to industrial-scale hog confinements have a significantly increased prevalence of physician-diagnosed asthma.[32] Adults living next to them have more eye irritation, wheezing, and difficulty breathing. Perhaps of little surprise, the air breathed by those living next to hog CAFOs has a level of hydrogen sulfide concentration that exceeds the Environmental Protection Agency's recommended community standards.[33]

Hog CAFOs, like those subject to the lawsuits filed by Lincoln Township and Mr. Lewis, are devastating not only for neighbors but likewise for the animals themselves. The hog production system now tightly contains production to different stages at different sites, with gestation facilities arguably the most inhumane. Hogs confined in such facilities chew incessantly on the bars, trying to get out. Once a gilt (a female who has not birthed piglets) is seven months of age, she is artificially inseminated with semen extracted from boars. (Boars too live in confinement, but typically at a different facility.)[34] As the piglets grow, the gilt is trapped in a gestation crate a few feet wide and six feet long, allowing the animal only inches to move. Right after birth, the sow moves to a farrowing crate, where she is pinned on her side as the piglets nurse. Once the piglets are weaned, the sows are bred again, and the process starts over. Sows that don't have enough piglets the first time are sent straight to slaughter. For those that survive to have their first litter, sometimes their legs give out, denied the opportunity to build muscle strength by walking. A sow's life in confinement is brutal and short: only about two years, much shorter than hog farmers expected when the animals had more outdoor access before the widespread use of gestation crates.[35]

The treatment of food as a public good goes some way to explain how CAFOs can win so often and residents so seldom. By framing agriculture and food as a public good, legislators have been able to effectively push for exceptions from the rules, even for unwelcome CAFOs. An agriculture of mass production has resulted, rather than an integrated and local agriculture that is part of community, home, or family. This particular vein of exceptionalism, and its co-optation by the largest operations, rather than ensuring stable, place-supportive food production, has in fact reversed it by enabling the most extractive and consolidated of industries to plunder without recourse. Most notably, this shift has materialized in agricultural exemptions from local zoning, land use, and property laws, giving so-defined operations the capacity to forcibly take property rights from others without their consent and without providing them just compensation. In practice, agricultural exceptionalism has become corporate exceptionalism, as CAFOs and business firms win the most against homeowners, residents, and landowners—in essence, those often in the open countryside without zoning laws or outside of incorporated towns or villages (see table 1.2). Business firms and CAFOs also do particularly well when groups of plaintiffs sue them and try to collectively exert their property rights or protect their health.

On the other hand, as mentioned above, smaller-scale agriculture, like sole proprietor farmers who act by their own name and personhood, win the least often of any party type. CAFOs and business firms gain market advantage through RTF laws. By disadvantaging local places—especially homeowners and farmers who operate by name—RTF laws advantage absentee and foreign ownership, like that of Smithfield Foods and WH Group Ltd. In 1982, on the cusp of the RTF wave, there were 2.24 million farms spanning 987 million acres.[36] Since then, the overall number of farms has declined by 10 percent to just over 2 million, covering only 895 million acres.[37]

The decline of farm operators when considered by sector is even more startling. Since 1978—just when RTF laws were beginning to be adopted across the country—the number of corn, wheat, dairy, and hog farms has dropped by more than half. Hog farmers have experienced the starkest decline, with the number of operators dropping by 87 percent since 1978 (see table 1.4). The relationship cannot be overstated. Nearly nine out of every ten hog farmers have exited the business, and with their absence the conditions have become progressively crueler for workers, communities, and the hogs themselves.

Sole proprietor farmers, the closest match to the iconic farmer, also does the poorest of any party type as a plaintiff, winning none of their nine RTF-related cases (table 1.2). In a 2016 Missouri case—the same state where Smithfield Foods' Premium Standard Farms successfully used the state's RTF law to invalidate a township's attempted oversight of its twelve manure lagoons spanning over fifty-eight acres each—farmer Eric Vimont, who notably called himself by name, was not allowed to sell raw milk at his county farmers' market. The Christian County Health Department, which Vimont sued, allowed raw milk to be sold on the farm but not elsewhere. By this time, nineteen years since the Premium Standard ruling, Missouri had even extended the RTF legislation to include a constitutional protection for the RTF.[38] The thirty-fifth constitutional amendment provides "that agriculture which provides food, energy, health benefits, and security is the foundation and stabilizing force of Missouri's economy. To protect this vital sector of Missouri's economy, the right of farmers and ranchers to engage in farming and ranching practices shall be forever guaranteed in this state, subject to duly authorized powers, if any, conferred by article VI of the Constitution of Missouri."[39]

Eric Vimont tried to sue the Christian County Health Department, claiming it violated his constitutional right to farm. The court disagreed and upheld the health department's ordinance barring the sale and distribution of raw milk.[40] Missouri's constitutional farming rights, the court ruled, are subject to a county commission's authority to create public health rules and ordinances.[41] Three years later, the Missouri legislature in 2019 passed a bill that barred county commissions or health centers from imposing standards on agricultural operations more stringent than state law.[42] Health ordinances formerly were a crucial means for Missouri rural communities to protect themselves from CAFOs, as state law limits zoning of farm buildings and structures.

12 THE NATIONAL IMPACT OF RIGHT-TO-FARM LAWS

Table 1.4 Change in Number of Farm Operations by Sector, 1978–2017

	Number of operations									% change 1978–2017
	1978	1982	1987	1992	1997	2002	2007	2012	2017	
Wheat	383,367	446,075	352,237	292,464	252,922	169,528	160,810	147,632	104,792	−72.67
Corn	919,297	779,743	788,326	797,713	550,019	452,211	375,631	376,179	328,101	−64.31
Soy	550,640	511,229	441,899	381,000	367,300	317,611	279,110	302,963	303,191	−44.94
Hay	1,200,551	1,050,992	994,551	905,296	888,597	870,514	845,050	781,899	728,156	−39.35
Beef	1,032,952	951,698	841,778	803,241	899,756	796,436	764,984	727,906	729,046	−29.42
Hogs	512,292	329,833	243,398	191,347	124,889	78,895	75,442	63,246	66,439	−87.03
Dairy	221,007	199,602	162,555	132,092	99,238	78,963	69,763	50,556	40,336	−81.75
Poultry	368,181	256,014	184,071	150,051	140,484	146,206	187,420	233,770	267,294	−27.40
Fruits, nuts, and berries*	94,094	90,291	96,908	89,417	85,973	107,707	112,690	105,737	109,994	+16.90
Vegetables, sweet corn, and melons**	72,869	68,725	60,753	61,924	53,641	59,044	69,100	72,267	75,320	+3.36
Nursery and greenhouse products***	60,627	54,207	37,298	47,425	67,816	56,070	50,784	52,751	46,970	−22.53

* After 2002, includes tree nuts.
** After 2002, includes potatoes and sweet potatoes.
*** After 2002, includes floriculture and sod.

Source: U.S. Department of Agriculture, *2017 Census of Agriculture*. For more details, please see the appendix.

Simultaneous to disadvantaging sole proprietor farmers in rural contexts, RTF laws on the aggregate have not enabled urban agriculture or small-scale farming in city spaces that may be perceived as unwelcoming to agriculture. Rather, property owners in towns and villages with unclear agricultural ties try to use RTF laws to protest local zoning laws or ordinances. Often, they lose and the government wins in these cases, which in part accounts for why, after CAFOs and business firms, the government is the most successful party type. Examples of such cases include an Alaskan homeowner trying to defend the building of a fence in a city right-of-way, a California homeowner attempting to counter that his junkyard was not blight, and a Massachusetts grocery store and restaurant owner who tried to avoid a city requirement to reduce the size of his electronic business sign.[43] Six of the sixty-three cases where the government won pertained to horses in town or to horse racing, and eight cases attempted to claim agriculture exceptions for waste or composting sites. None of these cases had a clear urban food benefit, where the food that people eat stands at risk from overly sensitive neighbors.

There are, however, a few cases where the government constrained urban farming or tried to defend food production against those annoyed by the more gentle, everyday sounds of agriculture. In one California case, the County of Solano, which is proximate to San Jose, San Francisco, and Oakland, passed an ordinance that hampered small-scale chicken farming. The court ruled that the poultry farmers could not use the RTF defense for their eighty-acre farm because they were not commercial farmers. Like California, most states stress that operations must be commercial to receive RTF protections, which in practice disadvantages the 89 percent of farms nationally that are small and that mostly rely on off-farm income.[44] The poultry "hobby" farmers were not considered "legitimate" by the court and thus had to adhere to a recently passed ordinance that required them to reduce their herd from sixty roosters to fewer than four.[45] Denigration of those who make less money farming often comes up in cases where retired or part-time farmers try to defend their homes. In Indiana, the Parkers also fell into the category of "weekend farmers" or "hobby farmers," titles used to deflate their importance and, in court, their power under RTF laws.[46]

Governmental bodies also do not necessarily oppose farmers. Sometimes they act as codefendants. For example, in one case a neighbor sued sole proprietor farmers for using Great Pyrenees to protect their livestock. The neighbor thought the dogs barked too much. The New York State Department of Agriculture and Markets was also named as a defendant, and

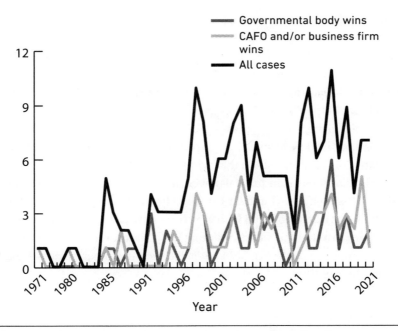

Figure 1.1 Timeline of RTF case law showing a general increase of RTF litigation over time and trends in governmental body wins and CAFO and/or business firm wins.

ultimately the state and the farmers together won, establishing that keeping the Great Pyrenees was a sound and long-established effective agricultural practice. The dogs, indeed, did not have to go.[47]

CAFOs, business firms, and governmental bodies rely on strikingly different arguments to win RTF cases. Governmental bodies tend to win when they reframe agriculture as similar to any other industry. In these cases, residents or commercial industries are required to follow the rules like any other person or entity. Even claims by CAFOs and business firms that RTF laws supersede governance can fall short in cases where governmental bodies effectively convince the court that agriculture is not exempt from the rules. However, some state RTF amendments put substantial constraints on this approach. Most notably, the explicit protection of processing in RTF laws allows industries to claim agricultural exemptions from nuisance laws even when, for example, processing meat by-products or paper at a plant.

An RTF law's treatment of time and longevity—with regard to which operations receive protection—facilitates vastly different case outcomes for governmental bodies versus CAFOs and other businesses. More than any other statutory feature, CAFOs and business firms draw on one-year immunity from lawsuits to win, while governmental bodies mostly draw on the "there first" provision—meaning the agricultural operation has to be established in a specific location first, before a homeowner or a resident, for example—to receive RTF immunity from lawsuits. CAFOs that win with RTF laws also utilize the statutory provision that they are immune from culpability if a locality changes or if they undergo technology and ownership changes. Sometimes, a CAFO is also a business firm. Combining CAFOs and business firms as party types eliminates cases where party types overlap (that is, an operation that is both a CAFO and a firm) and simultaneously identifies the industrial players that benefit most from RTF laws.[48] When wins by a CAFO and/or business firm (sixty-eight cases between 1971 and 2021) are compared with government wins (sixty-three cases over the same period), it becomes clear that the government has been winning less recently (see figure 1.1). Altogether, RTF-related litigation has generally increased over time.

Geopolitical Extraction

The party types that win the most when they go to court—CAFOs, business firms, and governmental bodies—do so in geopolitical contexts that, while in the same nation, are worlds apart. Courts face starkly different legal apparatuses across the country, leaving them with highly differentiated capacities to protect communities and smallholders from large corporate agribusinesses. The starkest differences in party type wins play out in the Northeast, Midwest, and Southeast (see figure 1.2). In the Southeast, business firms win 3.75 times more often than governmental bodies. In the Northeast, the trend is very different: governmental entities win twice as often as firms and fourteen times more often than CAFOs. Nationally, the bulk of litigation continues to unfold in the Midwest. When CAFOs go to court in the Midwest, they are the most likely of any party type to win. However, government entities—while less likely to prevail when they go to court—on aggregate win the most cases in the Midwest because they go to court more often, particularly in Michigan. Notably, the wealthier Northeast has more governmental wins than any other region. Governmental bodies provide a signifier of the strength of democracy, where elites remain accountable for their actions. Regions where persistent poverty and resource dependency reign stand in stark contrast. There the haves rule local governance, disenfranchising the have-nots, acutely so in parts of Appalachia and the Black Belt.[49]

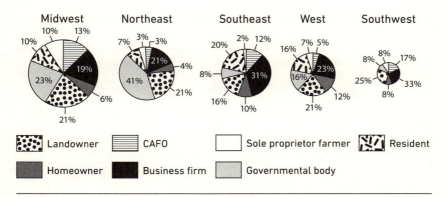

Figure 1.2 Regional shares of RTF case law by party type wins. This proportional visualization shows party type wins by region, from largest (Midwest) to smallest (Southwest). Percentages are rounded up or down to the nearest numerator for each party type, accounting for total regional percentages ranging from 99 to 102.

Specific states with near-opposite case-law outcomes provide a window into more exact RTF statutory provisions that enable corporate and agribusiness expansion (see table 1.5). In Indiana, where CAFOs are winning the most, no governmental entity has yet to even be a party in an RTF case, let alone win one. In contrast, governmental entities have won every case they have been party to in Massachusetts. Indiana cases have heavily drawn on a suite of provisions that expanded the protection for operations that have been in existence continually for more than one year. For example, Indiana protects such operations if their boundaries or size changes; if the locality around them changes; if they use a new technology; if they change the product they produce; and if there is a change in the operation's ownership. Indiana's law also extends these protections to industrial and mining operations more generally, in essence deflating the capacity to differentiate between food and industry at large. Massachusetts, while providing the same one-year immunity provision, does not include any accompanying protections like those in Indiana when an operation changes. Further, the one-year provision—which benefits firms and CAFOs the most—has yet to be used as a defense by any party in Massachusetts RTF cases, reflecting the prevalence of smaller farms and the absence of larger operations.

The prevalence of concentrated, powerful industries helps explain the domestic core and periphery dynamics that leave states like Massachusetts upholding local governance and states like Indiana bearing the brunt of corporate encroachment. The Midwest and the Southeast serve as periphery zones for protein and timber production, with most products exported

Table 1.5 State-Specific Number of Case Wins by CAFOs and/or Firms and Governmental Bodies

Region	CAFO and/or business firm wins	Governmental body wins
Midwest	Illinois (1), Indiana (7), Iowa (2), Michigan (3), Minnesota (2), Missouri (3), North Dakota (1), Ohio (3)	Illinois (1), Kansas (4), Michigan (13), Minnesota (2), Missouri (2), Wisconsin (1)
Southeast	Alabama (3), Florida (1), Georgia (1), Louisiana (2), Mississippi (4), North Carolina (5)	Kentucky (1), North Carolina (1), Virginia (2)
West	California (2), Hawaii (2), Idaho (2), Montana (1), Oregon (2), Washington (2)	Alaska (1), California (2), Idaho (2), Oregon (1), Washington (1)
Southwest	Texas (5)	Texas (1)
Northeast	Maine (1), Massachusetts (4), New Jersey (1), New York (1), Pennsylvania (4), Rhode Island (3)	Connecticut (3), Maine (2), Massachusetts (11), New Hampshire (2), New Jersey (4), New York (2), Pennsylvania (2), Rhode Island (2)

globally. CAFOs and/or business firms do particularly well in states that are in the top five for multiple animal sectors (broilers, cattle, dairy, hogs, layers) or timber.[50] Indiana, for example, is fourth in hogs and third in layer inventory, whereas Massachusetts is not in the top five for any animal inventory (see table 1.6).[51] Like Indiana, other states are listed multiple times in the top five: Iowa (hogs and layers); Texas (milk cows, layers, and beef); North Carolina (hogs and broilers); Nebraska (hogs and beef); California (milk cows and beef); and Georgia, Alabama, and Mississippi (timber and broilers).

CAFOs win, in part or in full, every single case that they are party to in the top five states for broilers and timber. CAFOs win 83 percent of the cases they are party to in the top five dairy states. CAFOs as a party type win more cases in total in the top five hog states than in any other top-five state sector, and they win 72 percent of the time that they go to court. In the top five hog states, out of all party types, CAFO wins are the most common.[52] Hogs and poultry are also the industries with the highest levels of contract agriculture, leaving local farmers no, or severely constrained, access to markets.[53] The biggest winners for total cases in the remaining sectors are business firms in top five broiler states; landowners in the top five cattle

18 THE NATIONAL IMPACT OF RIGHT-TO-FARM LAWS

Table 1.6 States with Top Five Animal and Timber Inventories

	Hogs	Milk cows	Beef cattle	Broilers	Layers	Timber harvested
Alabama				•		•
Arkansas				•		
California		•	•			
Georgia				•		•
Idaho		•				
Illinois	•					
Indiana	•				•	
Iowa	•				•	
Kansas			•			
Mississippi				•		•
Nebraska	•		•			
New York		•				
North Carolina	•			•		
Ohio					•	
Oklahoma			•			
Oregon						•
Pennsylvania					•	
Texas		•	•		•	
Washington						•
Wisconsin		•				

states; governmental bodies and business firms in the top five dairy states; business firms in the top five layer states; and business firms in the top five timber states (table 1.7).

The dominance of business firms is even more striking when considering how often they win a case when they go to court. Business firms that can claim grower, producer, processing, or industrial status win 90 percent of the time in the top five states for layers, 75 percent of the time in the top five broiler states, 71 percent of the time in the top five hog states, 69 percent of the time in the top five timber states, 67 percent of the time in the top five dairy states, and 50 percent of the time in the top five cattle states.[54] In every sector except cattle, business firms win as much or more than the national rate (table 1.2). When compared to the national rates for wins by party type, only in cattle and dairy states do governmental entities win at a higher or comparable level: 78 percent and 66 percent, respectively. Otherwise, governmental entities rarely engage with and win less than half of the time in RTF litigation in timber-, hog-, broiler- or layer-dominated states. Landowners win only over half the cases they are party to in the top five cattle states (50 percent) and the top five hog states (56 percent). The least successful party type in the top five sectors is sole proprietor farmers in broiler states, where they lost the only case that they were party to (table 1.7).

The dominance of CAFOs in RTF cases where state animal inventories are the highest suggests two ongoing trends. On the one hand, townships, resident farmers, and smaller landholders are fighting vertically integrated operations through nuisance, trespass, and negligence litigation, as attempted by Lincoln Township in Missouri and by the Parkers in Indiana. On the other hand, despite their efforts to go to court to stop these operations, these parties—on the aggregate—are not winning, as CAFOs win fully or in part 69 percent of the time when they are parties to a case. These case outcomes and related statutory amendments disincentivize the use of courts to achieve justice, especially for residents, homeowners, and sole proprietor farmers. Three of the top five hog states (Iowa, Illinois, and Indiana) stipulate that court costs be awarded to the winning defendant only. This provides a significant advantage for corporate agriculture, as CAFOs generally are defendants but not plaintiffs, whereas homeowners nearly always are plaintiffs (see table 1.2). The same states also have provisions allowing the courts to determine whether the action brought was frivolous. If a court finds it was frivolous, then court costs can be charged against the party who brought the case. The meaning of "frivolous" is not defined by the law but instead often left to court interpretation.[55] These statutory provisions not only help

Table 1.7 Case Wins by Party Type, Based on Animal or Timber Sector

	Total # of cases	Governmental body	CAFO	Business firm	Landowner	Homeowner	Resident	Sole proprietor farmer
Top five broiler states	20	1	6	12	3	4	6	0
Top five cattle states	24	7	3	5	7	3	1	1
Top five dairy states	26	8	5	8	7	3	2	3
Top five hog states	30	2	13	12	9	4	6	2
Top five layer states	35	3	12	18	9	3	5	2
Top five timber states	25	2	2	11	5	5	8	3
Nation	197	63	25	62	55	20	32	17

Note: In comparison, table 1.2 shows the number of wins and the winning rate nationally by party type. As in table 1.1, party types are not mutually exclusive, meaning that there can be multiple party types for each case.

defendants like CAFOs win in court but also place a disproportionate risk on the lawyers and their plaintiffs, like the Parkers and Mr. Lewis, who try to defend their rights in court. This risk can also deter would-be plaintiffs from engaging in litigation to begin with, defeating them before they even start.

Even with disproportionate wins in court, some states continue to adopt RTF amendments that further narrow the capacity of parties like residents and homeowners to file suits. In direct response to Murphy-Brown LLC's losses in court, the North Carolina General Assembly amended the RTF law with two particularly chilling provisions to limit who could file lawsuits. The first amendment limited standing to bring a lawsuit to "legal possessors of real property," thus excluding family members from bringing a nuisance lawsuit even if they also lived on the property and were exposed to the same pollution and impacts. The justice implications of such statutes in North Carolina are stark, as North Carolina's hog confinement facilities are located disproportionately in communities with higher levels of poverty and higher numbers of nonwhite residents.[56]

The amendment directly impacted Mr. Lewis's power in court. Lawyers for Murphy-Brown LLC argued that Mr. Lewis had no standing to bring the lawsuit in the first place because his mother owned the property.

"He has alleged only that he is an heir to his mother's estate," the lawyers wrote in the first reply. "Bladen County tax records confirm that Mr. Lewis is not a legal possessor of the property. . . . As a result, Lewis may not bring this action."[57]

Murphy-Brown LLC's lawyers also drew on a second 2018 amendment, which barred anyone who lives over a half mile away from the alleged nuisance from filing a nuisance suit. They asserted that Mr. Lewis lived 1.23 miles, rather than 600 yards, from the alleged nuisance and thus had no standing to file the lawsuit. In the verdict, the court did not weigh in on Lewis's standing as a real property owner or the distance of the property from the nuisance. Rather, the judge dismissed Lewis's case because of a third 2018 amendment. Drawing on the statute that CAFOs and business firms use the most to win, the court concluded the lawsuit had to be dismissed because the CAFO had been up and running for more than one year before Mr. Lewis filed the lawsuit.

The Midburden and the Path to Poverty

State-level trends in rural poverty and rural racial minority levels—typical proxies for burden and exploitation—tend to follow mediums when it comes to RTF court outcomes. We call this the midburden, a process of poverty-making and exploitation, where people seek to exert their rights and to prevent their dispossession while they still have the means to do so. Existing research, albeit not nationally comprehensive, suggests that lawyers are the most difficult to access in the rural Midwest and in the rural South, with the starkest shortage in the Midwest.[58] The prevalence of RTF-related cases in the Midwest suggests an attempt to preserve local agriculture, community, local economies, and sustenance in the face of extraction, even despite a lawyer shortage.

Most RTF cases take place in states with medium levels of rural poverty as part of the midburden (see figure 1.3).[59] The states with medium levels of poverty—which happen to be every midwestern state—account for 76 percent of all cases pertaining to RTF laws. Nationally, 89 percent of CAFO cases and 77 percent of business firm cases also take place in these states with medium rural poverty levels, with business firms the party type that wins the most cases overall.[60] In contrast, only 7 percent of litigation takes place in states with high levels of rural poverty and 17 percent in those with low levels of rural poverty.[61] The midburden, taking from the many to accumulate for the few, has a substantive impact on community well-being. On the one hand, dispossession of rural residents grows through taking of environmental and human health dimensions of property rights. On the other hand, rates of rural poverty in the Midwest have increased during the same general time period of RTF enactment and litigation. From 1980 to 2020, poverty rates increased in 33 percent of rural counties in the Midwest.[62]

The midburden paves the way to more acute poverty. On the aggregate, less RTF litigation over the last half century has taken place in the states where rural people have the least. Most litigation takes place in states with moderate but not high levels of rural racial minorities (see figure 1.4). Black Americans have a long history of being exploited through the court system, still often dominated by white elites. They tend to avoid the courts over matters pertaining to land in other contexts, with North Carolina being a notable exception in our study.[63] Taken together, 56 percent of RTF litigation takes place in states with relatively low rural racial minority levels, 22 percent in states with moderately high rural racial minority levels, and 21 percent in states with high racial minority levels.[64]

Business firms, however, win even more often when they go to court in states with high rural poverty and high rural racial minority levels. In contrast, governmental bodies are the party type that prevails the most in states with low poverty levels. In Mississippi, for example—a state with both high

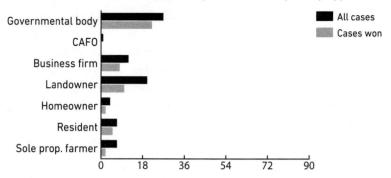

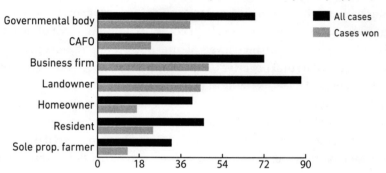

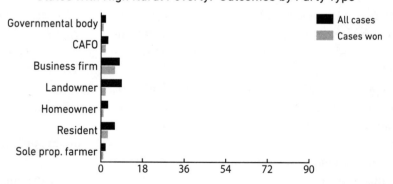

Figure 1.3 Comparison of the amount of litigation that takes place according to state levels of low, medium, and high rural poverty. Most litigation takes place at medium rural poverty levels.

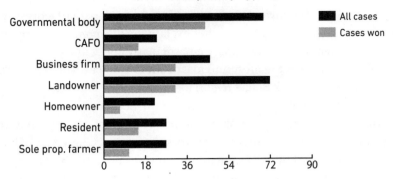

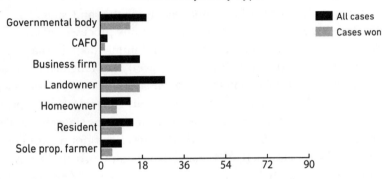

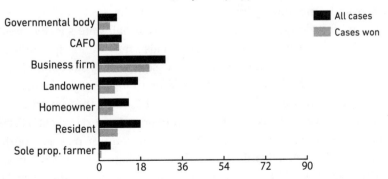

Figure 1.4 State-level comparison of the amount of litigation and wins by party type according to state levels of moderately low, moderately high, and high rural racial minority levels. No states have low rural minority levels. Most litigation takes place in states with moderate racial minority levels.

rural poverty and high rural racial minority levels—hog CAFOs tend to be located in areas with high percentages of African Americans and persons in poverty.[65] Timber inventory numbers, for which Alabama, Georgia, and Mississippi are in the top five, further explain the divergence in party type wins, as timber processing firms are particularly adept at using RTF laws to their advantage in the most unequal of circumstances. These states are also home to the Black Belt, a region identified by W. E. B. Du Bois as the "Egypt of the Confederacy," accounting for the deep suffering and cruelty weathered by slaves freed in name but not in economic or civic power.[66] High and persistent rates of rural poverty still remain as the legacy of inequitable agricultural practices, including both slavery and sharecropping, continues to shape racial exploitation and concentration of land ownership. For example, 61 percent of timberland in rural Alabama is owned by legal entities or people who do not live in the same county, with 36 percent of that total owned by those who do not even live in the same state.[67]

RTF laws are the latest enunciation of ongoing processes of corporate extraction and accumulation by forcible and unjust takings, playing out most acutely in the Midwest. The path to poverty has long been paved by dispossessing people of their homes and self-security through various legal rights: personhood, mineral, surface, and land. The forced and repeated removal of Indigenous peoples set the stage for ongoing state creation and colonization. The racialization and othering of various groups, from Appalachian whites to southern Blacks, enabled the treatment of these groups as lesser in order to take their property, deny property in the first place, or treat these racialized groups as property. Now, those in the middle of the United States experience the most acute takings in court, with medium levels of poverty and a moderately low rural racial minority level.

The midburden is not only a matter of internal, state-specific dynamics. Federal governmental structures can also reify the peripheralization of states, regions, and rural spaces. RTF cases typically start at trial courts and work their way up to higher courts when rulings are appealed. No RTF case has yet to be heard at the very highest U.S. court, the Supreme Court. However, CAFOs and business firms dominate at the next highest U.S. court level: federal appellate (see tables 1.8 and 1.9). In contrast, no sole proprietor farmer case has been heard by the federal appellate court. CAFOs that are also business firms have won in whole or in part every case they have been party to at the federal district and federal appellate court level, whereas sole proprietor farmers have yet to win a case at the federal district level (see table 1.9). Since we analyzed only the highest level of any court case,

Table 1.8 Prevalence of Party Types per Court Level

	All cases	Governmental body	CAFO	Business firm	Homeowner	Landowner	Resident	Sole proprietor farmer
State trial	21	16	1	9	2	15	5	2
State intermediate appellate	111	60	17	40	26	64	25	33
State highest	41	16	9	22	11	27	16	5
Federal district	20	4	6	18	8	11	10	No cases
Federal appellate	2	No cases	2	2	No cases	No cases	2	No cases

Note: More than one party type can appear per case.

Table 1.9 Percentage of RTF Cases Won by Each Party Type by Court Level

	Governmental body	CAFO	Business firm	Homeowner	Landowner	Resident	Sole proprietor farmer
State trial	81%	0%	67%	50%	60%	80%	0%
State intermediate appellate	60%	76%	65%	38%	39%	52%	52%
State highest	69%	56%	73%	55%	70%	63%	0%
Federal district	50%	83%	67%	38%	18%	40%	No cases
Federal appellate	No cases	100%	100%	No cases	No cases	50%	No cases

Note: To calculate, we divided the number of total cases where that party type won by the number of cases that party type was involved with at each court level.

this also reveals that when CAFOs do lose at the trial court level, they appeal to higher courts with more success. In essence, this means that when they appeal to higher-level courts, corporate CAFOs win more than any other party type. These cases, while limited in number, are more impactful because they address issues pertaining to the U.S. Constitution or federal statutes or otherwise set regional and national precedents.[68]

The two corporate CAFO cases heard in the federal appellate court originated in Indiana and North Carolina, the states most heavily burdened with RTF litigation. In Indiana, Country View Family Farms LLC, an absentee owner of various entities, converted a long-standing grain farm into a hog CAFO. In 2013, the federal court drew on Indiana's RTF law to conclude that the agricultural use was general and the change to a hog CAFO from a grain farm was not substantial. Further, the court also dismissed the plaintiffs' claim that the CAFO was negligent, meaning it could farm in a more reasonable way with fewer impacts on neighbors but did not bother to. The court argued that it mattered little if the hog CAFO itself was a nuisance; rather, the issue was whether or not the nuisance resulted from negligence itself. A CAFO, the court presumed, could not be a nuisance simply of its own accord. The judge wrote, "Without any effort to show that a well-run pig farm is not a nuisance, or even any effort to show that the shortcomings plaintiffs see in defendants' operations contribute materially to how surrounding landowners perceive the farm's odors, there is nothing for a jury to determine."[69] In effect, the court assumed CAFOs to be the only type of pig farming possible and in doing so reified industrial power by limiting the plaintiffs' argument to technological adoptions or remediations at that intensive scale.

In the other federal appellate case, a group of North Carolina residents (not including Mr. Lewis) lost in part and won in part on appeal in 2020. Murphy-Brown LLC, part of WH Group, as well as its co-named parties, including the American Farm Bureau Federation, the National Pork Producers Council, the North American Meat Institute, and the National Association of Manufacturers, teamed together in the case. The split verdict allowed for what are called punitive damages, designed to punish defendants monetarily whose conduct is considered grossly negligent or intentional. But the court reduced the damages substantially from the lower court, arguing that the parent companies' financial information (Smithfield Foods Inc. and WH Group Ltd.) should not have had a bearing on the damages awarded but instead that the damages should be limited specifically to the subsidiary, Murphy-Brown LLC. The federal court reified the lack of financial culpability for corporations by citing federal law and in effect enabled corporate takings.

The outcomes of the twenty federal district court cases are similar—CAFOs and business firms mostly win while government entities have less success (see table 1.9). In one such case, more than 300 residents of Prattville, Alabama, tried to take on a mill, International Paper, suing for nuisance. They argued that they had difficulty breathing, ocular disorders, frequent headaches and sore throats, and upper respiratory syndromes. They alleged that fine particulate matter and chemicals corroded their homes, making their case with expert testimony. In the ruling in favor of International Paper, the federal district court threw out the evidence the residents had supporting their various claims. In particular, the judge cited Alabama's RTF law to rule that residents who lived there after the start of the mill's operation in 1967 could not claim nuisance compensation: "The mill has been in operation since 1967 and there is no indication that, within its first year of operations, the mill was adjudicated a nuisance by any court of competent jurisdiction."[70] The one-year statutory provision again proved most beneficial to corporate power, rendering obsolete the local social ecology for those most deeply embedded in it.[71]

Agricultural, Rural, and Environmental Justice

Mr. Parker's deposition was just about over. The questions about the longevity of his wife's depression, his children's professions, the value of his house, and his history of farming seemed to mercifully be at an end. Mr. Janzen, the Indianapolis attorney representing Obert's Legacy Dairy LLC and Indiana's Dairy Producers, thought for a moment he was finished.

"Well, wait a minute," Mr. Janzen said, deciding that he wasn't quite through. "I assume that you drink milk; is that right?"

"Very little," Parker answered.

"Very little?" Janzen returned, incredulously.

"It's not my—not on my high list of things I like. I'm sorry, but—"

Parker didn't have a chance to finish.

"But you eat dairy products?" Janzen asked.

"Really now," Mr. Parker's lawyer interjected, for a moment derailing Janzen's belittlement. Then he allowed it to continue. "Go ahead."

"I eat some cheese, it's pretty hard not to—" Mr. Parker started to answer.

"Okay," Mr. Janzen interrupted again.

"—if you eat pizza," Mr. Parker finished.

RTF LAWS HAVE BENEFITED FROM DIVISION: the eater from the grower, the dweller from the farmer, the feeder from the fed, the agri- from the -culture. In doing so, RTF laws have benefited the takers—large-scale corporate agribusiness—at the expense of the doers, people who live and dwell proximate to where they grow food. By creating a false opposition between the goodness of eating, growing, and living, the largest and most wealthy of operators have been able to sow deep divisions to their acute benefit.

RTF laws are not working in the way they were purportedly designed. Corporations and other incorporated entities alongside CAFOs are using the laws most to their advantage through denigration and division. Acute burdens exist for those in the Midwest and the Southeast, as well as in states where most hogs, poultry, and cattle reside. There remain substantial variations within specific states, where RTF laws interact uniquely with other state laws.

In the next section, we present state-specific summaries of RTF laws to help provide a more comprehensive picture and analysis of how they operate at the state level. These summaries are designed for educational purposes and are not a substitute for expert legal advice. We also provide tables to give a sense of how each state compares with the rest of the nation on key statutory provisions. Our final section of the book builds on our analysis of national trends in RTF laws to consider how to democratize agriculture by reforming or abolishing RTF laws, distributing market power in agriculture, stripping away federal subsidization of absentee and concentrated agriculture, and amending constitutions for a more just tomorrow.

NOTES

1. Complaint at 8, *Lewis v. Murphy Brown, LLC*, No. 7:19-CV-127-BR, 2019 WL 5606237 (E.D.N.C. Aug. 19, 2019).
2. *McKiver v. Murphy-Brown, LLC*, 980 F.3d 937, 946 (4th Cir. 2020).
3. Bloomberg Finance L.P. Security Ownership graph for WH Group Ltd. and RELS code direct subsidiaries Smithfield Foods Inc. Accessed via Bloomberg terminal, 2022.
4. *Parker v. Obert's Legacy Dairy, LLC*, 988 N.E.2d 319, 321 (Ind. Ct. App. 2013). The Parkers' home was 1,500 feet away from the CAFO. The property was permitted to house up to 900 milking cows. The Obert family had farmed in the area since the 1830s, and the Parker family had resided there since 1932. The ownership of the cows is unclear: 70 percent were owned by another corporation with unclear beneficiaries—Obert's Farms, Inc.—and 15 percent of the cows are owned by Wes and Kling Obert (Def. Obert's Legacy Dairy, LLC's Brief in Support of Motion for Summary Judgment at 5–6, *Parker v. Obert's Legacy Dairy, LLC*, No. 26001-1106-PL-14 (Gibson Superior Court, April 25, 2012)). Separately from this, the Oberts formed a limited liability company called Obert's Legacy Dairy, LLC, that would own the land and buildings for the expansion (Defendant Obert's Legacy Dairy, LLC's Brief in Support of Motion for Summary Judgment, at 3, *Parker v. Obert's Legacy Dairy, LLC*,

No. 26001-1106-PL-14 (Gibson Superior Court, April 25, 2012)). Specific documents cited here can be obtained from the county clerk.

5. Deposition of Glenn Parker at 25–28, Evidence in Support of IT Motion for Summary Judgment, *Parker v. Obert's Legacy Dairy, LLC*, No. 26001-1106-PL-14 (Gibson Superior Court, February 17, 2012).

6. For the histories and specific legal context of each state, please see our state-specific summaries in the next section. Our chronology here references the enactment of laws that used specific RTF rhetoric in their justification.

7. This dynamic, spanning millennia, is laid out in Michael Bell, *City of the Good: Nature, Religion, and the Ancient Search for What Is Right* (Princeton: Princeton University Press, 2018).

8. Rick A. Richards. "State's Right-to-Farm Law Is Upheld," *Merrillville (Ind.) Post-Tribune*, August 17, 1987.

9. For more on the relationship between common law and private property rights, see Danielle Diamond, Loka Ashwood, Allen Franco, Aimee Imlay, Lindsay Kuehn, and Crystal Boutwell, "Farm Fiction: Agricultural Exceptionalism, Environmental Injustice and U.S. Right-to-Farm Law," *Environmental Law Reporter* 52 (Sept. 2022): 10727–48; and Loka Ashwood, Danielle Diamond, and Fiona Walker, "Property Rights and Rural Justice: A Study of U.S. Right-to-Farm Law," *Journal of Rural Studies* 67 (2019): 120–29. This book is based on analysis that updates and refines data from these articles, while building on the earlier analyses presented in these publications.

10. Quote in April Simpson, "Right-to-Farm Laws Strengthened in Several States," *Free Press* (Mankato, Minn.), June 1, 2019.

11. See 2004 Minn. Laws 254 (S.F. 2428); 2001 Minn. Laws 128 (S.F. 1659); and 1994 Minn. Laws 619 (H.F. 2493) (each amending Minn. Stat. § 561.19).

12. States that extend labor and employment immunity are Alabama, Florida, Georgia, Hawaii, Iowa, Maine, Michigan, Montana, New Hampshire, New York, Tennessee, Washington, and Wisconsin.

13. Ian R. Carrillo and Annabel Ipsen, "Worksites as Sacrifice Zones: Structural Precarity and Covid-19 in US Meatpacking," *Sociological Perspectives* 64, no. 5 (2021): 726–46.

14. *Parker*, 988 N.E.2d at 321–22.

15. Some states also have acreage minimums for operations to receive RTF protections: Nebraska (ten acres), Neb. Rev. Stat. § 2-4402(1) (2021); New York (seven acres), N.Y. Agric. & Mkts. Law § 301(4) (2021); and Pennsylvania (ten acres), 3 Pa. Stat. § 952 (2021). The Kentucky RTF law defines agricultural use, referencing five acres in its definition to "typically qualify for agricultural use," Ky. Rev. Stat. § 100.111(2) (2020).

16. *Born v. Exxon Corp.*, 388 So. 2d 933, 934 (Ala. 1980) (citing Ala. Code § 6-5-127(a) (1975)).

17. *Gilbert v. Synagro Cent., LLC*, 634 Pa. 651, 654–55 (2015).

18. *Gilbert*, 634 Pa. at 683–84 (citing § 952 of Pennsylvania's RTF law).

19. *Leaf River Forest Prods. v. Ferguson*, 662 So. 2d 648 (Miss. 1995).

20. *Collett v. Weyerhaeuser Co.*, No. 19-11144, 2020 WL 6828613, at *22–23 (E.D. La. Nov. 19, 2020). Since the relief sought was injunctive, the RTF law could be used. This action was brought under a specific Louisiana law that allowed for damages for negligence actions and injunctions for nuisance actions. Because the RTF law expressly does not apply to negligence, the court allowed the defense only insofar as it related to the claim for an injunction.

21. Alaska Stat. § 09.45.235(c) (2021).

22. This captures a range of ways in which RTF laws can supersede local governance that we detail more specifically in our state summaries. However, we use this figure to capture ways in which local governance loses power, including when an RTF law supersedes entirely without qualification; supersedes when specific to nuisances; supersedes municipal ordinances specifically; supersedes when adhering to best management practices; supersedes

as long as facilities meet air and water control programmatic standards; supersedes local protection of well water; supersedes so long as it is not negligent; supersedes if it adheres to other nutrient management criteria; supersedes if nuisance at hand is within specific distance; supersedes unless it anticipates negative environmental or public health, then the state committee will review; supersedes regulation of affiliated buildings and structures; supersedes unless operation was built before 1979 in a city; supersedes township authority on parcels of five acres; supersedes if defined as local agriculture, unless it has impact on public health and safety or adheres to nutrient management act; supersedes ordinances unless identical to state laws and regulations, and unless risking health and safety of residents and governmental entities. The thirty-one states with such provisions does not include New York, which removes government power only in agricultural zones.

23. *Premium Standard Farms v. Lincoln Twp.*, 946 S.W.2d 234, 235–36 (Mo. 1997). Also see Bill Draper, "Jury Awards Plaintiffs $11M Total in Hog Lawsuit," Associated Press, March 4, 2010.

24. *Premium Standard Farms*, 946 S.W.2d at 236 (quoting Mo. Rev. Stat. § 65.677).

25. *Premium Standard Farms*, 946 S.W.2d at 240.

26. From this point forward, when we state "win," we refer to full wins as plaintiff or defendant or split rulings where that party prevailed on some of the merits of the case. In terms of party types, "landowners" include people or legal entities that own land as explicitly stated in the cases. "Governmental bodies" are places like towns and cities, where they are incorporated residential spaces. "CAFOs" are those animal operations referred to as such or where evidence was provided to identify a confined or concentrated animal feeding operation. "Sole proprietor farmer" most closely aligns to the traditional idea of a farm—where the farm bears the same name as the people who operate it and are named in the lawsuit. "Resident" refers to those who live on the property subject to the lawsuit, while "homeowners" are people who own as well as live in the home. These descriptors we use for parties in litigation related to RTF laws are not necessarily mutually exclusive. For example, a business firm can also be a landowner, and a landowner can also be a resident. A firm, however, cannot be a resident or a homeowner. Likewise, firms, for example, can sue one another, which can make the same case enter into multiple categories for party type as plaintiff, defendant, or split.

27. For more details, see the section "Farm Legal Organization" in U.S. Department of Agriculture, *America's Diverse Family Farms: 2018 Edition*, Economic Information Bulletin No. 203 (Washington, D.C.: Economic Research Service, 2018), 18.

28. Steve Wing, Rachel Avery Horton, Stephen W. Marshall, Kendall Thu, Mansoureh Tajik, Leah Schinasi, and Susan S. Schiffman, "Air Pollution and Odor in Communities Near Industrial Swine Operations," *Environmental Health Perspectives* 116, no. 10 (2008): 1362–68.

29. Mansoureh Tajik, Naeema Muhammad, A. Lowman, Kendall Thu, Steve Wing, and Gary Grant, "Impact of Odor from Industrial Hog Operations on Daily Living Activities," *New Solutions: A Journal of Environmental and Occupational Health Policy* 18, no. 2 (2008): 193–205.

30. Ellen K. Silbergeld, Jay Graham, and Lance B. Price, "Industrial Food Animal Production, Antimicrobial Resistance, and Human Health," *Annual Review of Public Health* 29, no. 1 (2008): 53.

31. Ana M. Rule, Sean L. Evans, and Ellen K. Silbergeld, "Food Animal Transport: A Potential Source of Community Exposures to Health Hazards from Industrial Farming (CAFOs)," *Journal of Infection and Public Health* 1, no. 1 (2008): 33–39.

32. Sigurdur T. Sigurdarson and Joel N. Kline, "School Proximity to Concentrated Animal Feeding Operations and Prevalence of Asthma in Students," *Chest* 129, no. 6 (2006): 1486–91.

33. Kelley J. Donham, Joung Ae Lee, Kendall Thu, and Stephen J. Reynolds, "Assessment of Air Quality at Neighbor Residences in the Vicinity of Swine Production Facilities," *Journal of Agromedicine* 11, no. 3–4 (2006): 15–24.

34. For more details on the corporate network and facilities used in industrial hog production, see Loka Ashwood, "'No Matter If You're a Democrat or a Republican or Neither': Pragmatic Politics in Opposition to Industrial Animal Production," *Journal of Rural Studies* 82 (2021): 586–94; and Loka Ashwood, Danielle Diamond, and Kendall Thu, "Where's the Farmer? Limiting Liability in Midwest Industrial Hog Production," *Rural Sociology* 79, no. 1 (2014): 2–27.

35. See Ted Genoways, *The Chain: Farm, Factory, and the Fate of Our Food* (New York: Harper Collins, 2014); and Matthew Scully, "Fear Factories: The Case for Compassionate Conservatism—for Animals," in *The CAFO Reader: The Tragedy of Industrial Animal Factories*, ed. Daniel Imhoff (San Rafael, Calif.: Earth Aware, 2010), 11–21.

36. U.S. Department of Agriculture, National Agricultural Statistics Service, "Table 1. Historical Highlights: 2012 and Earlier Census," in *2012 Census of Agriculture* (Washington, D.C.: United States Department of Agriculture, 2014).

37. The most recent farm numbers pertain to 2021. See Economic Research Service, table "Farm, Land in Farms, and Average Acres per Farm, 1850–2021," *Farming and Farm Income* (USDA Economic Research Service, September 2022), https://www.ers.usda.gov /data-products/ag-and-food-statistics-charting-the-essentials/farming-and-farm-income.

38. Missouri and North Dakota are the only two states that have constitutional amendments pertaining to the right to farm. Missouri's amendment explicitly uses right-to-farm language in its protections (Mo. Const. art. I, § 35), while the North Dakota Constitution provides that no law can be enacted that abridges the right of farmers and ranchers to use "agricultural technology, modern livestock production, and ranching practices" (N.D. Const. art. XI, § 29).

39. Mo. Const. art. I, § 35.

40. *Vimont v. Christian Cty. Health Dep't*, 502 S.W.3d 718, 720 (Mo. Ct. App. 2016).

41. *Vimont*, 502 S.W.3d at 719–20.

42. Missouri Senate, *SB 391: Modifies Provisions relating to Agricultural Operations*, S1708, August 28, 2019, https://www.senate.mo.gov/19info/BTS_Web/Bill.aspx?SessionType =R&BillID=3780907.

43. *Gates v. Tenakee Springs*, 822 P.2d 455, 463 (Alaska 1991); *Gray v. Cty. of Riverside*, No. E036288, 2006 WL 905953 (Cal. App. Apr. 10, 2006); *Bruni v. Gambale*, 16 LCR 534, 538 (Mass. Land Ct. 2008).

44. Economic Research Service, table "Farms and Their Value of Production by Farm Type, 2021," *Farming and Farm Income* (USDA Economic Research Service, September 2022), https://www.ers.usda.gov/data-products/ag-and-food-statistics-charting-the-essentials /farming-and-farm-income.

45. *Rivera v. Cty. of Solano*, No. A133616, 2012 WL 3871930 at *24–26 (Cal. Ct. App. Sept. 7, 2012).

46. Affidavit of Steve Obert, Evidence in Support of IT Motion for Summary Judgment, *Parker v. Obert's Legacy Dairy, LLC*, No. 26001-1106-PL-14 (Gibson Superior Court, April 25, 2012).

47. Matter of *Groat v. Brennan*, 831 N.Y.S.2d 353, 353 (Sup. Ct. 2006).

48. In graph 1.1, we combine CAFOs and business firms as party types, meaning we analyze cases where CAFOs and/or firms are parties. Table 1.2, however, lists CAFOs and business firms separately. In nineteen of the case wins in table 1.2, the CAFO and business firm party types overlap. This means that only six of the twenty-five winning CAFOs were not also explicitly business firms. This combination of party types helps identify the most powerful industrial and business interests exerted through RTF laws.

49. Cynthia M. Duncan, *Worlds Apart: Poverty and Politics in Rural America* (New Haven: Yale University Press, 2015).

50. Please see the appendix for more details about how these data were acquired for this analysis.

51. Cases could appear multiple times for states that are in different sectors; for example, a case that played out in a top poultry layer and hog state appears in each respective category.

52. North Carolina is in the top five for broilers and hogs. See table 1.6.
53. Mary K. Hendrickson, Philip H. Howard, and Douglas H. Constance, "Power, Food and Agriculture: Implications for Farmers, Consumers and Communities," Division of Applied Social Sciences Working Paper, University of Missouri College of Agriculture, Food and Natural Resources, The Bichler and Nitzan Archives, Toronto, 2017, https://philhowardnet .files.wordpress.com/2017/11/hendrickson-howard-constance-2017-final-working-paper -nov-1.pdf.
54. Please note that these percentages are not in table 1.7. We computed these percentages by dividing the total number of cases won by the total number of cases that included that party type in each top-five sector.
55. For an example, see *Merrill v. Valley View Swine, LLC*, 941 N.W.2d 10, 18 (Iowa 2020).
56. Steve Wing, Dana Cole, and Gary Grant, "Environmental Injustice in North Carolina's Hog Industry," *Environmental Health Perspectives* 108, no. 3 (2000): 225–31.
57. Motion to Dismiss at 14–15, *Lewis v. Murphy Brown, LLC*, No. 7:19-CV-127-BR, 2019 WL 5606237 (E.D.N.C. Aug. 19, 2019).
58. For details on the spatial dimensions of access to the law, see Lisa Pruitt, Amanda L. Kool, Lauren Sudeall, Michele Statz, Danielle M. Conway, and Hannah Haksgaard, "Legal Deserts: A Multi-state Perspective on Rural Access to Justice," *Harvard Law and Policy Review* 13 (2018): 15–156. Separately, Pruitt and Sobczynski write about how rural people are less likely to assert some types of legal rights, particularly those related to conservation. The prevalence of nuisance suit litigation in the Midwest may show a willingness to defend property rights that carry a different meta-narrative of rurality. See Lisa R. Pruitt and Linda T. Sobczynski, "Protecting People, Protecting Places: What Environmental Litigation Conceals and Reveals about Rurality," *Journal of Rural Studies* 47, Part A (2016): 326–36.
59. Data describing the percentage of racial minorities at the state level was collected from the U.S. Census Bureau's American Community Survey (ACS) 2020 five-year estimates. State-level rural poverty data was collected from the U.S. Census Bureau's 2021 ACS one-year estimates. See the appendix for details on how we calculated rural poverty and rural racial minorities thresholds.
60. The graphs on rural poverty show total number of cases, not percentages, but we calculate percentages in this paragraph.
61. More specifically, there were no CAFO wins in states with low rural poverty levels and two CAFO wins in states with high rural poverty levels. The remaining twenty-three CAFO wins took place in states with medium rural poverty levels.
62. These figures are based on our analysis of Decennial Census numbers. In total, 246 of 753 rural counties in the Midwest have higher poverty rates in 2020 than 1980.
63. See Thomas W. Mitchell, "Destabilizing the Normalization of Rural Black Land Loss: A Critical Role for Legal Empiricism," *Wisconsin Law Review* 557 (2005): 557–615; and Thomas W. Mitchell, "From Reconstruction to Deconstruction: Undermining Black Land-ownership, Political Independence, and Community through Partition Sales of Tenancies in Common," *Northwestern University Law Review* 95 (2001): 505–80.
64. In the Midwest, eight states have moderately low levels of minorities, and four states have moderately high levels of minorities.
65. Sacoby M. Wilson, Frank Howell, Steve Wing, and Mark Sobsey, "Environmental Injustice and the Mississippi Hog Industry," *Environmental Health Perspectives* 110, no. suppl. 2 (2002): 195–201.
66. W. E. B. Du Bois, *The Souls of Black Folk* (New York: Oxford University Press, 1903).
67. Conner Bailey and Mahua Majumdar, "Absentee Forest and Farm Land Ownership in Alabama: Capturing Benefits from Natural Capital Controlled by Non-residents," in *Rural Wealth Creation*, ed. John L. Pender, Bruce A. Weber, Thomas G. Johnson, and J. Matthew Fannin (New York: Routledge, 2014), 134–50.

68. This analysis includes 195 cases heard at the state trial, state intermediate appellate, state highest, federal district, and federal appellate court levels. Our entire data set, 197 cases, also includes two Illinois cases that appeared before the Illinois Pollution Control Board. We do not include these cases in court levels, as they did not play out in judicial court. For more details, see the appendix.

69. *Dalzell v. Country View Family Farms, LLC,* 517 F. App'x 518, 520 (7th Cir. 2013).

70. *Brantley v. Int'l Paper Co.,* No. 2:09-230-DCR, 2017 WL 2292767, at *48–49 (M.D. Ala. May 24, 2017).

71. By social ecology, we mean "the single commons of the Earth we humans share, sometimes grudgingly, with others—other people, other forms of life, and the rocks and water and oil and air that support all life." Michael Bell, Loka Ashwood, Isac Leslie, and Laura Hanson Schlachter, *An Invitation to Environmental Sociology,* 6th ed. (Thousand Oaks, Calif: Pine Forge Press, 2021), 5.

STATE SUMMARIES OF RIGHT-TO-FARM LAWS

Alabama

In 1978, legislators proposed a right-to-farm law in Alabama as a tool to prevent the loss of farmland and to protect family farms.[1] Since that time, the number of farms in the state has dropped by 33 percent, and today 29 percent fewer acres are being farmed.[2] So what does this legislation do in practice?

Alabama's RTF Law at a Glance

Alabama's RTF law provides no explicit protection for farmland or family farmers. Rather, Alabama's RTF law, like those present in the other forty-nine states, centers on protecting certain types of operations from nuisance suits when they impact neighboring property, for example through noise or pollution. This special protection applies to many types of production, ranging from silviculture to processing. Alabama's initial 1978 RTF law included manufacturing and other industrial plants as protected operations, and later amendments expanded to include racetracks as warranting protection from nuisance suits. Later statutory revisions clarified that the RTF law prevails over local governments when they pass ordinances that try to stipulate otherwise.[3]

Conditions and Activities

In 1990, a couple sued a neighboring poultry operation, claiming that odors from a disposal pit for dead chickens and litter applied near their trailer hampered the enjoyment of their property. They lost their case at the Pickens County circuit court, which ruled that the RTF law protected the corporate operation from nuisance suits. The case was appealed to the

Table 2.1 Alabama's Key RTF Provisions and National Comparison

Alabama's key RTF provisions		% U.S. states with similar RTF provisions
Operations are immune from lawsuits . . .	once in operation for a year.	48%
	if boundaries or size of operations change.	34%
	if there is a change in locality.	46%
	if they produce a different product.	26%
	if there is an ownership change.	26%
Operations are not immune from lawsuits . . .	if they are a nuisance from the start.	38%
	if they are negligent.	46%
	if they do not comply with federal laws.	62%
	if they do not comply with state laws.	66%
	if they do not comply with county laws.	42%
	if they pollute water.	36%
Other important details	RTF supersedes local ordinances and laws.	62%
	RTF protects processing.	48%

Alabama Supreme Court, which instead ruled that since the chicken house was built after the couple started living there, RTF protections did not apply.

Since that time, the Alabama legislature has added a series of conditions, including one that no longer requires operations to predate local property owners, just that they be in operation for one year.[4] When operations meet such conditions, they cannot be deemed a nuisance under state or local laws.[5] If conditions around the facility change after it starts operating, the protections for the operation still hold.[6] If operations use generally accepted agricultural practices, they are protected. However, what constitutes accepted practices is not clear.

Certain activities, though, are not protected in Alabama's RTF law. When an operation is negligent (meaning it fails to use proper care) or pollutes the water, it is not protected from nuisance suits.[7] However, some state and federal environmental rules and regulations exempt agricultural operations from standards required of other industries.[8] Air pollution, like odor, is not mentioned.

Local Government

Alabama's RTF law prevails over municipal ordinances that local governments try to enforce. More specifically, local governments cannot declare an operation a nuisance or require it to stop as long as it is not negligent and meets the aforementioned criteria.[9]

Other Important Aspects

By drawing on statutes separate from the state's RTF law, those who file nuisance suits and their attorneys can be required to pay attorney fees and costs if the court determines there was not substantial justification for the suit.[10]

NOTES

1. See Markeshia Ricks, "Measure Would Protect Farms from Nuisance Declarations," *Anniston (Ala.) Star*, March 13, 2003; Amy Sieckmann, "Bills to Protect Farms from Lawsuits and Ban Indoor Fireworks Pass Committee," *Anniston Star*, April 24, 2003.
2. U.S. Department of Commerce, "Table 1. Farms, Land in Farms, and Land Use: 1945–1978," in *1978 Census of Agriculture, Volume 1: Geographic Area Series, Part 1: Alabama State and County Data, Chapter 1: State Data* (Washington, D.C.: U.S. Bureau of the Census, 1981), https://agcensus.library.cornell.edu/wp-content/uploads/1978-Alabama-CHAPTER_1 _State_Data-181-Table-01.pdf; "2021 State Agriculture Overview: Alabama," U.S. Department of Agriculture, National Agricultural Statistics Service, accessed October 21, 2022, https:// www.nass.usda.gov/Quick_Stats/Ag_Overview/stateOverview.php?state=ALABAMA.
3. Ala. Code § 6-5-127 (2021).
4. Alabama Family Farm Preservation Act, 2010 Ala. Acts 397 (S.B. 61).
5. Ala. Code § 2-6B-3 (2021). The criteria in table 2.1 are summarized. See the Alabama Family Farm Preservation Act for exact language and more in-depth information.
6. Ala. Code § 2-6B-3 (2021).
7. Ala. Code § 6-5-127 (2021).
8. Danielle Diamond, Loka Ashwood, Allen Franco, Aimee Imlay, Lindsay Kuehn, and Crystal Boutwell, "Farm Fiction: Agricultural Exceptionalism, Environmental Injustice and U.S. Right-to-Farm Law," *Environmental Law Reporter* 52 (Sept. 2022): 10727–48.
9. Ala. Code § 2-6B-3 (2021).
10. Ala. Code § 12-19-272 (2021).

Alaska

Advocates view Alaska's RTF law as a tool to protect farmers from nuisance lawsuits when people come "in from the city" and build near farms.[1] Since the law passed in 1986, the number of farming operations has increased by 83 percent, while the acres of farmland have decreased by 17 percent.[2] So what does this legislation do in practice?

Alaska's RTF Law at a Glance

Alaska's RTF law does not explicitly protect farmers or farmland. Rather, Alaska's RTF law, similar to other such statutes nationally, centers on protecting agricultural operations and facilities from nuisance lawsuits over matters like pollution.[3] The law expansively defines operations, which includes aquatic, livestock, and crop production; the raising, slaughtering, and processing of livestock; timber harvesting, manufacturing, and processing; and the application and storage of pesticides, herbicides, animal manure, treated sewage sludge, or chemicals. In the RTF law, protected facilities are those that engage in commercial production or processing that pertains to "any land, building, structure, pond, impoundment, appurtenance, machinery, or equipment" related to crops, livestock, livestock products, or aquatic farming.[4]

Conditions and Activities

Alaska's right-to-farm law protects agricultural facilities and agricultural operations from nuisance suits when conditions change nearby, as long as the facility was not a nuisance when it began.[5] A facility cannot be a private nuisance if it is operated consistent with a soil conservation district plan.[6] In 2001, legislators amended the definition of "agricultural operations" to

42

Table 2.2 Alaska's Key RTF Provisions and National Comparison

Alaska's Key RTF provisions		% U.S. states with similar RTF provisions
Operations are immune from lawsuits ...	if boundaries or size of operation change.	34%
	if there is a change in locality.	46%
	if they use a new technology.	30%
Operations are not immune from lawsuits ...	if they are a nuisance from the start.	38%
Other important details	RTF supersedes local ordinances and laws.	62%
	RTF protects processing.	48%

protect those that change or utilize new technology, practices, processes, or procedures, as well as those related to the activities of "agricultural facilities."[7] Further, their beginning date does not restart regardless of any expansion or use of new technology. The amendment also removed the stipulation that operations be in existence for three years before they could receive protection from nuisance suits. Operations remain liable, however, for improper, illegal, or negligent conduct of their agricultural operations or when the operation causes flooding.[8]

The Supreme Court of Alaska has heard only one RTF case, where debate settled around questions of timing and what constituted an agricultural operation.[9] An operator owned land where he kept farming equipment, livestock, and lagoons for storing septage waste collected by his company and another one. A real estate developer, who owned land adjacent to the defendant's property where he built and sold new homes, sued the defendant for alleged nuisance in the form of odors and negligence. The developer sought a court order for the agricultural operation to stop, while the operator claimed that the RTF law protected him from such complaints. The court ruled that even though the RTF law lists sewage application as a protected activity, the operator did not use or intend to use the septage for farming because the spreading of the waste on pastures began only *after* the neighbors were impacted. The court wrote that "the [Right-to-Farm] Act was meant to protect commercial agricultural facilities or operations that would otherwise become nuisances, not nuisances that may later become agricultural facilities or operations."[10]

ALASKA 43

RTF and Local Governance

Alaska's RTF law prevails over municipal ordinances, resolutions, or regulations that local governments try to enforce.[11] However, this is specific only to cases that pertain to nuisance. For example, in a 1991 case, a property owner built a fence and gate, which the city later removed, saying it was a right-of-way encroachment. The property owner sued, claiming an RTF defense. However, the court ruled that the RTF statute was a defense specifically tailored to nuisance, not to permit violations pertaining to local ordinances. In conclusion, the RTF defense did not apply.[12]

NOTES

1. See Zaz Hollander, "Alaska Supreme Court Goes to Valley School to Hear Case of Smelly Septage—Students Heard Oral Arguments in the Case Pitting a Farmer Who Uses Septage on His Crops against a Next-Door Developer Who Complained about the Stink," *Alaska Dispatch News* (Anchorage), October 20, 2016.
2. U.S. Department of Commerce, "Table 1. Historical Highlights: 1987 and Earlier Census Years," in *1987 Census of Agriculture, Volume 1: Geographic Area Series, Part 2: Alaska State and County Data, Chapter 1: State Data* (Washington, D.C.: U.S. Bureau of the Census, 1989), https://agcensus.library.cornell.edu/wp-content/uploads/1987-Alaska-CHAPTER_1_State_Data-3-Table-01.pdf; "2021 State Agriculture Overview: Alaska," U.S. Department of Agriculture, National Agricultural Statistics Service, accessed October 21, 2022, https://www.nass.usda.gov/Quick_Stats/Ag_Overview/stateOverview.php?state=ALASKA.
3. Alaska Stat. § 09.45.255 (2021).
4. Alaska Stat. § 09.45.235 (2021).
5. Alaska Stat. § 09.45.235(a) (2021).
6. Alaska Stat. § 09.45.235 (2021).
7. 2001 Alaska Sess. Laws ch. 28 (S.B. 60). See also Alaska Stat. § 09.45.235(d)(1) (2021) ("'agricultural facility' means any land, building, structure, pond, impoundment, appurtenance, machinery, or equipment that is used or is intended for use in the commercial production or processing of crops, livestock, or livestock products, or that is used in aquatic farming").
8. Alaska Stat. § 09.45.235(b) (2021).
9. Hollander, "Alaska Supreme Court Goes to Valley School to Hear Case of Smelly Septage."
10. *Riddle v. Lanser*, 421 P.3d 35 (Alaska 2018).
11. Alaska Stat. § 09.45.235(c) (2021).
12. *Gates v. City of Tenakee Springs*, 822 P.2d 455 (Alaska 1991).

Arizona

In 1981, legislators proposed the right-to-farm law in Arizona as a tool to prevent the premature removal of land from agricultural uses due to nuisance litigation.[1] Since that time, the number of farm operations in the state has grown by 144 percent, while the number of acres farmed has shrunk by 31 percent.[2] So what does Arizona's RTF law do in practice?

Arizona's RTF Law at a Glance

Arizona's RTF law provides no explicit protection for farmland against urban development. Instead, Arizona's RTF law, like those present in the other forty-nine states, centers on protecting certain types of agricultural operations from nuisance lawsuits. Arizona's statute protects owners, lessees, agents, and independent contractors or suppliers if they are engaged in activities "on any facility for the production of crops, livestock, poultry, livestock products or poultry products or for the purposes of agritourism."[3]

The state's RTF law, while changed in name to the "Agriculture Protection Act" in 1995, remained substantively unchanged until sweeping 2021 amendments, discussed further below.[4]

Conditions and Activities

To receive protection, operations must be conducted on farmland, defined as land devoted to commercial agricultural production. Operations must be established prior to surrounding nonagricultural land uses. In practice, this means that the operation has to predate its neighbors in order to receive protection, a once common but increasingly rare stipulation. Currently, most states either have amended their RTF laws to say that an operation does not have to predate its neighbors or have failed to include this limitation entirely.[5]

Operations are also required to use good agricultural practices in order to receive RTF protection, which are defined in the statute to mean those practices undertaken in conformity with federal, state, and local laws and regulations.[6] However, some state and federal environmental rules and regulations exempt agricultural operations from standards required of other industries.[7] In addition, Arizona's RTF statute creates a presumption that these so-defined good agricultural practices do not adversely affect public health and safety.[8] Burden of proof is placed on any litigant trying to contend otherwise.

Arizona separately regulates environmental nuisances, and it is not clear how Arizona's RTF law may interact with this administrative law. Arizona defines an environmental nuisance as "the creation or maintenance of a condition in the soil, air or water that causes or threatens to cause harm to the public health or the environment."[9] More specifically, this includes a breeding place for flies that transmit diseases in populous areas; waste that risks transmitting disease; spillage of excreta; and the contamination of domestic waters.[10] If a condition occurs, the director of the Department of Environmental Quality may bring an action to force the operation to stop the activity causing the environmental nuisance.[11]

Local Governance

The 2021 amendments to Arizona's RTF law took away local governments' ability to regulate agricultural operations, if the state Department of Agriculture or Department of Environmental Quality says otherwise. The law now stipulates that "a city, town, county, [or] special taxing district . . . may not declare an agricultural operation conducted on farmland to be a nuisance if the agricultural operation's practices are lawful, customary, reasonable, safe and necessary to the agriculture industry as the practices pertain to an agricultural operation's practices as determined by the agricultural best management practices committee established by § 49-457, the Arizona department of agriculture or the department of environmental quality."[12]

Attorney Fees and Limits on Damages

In 2021, the law was also amended to stipulate that attorney costs and fees be awarded to the prevailing party.[13] However, if the action is filed in bad

Table 2.3 Arizona's Key RTF Provisions and National Comparison

Arizona's key RTF provisions		% U.S. states with similar RTF provisions
Operations are immune from lawsuits ...	when they are there first.	44%
Operations are not immune from lawsuits ...	if they do not comply with federal laws.	62%
	if they do not comply with other laws.	50%
	if they do not comply with state laws.	68%
Other important details	Attorney fees are awarded to prevailing party.	14%
	RTF supersedes local ordinances and laws.	62%

faith, determined by whether or not it is grounded in fact or law or for an improper purpose, attorney costs and fees may be awarded to the other party.[14] The amendment also disallows punitive damages unless the agricultural operation was subject to criminal or civil action from a state or federal environmental or health regulatory agency.[15]

Other Related Agricultural Laws

Arizona allows producers, shippers, or an association that represents producers or shippers to bring action for damages or other relief when they suffer from malicious public dissemination of false information.[16] Although the term "malicious" is not specifically defined, individuals can be held liable under the statute if they knowingly disseminate false information with intent to harm. If individuals knowingly damage, destroy, or remove any crop or product used for commercial, testing, or research purposes, they are liable for up to twice the market value of what is damaged, up to twice the costs of the production, and the litigation costs of those bringing suit.[17]

Arizona also allows agricultural landfills on any farm or ranch of more than forty acres in an unincorporated area, as long as the landfill does not create an environmental nuisance (defined above).[18] These landfills can consist of solid household waste generated by those living on the farm or from the property at large's solid (but not hazardous) waste. These landfills must have a location map and general description filed with the board of

ARIZONA 47

supervisors.[19] In court, agricultural landfills may be treated differently than general agricultural operations that qualify for RTF protections. Because of this, registered agricultural landfills may not receive RTF protections.

NOTES

1. Ariz. Sess. Laws 1981 ch. 168, § 1 (H.B. 2273).
2. U.S. Department of Agriculture, *USDA Quick Stats Tool: June 1981 Survey, Arizona*, distributed by National Agricultural Statistics Service, accessed December 9, 2020, https://quickstats.nass.usda.gov/results/87B5D180-6454-325D-9213-8C99479BD53E; "2021 State Agriculture Overview: Arizona," U.S. Department of Agriculture, National Agricultural Statistics Service, accessed October 21, 2022, https://www.nass.usda.gov/Statistics_by_State/Arizona/index.php.
3. Ariz. Rev. Stat. § 3-111(1) (2021).
4. For more details on the context of Arizona's recent legislation, see Danielle Diamond, Loka Ashwood, Allen Franco, Aimee Imlay, Lindsay Kuehn, and Crystal Boutwell, "Farm Fiction: Agricultural Exceptionalism, Environmental Injustice and U.S. Right-to-Farm Law," *Environmental Law Reporter* 52 (Sept. 2022): 10727–48.
5. See the section "The History of RTF Laws" in the introduction.
6. Ariz. Rev. Stat. § 3-112(A)–(B) (2021).
7. See Diamond et al., "Farm Fiction."
8. Ariz. Rev. Stat. § 3-112(B) (2021).
9. Ariz. Rev. Stat. § 49-141(A) (2021).
10. Ariz. Rev. Stat. § 49-141(A)(1)–(6) (2021).
11. Ariz. Rev. Stat. § 49-142 (2021).
12. Ariz. Rev. Stat. § 3-112(E) (2021).
13. Ariz. Rev. Stat. § 3-122 (2021).
14. Ariz. Rev. Stat. § 3-122 (2021).
15. Ariz. Rev. Stat. § 3-122 (2021).
16. Ariz. Rev. Stat. § 3-113 (2021).
17. Ariz. Rev. Stat. § 3-114 (2021).
18. Ariz. Rev. Stat. § 49-766 (2021).
19. Ariz. Rev. Stat. § 49-766(A)–(B) (2021).

Arkansas

Arkansas legislators passed the state's right-to-farm law in 1981, advocating it as a tool to protect agricultural and forest land by reducing the loss of the state's agricultural resources.[1] Yet since first enacted, the state's number of farm operations has dropped by 27 percent and the land in farms by 14 percent.[2] So what does this legislation do in practice?

Arkansas's RTF Law at a Glance

Arkansas's RTF law provides no explicit protection for farmland or family farmers. Rather, Arkansas's RTF law, like those present in the other forty-nine states, centers on protecting certain types of operations from nuisance lawsuits when they impact neighboring property, for example through noise or pollution. Arkansas's RTF protections apply to either private nuisance suits (those brought by people, like neighbors) or public nuisance suits (those brought by the government on behalf of the general public).

Initially, only facilities received RTF protections in Arkansas, but amendments in 2015 extended protections to agricultural and farming operations at large, defined as those involved in silviculture, agriculture, or aquaculture. Protected operations include those engaged in the production of any plant or animal in freshwater or saltwater; the planting, harvesting, and processing of crops and timber; and the care and production of livestock and plants.[3]

Conditions and Activities

Once up and running for a year, the RTF law shields agricultural operations from nuisance claims that result from a change in the area surrounding the operation.[4] In other words, an agricultural operation, if established first, is protected from nuisance suits so long as the operation was not a nuisance at the time it began.[5]

In 2005, a series of amendments markedly expanded the protection afforded to agricultural and farming operations. Operations now receive protection if they utilize methods or practices "that are commonly or reasonably associated with agricultural production."[6] If an operation is using such practices, the court assumes that it is not a nuisance, unless proved otherwise.[7] This places the burden of litigation on anyone trying to sue an agricultural or farming operation.

The 2005 amendments do not define the meaning of common or reasonable agricultural practices, but if operations utilize such practices, they receive sweeping protection from nuisance suits.[8] Agricultural operations can change their ownership or size without restarting the one-year clock necessary for nuisance protection.[9] They can change the product they produce or use a new technology and retain the same start date.[10] They can cease or become interrupted as well as participate in a government-sponsored agriculture program without restarting the clock.[11]

In addition, the RTF law stipulates that agricultural operations be in compliance with state and federal laws to receive protection.[12] The RTF law also states that operations are not protected if they pollute water, cause a change in the condition of the waters of any stream, or cause any overflow of the lands of any person, firm, or corporation.[13] However, agricultural operations are exempt from air pollution standards in the Arkansas Water and Air Pollution Control Act, making it unclear what compliance with state and federal laws means in practice.[14] Agricultural operations are also exempt from the state's Solid Waste Management Act within the state's Environmental Compliance Resource Program, unless the agricultural operation creates an illegal dump site; a fire, health, or safety hazard; or a public or private nuisance.[15] However, the Arkansas RTF protection from public and private nuisance suits may mean agricultural operations are not liable when their solid waste is a nuisance.

Local Government

Arkansas's RTF law voids any municipal ordinance that attempts to declare an operation a nuisance or require an operation to stop a nuisance-causing activity if the farm or farm operation meets the statutory requirements.[16]

For example, Pilgrim's Pride Corporation operates Premium Protein Products, a twenty-six-acre animal by-product rendering plant, proximate

Table 2.4 Arkansas's Key RTF Provisions and National Comparison

Arkansas's key RTF provisions		% U.S. states with similar RTF provisions
Operations are immune from lawsuits . . .	if boundaries or size of operations change.	34%
	if there is a change in locality.	46%
	if they use a new technology.	30%
	if they produce a different product.	26%
	if there is an ownership change.	26%
	if there is a cessation or interruption in farming.	26%
	once in operation for a year.	48%
	when they are there first.	44%
Operations are not immune from lawsuits . . .	if they do not comply with federal laws.	62%
	if they do not comply with state laws.	68%
	if they pollute water.	36%
Other important details	Attorney fees are awarded to prevailing party.	14%
	RTF supersedes local ordinances and laws.	62%
	RTF protects processing.	48%

to the city of Russellville. The company sued the city over an odor ordinance it passed in response to complaints about smells up to 2.5 miles away from the facility. The facility collected nonedible poultry and animal by-products from butcher shops, poultry processors, and slaughterhouses. It then converted them into animal feed and organic fertilizers. In response to complaints from Russellville residents, the city passed an ordinance creating a fine of $1,000 for single offenses and up to $500 daily if the odor was continuous.[17] The corporation countered that the facility was an agricultural operation, which made such ordinances void. The city withdrew the ordinance in light of the costs imposed by the lawsuit.[18]

Some local organizations and governments have utilized methods outside of the courts to stop intensive agricultural operations. After a lengthy battle in both state and federal court, the Buffalo River Watershed Alliance worked with the Department of Arkansas Heritage and the governor's office to pay $6.2 million to close a controversial hog facility.[19] The group also successfully advocated a five-year ban on concentrated animal feeding operations in the Buffalo River watershed. However, the ban ended without renewal in July 2020.[20]

Attorney Fees

Arkansas's RTF law allows a court to award expert fees, reasonable court costs, and reasonable attorney's fees to the prevailing party in any action brought to assert that an agricultural operation is a public or private nuisance.[21]

NOTES

1. Ark. Code § 2-4-101 (1981).
2. U.S. Department of Agriculture, *USDA Quick Stats Tool: June 1981 Survey, Arkansas*, distributed by National Agricultural Statistics Service, accessed Dec. 13, 2020, https://quickstats.nass.usda.gov/results/56A292E9-F9F8-3C34-99C7-4D33941D4569; "2021 State Agriculture Overview: Arkansas," U.S. Department of Agriculture, National Agricultural Statistics Service, accessed October 21, 2022, https://www.nass.usda.gov/Quick_Stats/Ag_Overview/stateOverview.php?state=ARKANSAS.
3. Ark. Code § 2-4-102(1)(A)–(C) (2021).
4. Ark. Code § 2-4-107(a) (2021).
5. Ark. Code § 2-4-107(a) (2021).
6. Ark. Code § 2-4-107(c)(2) (2021).
7. Also known as a "rebuttable presumption." Ark. Code § 2-4-107(c)(2) (2021).
8. Ark. Code § 2-4-107(b)(1) (2021).
9. Ark. Code § 2-4-107(b)(2)(A) (2021).
10. Ark. Code § 2-4-107(b)(2)(D) (2021).
11. Ark. Code § 2-4-107(b)(2)(B)–(C) (2021).
12. Ark. Code § 2-4-107(c)(2) (2021).
13. Ark. Code § 2-4-106 (2021).
14. Ark. Code § 8-4-305(1)–(8) (2021).
15. Ark. Code § 8-6-2019 (2021).
16. Ark. Code § 2-4-105 (2021).
17. Linda Satter, "Arkansas Plant Files Suit to Toss Odor Ordinance," *Arkansas Democrat Gazette* (Little Rock), May 30, 2017.
18. Sean Ingram, "PPP Lawyers File Second Amended Suit," *Russellville (Ark.) Courier*, June 16, 2017; Linda Satter, "Arkansas Rendering Plant Stops Suit after City Agrees to Look for a New Way to Fight Stink," *Arkansas Democrat Gazette*, September 25, 2017.
19. Settlement Agreement, C&H Hog Farm, Inc., and State of Arkansas, June 13, 2019, on Buffalo River Watershed Alliance website, https://buffaloriveralliance.org/resources/Documents/closure.pdf.
20. Michael M. Wickline, "Proposal to Ban Hog Farms near Buffalo River Tossed Out," *Arkansas Democrat Gazette*, June 20, 2020.
21. Ark. Code § 2-4-107(d) (2021).

California

∙ ∙

Advocates at the state and county level contend that California's right-to-farm law protects farmland by safeguarding agricultural practices.[1] Yet since the state's RTF law was passed in 1981, California has lost 16 percent of its farms and 28 percent of its farmland.[2] So what does this legislation do in practice?

California's RTF Law at a Glance

California's RTF law provides no explicit protection for farmland. Rather, California's RTF law, like those present in the other forty-nine states, centers on protecting certain types of operations from nuisance suits when they impact neighboring property, for example through noise or pollution. California's RTF protections apply to either private nuisance suits (those brought by people, like neighbors) or public nuisance suits (those brought by the government on behalf of the general public).

While California's farmers and ranchers are broadly concerned with the loss of farmland due to urban growth, their support of measures to protect land from development through easements, trusts, and zoning has been mixed.[3] Instead, advocates have introduced and passed RTF laws with broad support at the state level since 1981 and since then through county-level ordinances.[4]

The state's RTF law generally protects any practices performed by a farmer or on a farm, such as the preparation, delivery, and storage of agricultural commodities incident to or in conjunction with those farming operations. The statute specifically protects the cultivation and tillage of soil, dairy operations, and the production of any agricultural commodity, including timber, viticulture, apiculture, horticulture, livestock, fur-bearing animals, fish, and poultry.[5]

53

Conditions and Activities

Only commercial agricultural operations, activities, and facilities receive California's RTF protections. In 2012, the owners of an eighty-acre parcel sued their county over an ordinance that mandated the removal of their sixty roosters and forty hens within the county's unincorporated area, claiming RTF defense. However, the court ruled that their activities did not qualify as commercial, neither in terms of a local county ordinance nor in terms of the state's RTF law. Further, the court ruled that the county had the right to pass such an ordinance. Even though the owners had raised chickens for a decade, the court stated that "poultry hobbyists" who raised chickens for hobby, pleasure, and show were not afforded RTF protections.[6]

For commercial operations to receive protections, they must use generally accepted practices similar to those used by other operations. What constitutes accepted practices is not defined in the statute but rather plays out in court. In a 1996 case, when ranch owners did not provide evidence that their bird farming activities met acceptable standards or were in existence for three years, they did not receive RTF protections.[7] However, in a 2019 case, Olivera Egg Ranch LLC, which housed between 650,000 and 700,000 hens, produced about 468,000 eggs daily, and generated about 142,670 pounds of chicken manure daily, was able to effectively claim RTF as a defense. Here, the court ruled that "despite the number of complaints about odor and flies," the operation provided "substantial evidence to suggest that the ranch operated within the norms of the agricultural region and eventually implemented manure management measures that surpassed local standards."[8]

Agricultural operations receive RTF protections after they have been in operation for three years. If the conditions in or around the facility change after that time period and the operation was not a nuisance at the time it began, the operation still receives RTF protections.[9] Agricultural operations that change their methods or the commodity they produce have effectively claimed an RTF defense in court, even though such protection is not explicitly provided in California's RTF law. In court, agricultural operations that experienced increased irrigation runoff after introducing a new crop used an RTF defense in order to not be found a nuisance or negligent and to evade requests for injunctive relief based on claims of alleged property damage from adjacent landowners.[10]

Nonetheless, agricultural operations remain subject to other applicable state and federal statutes and regulations.[11] In a 2007 court ruling over a

Table 2.5 California's Key RTF Provisions and National Comparison

California's key RTF provisions		% U.S. states with similar RTF provisions
Operations are immune from lawsuits . . .	if there is a change in locality.	46%
	once in operation for three years.	2%
Operations are not immune from lawsuits . . .	if they are a nuisance from the start.	38%
	if they do not comply with state laws.	68%
Other important details	RTF supersedes local ordinances and laws.	62%

private nuisance suit, a composting operation did not receive RTF protection because it did not comply with its use permits or requests from regulatory agencies to take measures to reduce its odor and suppress its dust.[12]

However, California's statutes and regulations related to health and safety sometimes provide exceptions for agricultural operations not afforded to other industries. For example, the state's health and safety code bars the discharge of air contaminants and other materials that "endanger the comfort, repose, health or safety of any of those persons or the public." Yet, the law makes an exception for agricultural operations, saying that the law does not apply to their odors, animal waste products, compost green material, or compost facilities and operations.[13]

Courts have also interpreted the state's RTF law to bar nuisance action brought by one commercial agricultural entity against another, although this is not explicitly stated in the RTF statute.[14]

Local Government

California's RTF law supersedes any local regulations. However, many counties have passed ordinances that bolster the state's RTF law, providing even further protections for agricultural operations. These county-level ordinances often hold up in court. In 2002, an environmental organization lost a suit against a county board of supervisors for adopting a revised version of the RTF law. The organization had tried to claim that the RTF law violated an environmental state law.[15]

California delegates the responsibility to implement state and federal environmental laws to counties or regional boards. The state's water quality control law asserts that a regional board should, "in its judgement[,] . . . ensure the reasonable protection of beneficial uses and the prevention of nuisance."[16] This gives regional boards flexibility in establishing their own standards, which means some counties may have more or fewer exemptions for agricultural operations depending on what standards are set by their regional boards.

California elsewhere treats "excess pesticide residue as public nuisance" in its agricultural code.[17] County-level district attorneys can take civil action to abate such nuisances. It is not entirely clear how this statute interacts with the state's RTF law.

In 1992, the RTF law was amended to allow cities and counties to require that prospective homeowners be given notice that certain properties are proximate to nuisance-causing agriculture activities.[18]

NOTES

1. Dennis Wyatt, "Raising a Stink over Farming? Time to Chill," *Manteca (Calif.) Bulletin*, December 30, 2016; Tom Hannigan, "Capitol Report," *Sacramento News-Ledger*, April 1, 1981.
2. U.S. Department of Agriculture, *USDA Quick Stats Tool: June 1981 Survey, California*, distributed by National Agricultural Statistics Service, accessed November 30, 2020, https://quickstats.nass.usda.gov/results/F1947FFA-F7E0-3BE8-A52B-F3B2C62D5AEF; "2021 State Agriculture Overview: California," U.S. Department of Agriculture, National Agricultural Statistics Service, accessed October 21, 2022, https://www.nass.usda.gov/Quick_Stats/Ag_Overview/stateOverview.php?state=CALIFORNIA.
3. Laura Holson, "Farms Fear Urban Encroachment, FSU Study Says," *Fresno (Calif.) Bee*, October 15, 1992; Ket Miller, "Housing or Farms: A Clash of Dreams," *Santa Maria (Calif.) Times*, January 30, 2005.
4. Henry Schacht, "The Push for Farmland Preservation in California," *San Francisco Chronicle*, March 11, 1993; John Holland, "National Leaders in Ag Preservation Gather in Modesto," *Modesto (Calif.) Bee*, October 4, 2015; Thy Vo, "Program Aims to Keep Farmland for Farms—County Would Buy Easements to Block Development on the Properties," *Mercury News* (San Jose, Calif.), January 28, 2019.
5. Cal. Civ. Code § 3482.5(e) (2021).
6. *Rivera v. County of Solano*, No. A133616, 2012 WL 3871930 (Cal. Ct. App. Sept. 7, 2012).
7. *Mohilef v. Janovici*, 51 Cal. App. 4th 267 (1996).
8. *Acoba v. Olivera Egg Ranch, LLC*, No. H041585, 2019 WL 5882157 (Cal. Ct. App. Nov. 12, 2019).
9. Cal. Civ. Code § 3482.5(a)(1) (2021).
10. *Basor v. Rocha*, No. H023805, 2004 WL 859285 (Cal. Ct. App. Apr. 22, 2004); *Rancho Viejo, LLC v. Tres Amigos Viejos, LLC*, 100 Cal. App. 4th 550 (2002); *Souza v. Lauppe*, 59 Cal. App. 4th 865 (1997); *W&W El Camino Real, LLC v. Fowler*, 226 Cal. App. 4th 263 (2014).
11. Cal. Civ. Code § 3482.5(a)(1), (c) (2021).
12. *Preserve Country Neighborhoods v. Mendocino Cty. Bd. of Supervisors*, No. A109635, 2007 WL 1810692 (Cal. Ct. App. June 25, 2007).

13. Cal. Health & Safety Code § 41700(a), (b) (2021).
14. *Souza*, 59 Cal. App. 4th 865.
15. *Ad Hoc Comm. for Clean Water v. Sonoma Cty. Bd. of Supervisors*, No. A094056, 2002 WL 1454105 (Cal. Ct. App. July 8, 2002).
16. Cal. Water Code § 13241 (2021).
17. Cal. Water Code § 12642 (2021).
18. 1992 Cal. Stat. ch. 97 (Assemb. B. 1190) (amending Cal. Civ. Code § 3482.5(d)).

Colorado

When legislators first passed right-to-farm legislation in 1981, they advocated it as a tool to protect farmland and Colorado family farms.[1] Since that time, the number of farms in the state has increased by 43 percent, mostly in the small category, while the acreage in farmland has dropped by 5 percent.[2] So what does this legislation do in practice?

Colorado's RTF Law at a Glance

Colorado's RTF law provides no explicit protection for farmland or family farmers. Rather, like those RTF laws present in the other forty-nine states, it centers on protecting certain types of operations from nuisance suits when their activities impact neighboring property, for example through activities like noise or odor. Protected types of operations are all-encompassing, including horticulture, floriculture, viticulture, forestry, dairy, livestock, poultry, and bee operations, as long as two conditions are met. First, the operation must use methods or practices that are "commonly or reasonably associated with agricultural production." Second, the operation must have existed before surrounding nonagricultural activities began.[3]

Conditions and Activities

Colorado's RTF law allows operations to significantly change and still be considered to exist before their neighbors. The operation's ownership can change; the type of agricultural product being produced can change; or there can be an interruption or temporary cessation of farming, among other things. Operations can use a new type of technology or participate in a government-sponsored agricultural program. Agricultural operations

Table 2.6 Colorado's Key RTF Provisions and National Comparison

Colorado's key RTF provisions		% U.S. states with similar RTF provisions
Operations are immune from lawsuits ...	if they use a new technology.	30%
	if they produce a different product.	26%
	if there is an ownership change.	26%
	if there is a cessation or interruption in farming.	26%
	when they are there first.	44%
Operations are not immune from lawsuits ...	if they are negligent.	46%
	if they do not comply with county laws.	42%
	if they do not comply with environmental laws.	26%
	if they do not comply with federal laws.	62%
	if they do not comply with other laws.	50%
	if they do not comply with state laws.	68%
Other important details	Attorney fees are awarded to prevailing party.	14%
	RTF supersedes local ordinances and laws.	62%

can substantially increase in size or use methods or practices that are "commonly or reasonably associated with agricultural production."[4]

Taken together, RTF protections continue to apply across this suite of changes unless facilities use improper care (that is, negligence).[5] Further, RTF protections cannot restrict the state's Air Quality Control Program or the Water Quality Control Program for "commercial swine feeding operations."[6] These laws have enforceable provisions available to certain local governmental entities and citizens that may address nuisance-like impacts.

Local Government

Otherwise, local governments do not have the ability to limit or override any of the protections provided by Colorado's RTF law. For example, a court ruled that a board of county commissioners could not prevent a farmer from moving his mobile sprinkler system across a county road.[7] The court stipulated that prohibiting the farmer would be inconsistent with the state's policy of supporting agricultural operations. However, local governments can regulate agricultural operations located within the limits of any city or town as of July 1, 1981, or agricultural operations located on property that was voluntarily annexed to a municipality on or after July 1, 1981.

In addition, local governments can choose to pass ordinances or resolutions that protect agricultural operations even more than the state's RTF law does.[8]

Attorney Fees and Limits on Damages

Under Colorado law, recovery may be limited to either damages for the loss of land value from the nuisance or a permanent injunction to stop the nuisance, if irreversible damage is not already done.[9] In addition, whoever the court rules in favor of, either the defendant (typically an agricultural operation) or the plaintiff, can be awarded reasonable attorney fees and costs.[10]

NOTES

1. Colo. Rev. Stat. § 35-3.5-101 (2021).
2. U.S. Department of Commerce, "Table 1. Farms, Land in Farms, and Land Use: 1982 and Earlier Census Years," in *1982 Census of Agriculture, Volume 1: Geographic Area Series, Part 6: Colorado State and County Data, Chapter 1: State Data* (Washington, D.C.: U.S. Bureau of the Census, 1984), https://agcensus.library.cornell.edu/wp-content/uploads/1982 -Colorado-CHAPTER_1_State_Data-121-Table-01.pdf; "2021 State Agriculture Overview: Colorado," U.S. Department of Agriculture, National Agricultural Statistics Service, accessed October 21, 2022, https://www.nass.usda.gov/Quick_Stats/Ag_Overview/stateOver view.php?state=COLORADO. See Colorado State Demography Office, "Highlights from the 2017 Census of Agriculture," *Crosstabs* (blog), January 9, 2020, accessed October 1, 2020, https://demography.dola.colorado.gov/crosstabs/Census of Agriculture 2017/.
3. Colo. Rev. Stat. § 35-3.5-102 (2021).
4. 2000 Colo. Sess. Laws ch. 66 (S.B. 00-29); Colo. Rev. Stat. § 35-3.5-102 (2021).
5. Colo. Rev. Stat. § 35-3.5-102 (2021).
6. Colo. Rev. Stat. §§ 25-7-138, 25-8-501.1, 35-3.5-102 (2021).
7. *Bd. of Cty. Comm'rs v. Vandemoer*, 205 P.3d 423 (Colo. App. 2008).
8. Colo. Rev. Stat. § 35-3.5-102 (2021).
9. *Staley v. Sagel*, 841 P.2d 379 (Colo. App. 1992).
10. Colo. Rev. Stat. § 35-3.5-102 (2021).

Connecticut

Advocates of Connecticut's right-to-farm law promoted it as a legal tool that protects land from suburban sprawl and protects old-timers from urban newcomers.[1] Since the state law was first enacted in 1983, the number of farm operations in the state has grown by 28 percent, while 24 percent fewer acres are farmed.[2] So what does this law do in practice?

Connecticut's RTF Law at a Glance

Connecticut's state law provides no explicit protection for farmland. Rather, Connecticut's RTF law, like those present in the other forty-nine states, centers on protecting agricultural and farming operations from nuisance suits when they impact neighboring property, for example through noise or pollution. Connecticut's RTF protections apply to either private nuisance suits (those brought by people, like neighbors) or public nuisance suits (those brought by the government on behalf of the general public).

Connecticut's RTF law does not define agricultural and farming operations.[3] A 1997 amendment to the RTF law added the collection of spring and well water as protected agricultural activities.[4] The RTF law defines spring water as that obtained from an underground formation that naturally flows to the surface, while well water means natural water obtained from a hole bored, drilled, or otherwise constructed in the ground.[5] One court consulted a local zoning code to determine the meaning of agriculture when a spring water company tried to claim RTF status. Based on its code, the town demanded the company stop collecting and storing spring water. The court deferred to the town's definition of agriculture—which did not include water as food—to affirm that the company could not bottle water.[6]

Conditions and Activities

Once agricultural and farming operations are up and running for a year, Connecticut's RTF law protects them, so long as they use generally accepted agricultural practices. Inspection and approval by the commissioner of agriculture is taken as evidence that the operation, place, establishment, or facility follows such practices, unless proved otherwise.[7]

The law specifically protects operations from nuisance suits related to odor, dust, noise, and the use of chemicals.[8] To receive RTF protections, the method of chemical application must be approved by the commissioner of energy and environmental protection and, when applicable, the state commissioner of public health. The law also protects agricultural and farming operations from nuisance suits over water pollution from livestock or crop production, except when they pollute public or private drinking water. The commissioner of energy and environmental protection determines what constitutes acceptable management practices for water pollution.[9]

In one case, a city sued horse owners in part for having the horses fenced closer to the neighbor's property than allowed by city and state ordinances. The horses also were boarded proximate to an abandoned well. In a split ruling, the court ruled that the location of the fence line was in accordance with generally accepted practices and protected by the RTF law. However, the court ruled that the inactive well had yet to be properly abandoned, and RTF protections do not apply to private or public wells.[10]

The law also does not protect operations that cause a nuisance due to negligent (failing to take proper care), willful (done intentionally), or reckless (person knew or should have known their actions would cause harm) agricultural practices.[11] In one case, neighbors sued a dairy farm for not adhering to its waste management plan, failing to replace or repair broken pipes that disposed of waste, and housing more cows than permitted under special exemption. The jury found that the dairy farm had emitted offensive odors that unreasonably interfered with the residents' enjoyment of their property. The jury also found that the farm was negligent.[12] The couple was awarded $60,000 for permanent loss of the enjoyment of their home and $40,000 for noneconomic damages.[13]

Willfulness played a central role in a different case, when landowners erected a small sheep pen behind a subdivision home after the subdivision installed signs on the landowners' property, against their wishes. The owners of the sixteen acres admitted that they knew the homeowner in the subdivision did not like livestock when they placed five sheep and two

Table 2.7 Connecticut's Key RTF Provisions and National Comparison

Connecticut's key RTF provisions		% U.S. states with similar RTF provisions
Operations are immune from lawsuits . . .	once in operation for a year.	48%
Operations are not immune from lawsuits . . .	if they do not comply with other laws.	50%
	if they are negligent.	46%
	if they pollute water.	36%
Other important details	RTF supersedes local ordinances and laws.	62%

goats in the pen. In addition, the landowners painted a box truck with the depiction of a goat and the words "baa baa" on the side. The homeowner said the animal pen and box truck interfered with her peaceful enjoyment of her property and reduced its value. The court found that the defendants were likely not protected by the state's RTF law because their actions were willful.[14]

Local Government

Connecticut's RTF law provides protections from nuisance suits "notwithstanding" any general statute, municipal ordinance, or regulation to the contrary.[15] Courts have interpreted this to allow for local zoning as long as those ordinances do not try to regulate odor, dust, noise, and chemicals. Some local governments have responded by passing local right-to-farm ordinances.[16] However, most RTF litigation in Connecticut pertains to agricultural operations claiming RTF exemption from local laws.

In one case, a town issued a zoning citation against a farm for constituting a blight to adjacent property owners through deteriorating structures, improper storage of trash, and interference with the use and enjoyment of other properties in the area. The farm claimed that the town's zoning ordinance was unenforceable due to the restrictions on local government in the RTF law.[17] The court found that although the RTF law prohibits ordinances related to nuisance, it does not prevent towns from passing and enforcing ordinances related to safety, health, and the general welfare of residents.

In a similar case, a corporate tobacco farm on multiple occasions allowed a helicopter to take off and land on the property, violating a town's zoning ordinances. The operator claimed that the RTF law preempted the local ordinance. The court found that the RTF law did not apply because the town's opposition to the helicopter did not pertain to nuisance but rather to an illegal use of land. The court also ruled that the zoning ordinance did not prevent the farm from operating and thus did not violate the RTF law. The court stated that the RTF law was intended to protect "longstanding farms" in reference to how they were "historically operated." Last, the court noted that even if the ordinance had been in conflict with the RTF law, the helicopter had not been in use for more than one year, the amount of time an agricultural activity needs to have existed before RTF protection is given.[18]

NOTES

1. George Krimsky, "Here Comes the Neighborhood," *Waterbury (Conn.) Republican-American*, August 7, 2018; "Right-to-Farm Helps State/Editorials," *Hartford (Conn.) Courant*, June 4, 2013.
2. U.S. Department of Agriculture, *USDA Quick Stats Tool: June 1983 Survey, Connecticut*, distributed by National Agricultural Statistics Service, accessed December 13, 2020, https://quickstats.nass.usda.gov/results/7CE4E7BB-5D0E-36E5-BAE7-03B62981294F; "2021 State Agriculture Overview: Connecticut," U.S. Department of Agriculture, National Agricultural Statistics Service, accessed October 21, 2022, https://www.nass.usda.gov/Quick_Stats/Ag_Overview/stateOverview.php?state=CONNECTICUT.
3. *Wood v. Zoning Bd. of Appeals of Town of Somers*, 784 A.2d 354 (Conn. 2001).
4. A 1997 amendment to the RTF law added the collection of spring and well water as protected agricultural activities. 1997 Conn. Acts 11 (S.B 3004, Spec. Sess.) (adding, in relevant part, Conn. Gen. Stat. § 19a-341(b)).
5. Conn. Gen. Stat § 21a-150 (2021).
6. *Wood*, 784 A.2d 354.
7. Conn. Gen. Stat. § 19a-341(a) (2021).
8. Conn. Gen. Stat. § 19a-341(a)(1)–(4) (2021).
9. Conn. Gen. Stat. § 19a-341(a)(4) (2021).
10. *Havlicek v. Hills*, No. CV030102301, 2003 WL 22962871 (Conn. Super. Ct. Dec. 5, 2003).
11. Conn. Gen. Stat. § 19a-341(c) (2021).
12. *Petsey v. Cushman*, No. 530238, 1994 WL 720359 (Conn. Super. Ct. Dec. 15, 1994).
13. *Petsey v. Cushman*, No. X07CV 9470091, 2000 WL 157920 (Conn. Super. Ct. Jan. 28, 2000).
14. *Morytko v. Westfort*, No. CV04400600S, 2005 WL 1524799 (Conn. Super. Ct. May 31, 2005).
15. Conn. Gen. Stat. § 19a-341(a) (2021).
16. Lynn Mellis Worthington, "Farm Ordinance Going to Voters—Move to Guard Farmers from Nuisance Suits," *Waterbury (Conn.) Republican-American*, May 7, 2015; Jackie Nappo, "Ellington Selectmen Endorse Proposed 'Right to Farm' Ordinance," *Manchester (Conn.) Journal Inquirer*, January 16, 2019; Erik Hesselberg, "Town Eyes 'Right to Farm' Ordinance/East Hampton," *Hartford (Conn.) Courant*, June 3, 2013; Caitlin Dineen, "Right-to-Farm Vote Draws Outcry," *Willimantic (Conn.) Chronicle*, September 30, 2009.
17. *Pierczyk Straska Farm v. Town of Rocky Hill*, No. CV155016838, 2016 WL 673490 (Conn. Super. Ct. Jan. 7, 2016).
18. *Town of Enfield v. Enfield Shade Tobacco, LLC*, No. CV010809006, 2002 WL 1162815 (Conn. Super. Ct. May 8, 2002).

Delaware

In 1980, legislators passed Delaware's first version of a right-to-farm law and later justified it as a tool to protect the state's agricultural resources from nonagricultural land uses.[1] Since that time, the number of farms in the state has dropped by 34 percent, with 18 percent fewer acres of farmland.[2] So what does this legislation do in practice?

Delaware's RTF Laws at a Glance

Delaware's RTF-related statutes, like those present in the other forty-nine states, centers on protecting certain types of operations from nuisance suits when they impact neighboring property, for example through noise or pollution. The RTF statutes themselves provide no explicit protection for farmland or family farms. In practice, this means that land is not tied to RTF protections; rather, such protections apply generally to agricultural operations.[3] The state defines protected agricultural operations as those engaged in producing or raising crops, poultry, eggs, milk and related products, livestock, bees, horses, or forestry products or in the cultivation of land more generally.[4] Protected agricultural operations also include structures such as grain elevators and feed mills, as well as the transportation of agricultural products to and from various storage areas.

Delaware's RTF-related statutes also tie in to the state's 1991 Agricultural Lands Preservation Act, where property owners who agree not to develop their lands for at least ten years receive tax benefits, RTF protections, and an opportunity to sell their preservation easement to the state to permanently protect it from development.[5] An Agricultural Preservation District contains at least 200 usable and contiguous acres.[6] Any parcel of land that is less than 200 acres but within three miles of an established district can be enrolled (and thus expand the district).[7]

65

Conditions and Activities

Delaware law has two primary RTF statutes that provide protections to agricultural operations from either private nuisance suits (those brought by people, like neighbors) or public nuisance suits (those brought by the government on behalf of the general public).[8] One statute protects agricultural operations that have been operating for more than one year from being deemed a public or private nuisance by any changed conditions that occur in or around their location.[9] The one-year clock begins either with the start of the operation or when the operation changes, so long as the operation was not a nuisance when it began or when it changed. However, the statute does not define what constitutes a change in operation and thus what would restart the one-year clock. Under this statute, operations lose RTF protections if they are negligent (not acting with appropriate care), if they are conducted in an improper manner, or if they do not comply with federal, state, or local health or zoning requirements.[10] Moreover, this law does not protect operations against certain types of environmental damages. For example, federal, state, and local agencies may still enforce air, water quality, or other environmental standards against agricultural operations.[11] In addition, people, firms, or corporations can recover damages from an agricultural operation that causes overflow onto their land or if the operation pollutes and/or changes the condition of water.[12]

A separate Delaware statute similarly provides protections to agricultural operations, as well as forestry operations, that have been operating for more than one year.[13] These operations cannot be deemed a public or private nuisance by any changed conditions that occur in or around their location. This statute, however, was amended in 2010 to provide even greater protections to agricultural and forestry operations by also giving them an absolute defense from nuisance suits (meaning they are immune from liability) if they can prove they have been in operation for at least a year and so long as they are in compliance with all relevant state and federal laws, regulations, and permits.[14] The absolute defense from nuisance suits also applies to an operation's employees and principals.

Local Government

The RTF protections void any local governmental ordinance that attempts to regulate or stop agricultural nuisances. However, this law does not apply if there has been a significant change in the operation itself or if the nuisance

Table 2.8 Delaware's Key RTF Provisions and National Comparison

Delaware's key RTF provisions		% U.S. states with similar RTF provisions
Operations are immune from lawsuits ...	once in operation for a year.	48%
	if there is a change in locality.	46%
Operations are not immune from lawsuits ...	if they are negligent.	46%
	if they do not comply with county laws.	42%
	if they pollute water.	36%
	if they do not comply with federal laws.	62%
	if they do not comply with state laws.	68%
	if they are a nuisance from the start.	38%
Other important details	RTF supersedes local ordinances and laws.	62%
	RTF supersedes local ordinances and laws in agricultural zones.	12%
	Attorney fees are awarded to prevailing defendant.	34%

results from a failure to utilize "good agricultural practices."[15] Delaware law presumes that operations utilize good agricultural practices as long as they are in compliance with all applicable state and federal laws, regulations, and permits.[16] In addition, state or local law enforcement agencies cannot bring a criminal or civil action against an agricultural operation for any activity that complies with state and federal laws, regulations, and permits.[17]

Agricultural operations participating in Agricultural Preservation Districts receive further protection against claims of nuisance.[18] Property deeds in subdivisions within 300 feet of an Agricultural Preservation District come with a notice about agricultural chemicals, nighttime operations, manure, dust, noise, and other odors. The notice also states that "the use and enjoyment of this property is expressly conditioned on acceptance of any annoyance or inconvenience which may result from such normal agricultural uses and activities."[19] As long as lawful, the preservation statute treats agricultural uses and activities in such districts as "protected actions" that no existing or future municipal codes and ordinances can regulate.[20]

In addition, the state's agricultural preservation law requires that villages, when considering a new subdivision development, provide a fifty-foot setback from any Agricultural Preservation District.[21] For example, a developer sued the Delaware Agricultural Lands Preservation Foundation after the state agency approved an Agricultural Preservation District adjacent to a planned residential subdivision.[22] The developer argued that the fifty-foot setback required on the subdivision's property constituted an unconstitutional taking of property. Initially, the Delaware Superior Court ruled that the developer had to provide the setback.[23] However, the state's supreme court later ruled that because the development predated the proposed Agricultural Preservation District, the developer did not have to provide a setback.[24]

Attorney Fees

Delaware's two main RTF-related statutes do not provide any specific provisions for attorney fees. However, if a lawsuit alleging nuisance is filed against owners of lands in an Agricultural Preservation District and the owners prevail, the owners are entitled to recover costs and expenses related to the lawsuit, including attorney fees.[25] This, and similar language, may have a chilling effect on the filing of nuisance suits against industrial operators.[26]

NOTES

1. Del. Code tit. 3, § 1401 (1980). For the justification of later RTF amendments, see 71 Del. Laws 462 (1998) (H.B. 609) (adding Del. Code tit. 10, § 8141).
2. U.S. Department of Agriculture, *USDA Quick Stats Tool: June 1980 Survey, Delaware*, distributed by National Agricultural Statistics Service, accessed December 8, 2020, https://quickstats.nass.usda.gov/results/D719D06D-9F83-31CA-97F2-DBB82F081D68; "2021 State Agriculture Overview: Delaware," U.S. Department of Agriculture, National Agricultural Statistics Service, accessed October 21, 2022, https://www.nass.usda.gov/Quick_Stats/Ag_Overview/stateOverview.php?state=DELAWARE.
3. Del. Code tit. 3, § 1401 (2021); Del. Code tit. 10, § 8141(a) (2021).
4. Del. Code tit. 10, § 8141(a) (2021).
5. For the laws on Agricultural Preservation Districts, see Del. Code tit. 3, §§ 907–911 (2021). See also Antonio Prado, "65 Farms Permanently Preserved by Agricultural Lands Preservation Foundation," *Dover (Del.) Post*, January 4, 2013; and "Del. Hits Farm Preservation Milestone," *Delaware State News* (Dover), March 21, 2009.
6. Del. Code tit. 3, § 907(a) (2021).
7. Del. Code tit. 3, § 907(d) (2021); "Preservation Program Helps Protect Farmland, Open Space," *Middletown (Del.) Transcript*, April 4, 2013.
8. See generally Del. Code tit. 3, § 1401 (2021), and Del. Code tit. 10, § 8141 (2021).
9. Del. Code tit. 10, § 8141(c) (2021).
10. Del. Code tit. 10, § 8141(b)(1), (3) (2021).
11. Del. Code tit. 10, § 8141(b)(2) (2021).
12. Del. Code tit. 10, § 8141(d) (2021).
13. Del. Code tit. 3, § 1401 (2021).
14. 77 Del. Laws 376 (2010) (S.B. 265) (amending Del. Code tit. 3, § 1401).
15. Del. Code tit. 3, § 1401 (2021); Del. Code tit. 10, § 8141(e) (2021).

16. Del. Code tit. 3, § 1401 (2021).
17. Del. Code tit. 3, § 1401 (2021).
18. Del. Code tit. 3, § 910(b) (2021).
19. Del. Code tit. 3, § 910(a)(1) (2021).
20. Del. Code tit. 3, § 910(b) (2021).
21. Del. Code tit. 3, § 910(a) (2021).
22. *In re 244.5 Acres of Land in the Vill., LLC v. Del. Agric. Lands Found.*, 808 A.2d 753, 758 (Del. 2002).
23. *In re 244.5 Acres of Land in the Vill., LLC v. Del. Agric. Lands Found.*, No. Civ.A. 98C-02-021, 2001 WL 1469155 (Del. Super. Ct. Aug. 22, 2001).
24. *In re 244.5 Acres of Land in the Vill., LLC*, 808 A.2d at 758.
25. Del. Code tit. 3, § 910(b) (2021).
26. Cordon M. Smart, "The 'Right to Commit Nuisance' in North Carolina: A Historical Analysis of the Right-to-Farm Act," *North Carolina Law Review* 94, no. 6 (2016): 2097–154. For more on the chilling effect of such statutes, see the section "Geopolitical Extraction" in the introduction.

Florida

Legislators proposed a right-to-farm law in Florida as a tool to preserve the state's landscape and agricultural lands encroached upon by urbanization.[1] Since the law was first passed in 1979, the number of farm operators in the state has grown by 25 percent, while the acreage farmed has dropped by 28 percent.[2] So what does this legislation do in practice?

Florida's RTF Law at a Glance

Florida's RTF law provides no explicit protection of farmland from urban development, while it has nonetheless been promoted as a tool that does so.[3] Florida's RTF law, like those present in the other forty-nine states, centers on protecting certain types of operations from nuisance suits when they impact neighboring property, for example through noise or pollution. In 1979, Florida first introduced protections from nuisance suits for commercial agriculture and farming operations, places, establishments, and facilities. Shortly after, the statute was renamed the "Florida Right to Farm Act" in 1982, with a sweeping preamble that justified its purpose as promoting the "economic self-sufficiency of the people of the state" and "the encouragement, development, improvement, and preservation of agriculture," alongside the description of agricultural lands as "unique and irreplaceable resources of statewide importance."[4] The amendments defined protected farms as land, buildings, facilities, and machinery and its appurtenances and defined protected farm operations as all conditions or activities by the owner, lessee, agent, independent contractor, or supplier.[5] In 1987, an amendment added aquaculture to the definition of farm.[6]

The meaning of "farming operation" can be subject to debate in court. For example, a county accused a farmer of operating a junkyard in an agriculturally zoned area because he kept heavy machinery stored outside, including a Bush Hog and a bulldozer. Initially, the circuit court ruled that the farmer had thirty days to remove the machinery or pay a fine. On reconsideration, however, the district court of appeals ruled that the lower court violated the farmer's right to due process by not allowing him to present evidence showing his machinery was farm equipment, a point that, if proved, would have protected him under the RTF definition of a farm.[7]

Conditions and Activities

Since 1979, Florida's RTF law has protected operations once they are up and running for a year, as long as the operation was not a nuisance at the time it began.[8] In addition, farm operations receive such protections in the event the area around the operation changes.

The 1982 amendments markedly expanded the protections afforded to farm operations. Namely, a farm operation can expand within its boundaries and still maintain the same established date of operation. The amendments also allow the operation to maintain the original establishment date, even if the ownership or the type of product produced changes. The expansion is not protected if it results in a more excessive farm operation with regard to noise, odor, dust, or fumes when proximate to an established homestead or business.[9] This means the clock does not restart when a farm changes, for example, from a corn field to a concentrated animal feeding operation when it is proximate to an established homestead or business. The 1982 amendments also expanded protections by shielding farm operations from either private nuisance suits (those brought by people, like neighbors) or public nuisance suits (those brought by the government on behalf of the general public).[10]

The amendments also stipulate four conditions that result in forfeited RTF protections for operations: (1) untreated or improperly treated human waste, garbage, offal, dead animals, waste materials, or gases that harm humans or animals; (2) improper septic tanks, water closets, or privies; (3) keeping diseased animals, unless in accordance with disease control programs; and (4) the unsanitary slaughtering of animals.[11] The 1982 amendments also made protections subject to farms using generally accepted agricultural and management practices, and in 1993 the law added explicit protection to changes related to the adoption of best management practices.[12]

The meaning of "excessive" and "generally accepted agriculture practices" often plays out in court, as they are not defined in the law. In one case, Pasco County charged Tampa Farm Service Inc., a farm operation housing 1.5–2 million chickens, with violating its waste and garbage disposal ordinances. The county made the charge after the corporation started to apply wet instead of dry manure on its land. In return, the company filed suit against the enforcement of the ordinance. The trial court initially determined that the company's activities were protected under the Florida Right to Farm Act. However, the appellate court disagreed, arguing that it mattered how disruptive the agricultural practice was, stating, "Even if a practice is agriculturally acceptable, it may cause unreasonable degradation for the established neighborhood." The court ruled, however, that "excessive" does not include minor odor changes or minimal degradation. The case was remanded for a new trial to determine whether the change in methods substantially degraded the locale and, if so, whether the country regulations were valid regarding traditional nuisance suits.[13]

In a more recent class action case, property owners sued a sugarcane corporation over preharvest sugarcane burning, but the court used the RTF law to rule that burning was an acceptable agricultural practice, even though it also affirmed that burning emitted pollutants.[14] In a separate case, Northeast Concepts Inc. and a resident were ordered by the Department of Environmental Protection to stop burning brush and cutting woodlands in a buffer zone. In addition, an injunction was filed by the Town of Holland to stop the operation, but the Northeast Concepts company prevailed, successfully utilizing the RTF defense to claim agriculture was exempt.[15]

Local Government

In 2000, the RTF law was amended to specifically limit local government's power. The RTF law (and a related one) stipulates that local governments cannot adopt policies that limit the activities of a "bona fide farm operation" on land classified as agricultural.[16] However, this limitation of local government applies only when the farm activities utilize best management practices or other measures developed by the Department of Environmental Protection, the Department of Agriculture and Consumer Services, or water management districts. For example, a county issued a stop-work order to Mariculture Technologies International Inc., which was expanding its operations by digging more ponds. However, the corporation claimed its right to farm superseded the county's excavation ordinance, and the county later determined it had no legal authority to issue or maintain the stop-work order.[17]

Table 2.9 Florida's Key RTF Provisions and National Comparison

Florida's key RTF provisions		% U.S. states with similar RTF provisions
Operations are immune from lawsuits . . .	once in operation for a year.	48%
	if there is a change in locality.	46%
	if they produce a different product.	26%
	if there is an ownership change.	26%
Operations are not immune from lawsuits . . .	if they do not comply with state laws.	68%
	if they do not comply with federal laws.	62%
	if they do not comply with other laws.	50%
	if they do not comply with county laws.	42%
	if they are a nuisance from the start.	38%
	if they pollute water.	36%
	if they do not comply with environmental laws.	26%
Other important details	RTF supersedes local ordinances and laws.	62%
	RTF supersedes local ordinances and laws in agricultural zones.	12%
	Attorney fees are awarded to prevailing defendant.	34%

Still, local governments can protect wellfield areas, which are designated by local governments to protect the groundwater sourced by a well that people draw from.[18] In addition, urban counties with a population over 1.5 million people and more than twenty-five municipalities can enact ordinances, regulations, or other measures necessary to carry out environmental programs.[19]

However, a separate law called the Agricultural Lands and Practices Act prohibits counties from enforcing wetland, spring protection, or stormwater ordinances, regulations, or rules adopted after July 1, 2003. Such ordinances and the like can be upheld at the county level only if they adhere to state agency or water management district mandates.[20] In practice, the Agricultural Lands and Practices Act further constrains county-level capacity to adopt intensive agriculture ordinances.[21] Further, it is not clear how the difference between a wellfield and a spring are determined. As a result of the Agricultural Lands and Practices Act, the RTF statute, and other related laws, courts have ruled that local governments can only utilize ordinances restricting farming activities that existed before the RTF law.[22]

Nonetheless, the RTF law does not always prevail over local law. For example, buildings constructed on land classified as agricultural may be subject to residential zoning regulations, as long as the regulations do not limit the operations of the "bona fide" farm operation.[23]

Environmental Laws

Local government has limited authority to prevent the clearing of agricultural land, which has resulted in ample controversy.[24] For example, the Florida Wildlife Federation sued Collier County, alleging that it was impermissibly allowing "HHH Ranch" to perform agricultural land clearing on 604 acres of occupied Florida panther and red-cockaded woodpecker habitat in violation of the Endangered Species Act. The court dismissed the claim relative to HHH Ranch because the land was classified as agricultural.[25]

In accordance with the Florida Pesticide Law, no local government, agency, commission, or department can adopt laws, rules, or policies that determine whether pesticides are injurious to the environment. Only Florida's Department of Agriculture and Consumer Services can determine as much by adopting from the U.S. Environmental Protection Agency's pesticide rules.[26]

NOTES

1. Fla. Stat. § 823.14(2) (2021).
2. U.S. Department of Agriculture, *USDA Quick Stats Tool: June 1979 Survey, Florida*, distributed by National Agricultural Statistics Service, accessed December 10, 2020, https://quickstats.nass.usda.gov/results/5BC82FC8-4457-3366-A60B-DB3E8859704F; "2021 State Agriculture Overview: Florida," U.S. Department of Agriculture, National Agricultural Statistics Service, accessed October 21, 2022, https://www.nass.usda.gov/Quick_Stats/Ag_Overview/stateOverview.php?state=FLORIDA.
3. See Lisa Schuchman, "Development Endangering U.S. Farmland," *Palm Beach (Fla.) Post*, July 15, 1993. The article states that the American Farmland Trust advocated strengthening right-to-farm laws to preserve farmland.
4. Fla. Stat. § 823.14(2) (2021).
5. Fla. Stat. § 823.14(3)(a)–(b) (2021).
6. Fla. Stat. § 823.14(3)(a) (2021).
7. *Kupke v. Orange Cty.*, 838 So. 2d 598 (Fla. Dist. Ct. App. 2003).
8. Fla. Stat. § 823.14 (2021).
9. Fla. Stat. § 823.14(5) (2021).
10. Fla. Stat. § 823.14(4)(a) (2021).
11. Fla. Stat. § 823.14(4)(a)(1)–(4) (2021).
12. Fla. Stat. § 823.14 (4)(a)–(b) (2021).
13. *Pasco Cty. v. Tampa Farm Service*, 573 So. 2d 909 (Fla. Dist. Ct. App. 1990).
14. *Coffie v. Fla. Crystals Corp.*, 460 F. Supp. 3d 1297 (S.D. Fla. 2020).
15. Patty Lawrence, "Farmer Prevails in Case against Town; Exemption Allows Burning of Brush," *Sarasota (Fla.) Herald-Tribune*, May 1, 2010.

16. Fla. Stat. § 823.14 (2021); Fla. Stat. § 163.3162(3)(a) (2021).

17. *Mariculture Tech. Intl. v. Volusia Cty.*, No. 6:11-cv-996-Orl-31DAB, 2011 WL 4596457 (M.D. Fla. Oct. 3, 2011).

18. Fla. Stat. § 823.14 (2021); Fla. Stat. § 373.4592 (2021).

19. Fla. Stat. § 163.3162(3)(g) (2021).

20. Fla. Stat. § 163.3162(I)(1)(3)(i)(3) (2021).

21. Greg C. Brunos, "Agricultural Bill Causing a Stir," *Gainesville (Fla.) Sun,* May 31, 2003.

22. *Wilson v. Palm Beach Co.*, 62 So. 3d 1247 (Fla. Dist. Ct. App. 2011).

23. 2009-26 Fla. Op. Att'y Gen. (June 15, 2009); 2001-71 Fla. Op. Att'y Gen. (Oct. 10, 2001); see also Shemir Wiles, "AG Rules in Barn Exemption—State Official Ruling Leaves Final Decision Up to County Leaders," *Citrus County Chronicle* (Crystal River, Fla.), June 15, 2009.

24. Eric Staats, "Farm Loophole Allows Permits for Clearing Sensitive Land—Federal, State Agencies That Require Wildlife Protections Don't Review Requests Beforehand If County Deems They Fall under Right to Farm Act," *Naples (Fla.) Daily News,* August 26, 2006.

25. *Fla. Panthers v. Collier Co.*, No. 2:13-cv-612-FtM-29DNF, 2014 WL 2742826 (M.D. Fla. June 17, 2014).

26. Fla. Stat. § 487.011(1)–(2) (2021).

Georgia

Georgia legislators passed the right-to-farm law in 1980, proclaiming it a tool to reduce the state's loss of agricultural and forest land resources.[1] Yet since first enacted, the state has lost 30 percent of its farming operations, alongside 32 percent of its farmland.[2] So what does this legislation do in practice?

Georgia's RTF Law at a Glance

Georgia's RTF law provides no explicit protection for farmland. Rather Georgia's RTF law, like those present in the other forty-nine states, centers on protecting certain types of operations from nuisance suits when they impact neighboring property, for example through noise or pollution. Since its beginning, Georgia's RTF law has protected agricultural operations from either private or public nuisance suits. Nuisances in Georgia generally mean anything that causes hurt, inconvenience, or damage to another.[3] Georgia clarifies "public nuisances" as those that damage all people within the sphere of operations, with varying effects on individuals.[4] Private nuisances, then, are injurious effects limited to one or a few individuals.[5]

A 1988 amendment to the state's RTF nuisance suit now shields most production and processing activities related to agriculture from nuisance suits. Protected agricultural operations are defined sweepingly, including plowing soil and harvesting crops, applying chemicals, and all activities related to farm animals—from breeding to processing, producing, and packaging egg products, manufacturing feed, and commercial aquaculture.[6] The same amendment also extended protections to facilities, which among other things are defined as buildings, structures, ponds, or machinery used for the commercial production or processing of crops, livestock, poultry, and related products.[7] In a 2004 case, a couple operating a fourteen-head cattle breeding business at a loss were not able to claim an RTF defense, as

76

the court ruled that their cattle did not qualify as an agricultural operation because the couple made around $194,000 annually as airline pilots.[8]

More recently, a 2004 amendment extended protections again by broadly defining "agricultural areas" as places protected from nuisance suits. This includes agricultural areas declared so by zoning or regulations, but it also assumes that any land not zoned or regulated when the operation or facility starts qualifies as an agricultural area.[9] That same year, forest and related products were afforded protections, including agricultural support facilities like food processing plants or forest processing plants. However, rendering plant facilities—where animal tissues are used to make other materials—are explicitly not protected in the law, unlike in Arkansas.[10] For example, homeowners and residents sued a waste disposal facility and associated parties, including the farm that housed it. They alleged that the farm collected human and commercial waste and then sprayed it through a sprinkler system, generating odor, attracting pests, and damaging their ability to use and enjoy their adjacent properties. The facility tried to claim RTF protection, but the court ruled that the site in question was not an agricultural facility but rather a waste disposal facility.[11]

Prior to the 2004 amendment, a utility pole manufacturing plant tried to use the RTF law in its defense when a homeowner sued the company for interfering with her use of her property. The court found in 1985 that the agricultural inputs of the manufacturing plant were not enough to title the plant an agricultural operation.[12] However, after the 2004 amendment extended protections to agricultural support facilities, a similar case had opposite results, where the court ruled that a paper mill qualified for RTF protections as long as the plaintiffs could not prove it was operating illegally, improperly, or negligently.[13]

Two state amendments are remarkable for their unusual specificity and deviation from more traditional RTF protections. Georgia is the only state nationally that explicitly includes people (in this case, migrant farmworkers) as part of facilities. Georgia legislators in 1989 added farm labor camps or facilities for farmworkers to the list of entities protected from nuisance suits. In 2007, an amendment also added manufacturers, distributors, and those storing gypsum rock (used to make cement and plaster, among other things) to the list of those afforded RTF protections from nuisance suits.[14]

Conditions and Activities

Once agricultural operations are up and running for a year, Georgia's RTF law protects them from nuisance suits if the conditions around them change. Originally, Georgia's RTF law protected agricultural and farming operations that were there first. In a 1981 case involving a concentrated chicken and egg production facility, the court ruled that agricultural facilities had to be "in existence at least one year prior to the change in conditions in the locality in order to receive protection." The court interpreted this as protecting existing farming operations from encroachment by nonagricultural uses of land, but not protecting a change in farm operations while surrounding nonagricultural operations remained unchanged.[15]

However, the sweeping 1988 amendment provided protections for operations even if they expanded or adopted new technology. In practice, this can mean that neighbors are not considered to predate an operation if it changes from less to more intensive production. A 2002 amendment later defined changed conditions as the conversion of an area to residential use or an increased number of residences.[16] Changed conditions also can include improvements on neighboring land that come closer to an agricultural facility after its first year of operation.

Operations are not protected if a nuisance results from negligent (failing to take proper care), improper (not in line with honest standards), or illegal operations. One court found that "negligent" and "improper" do not include the emission of hydrogen sulfide gas from a Georgia-Pacific products plant, because such emissions do not violate any rule, regulation, or standard.[17]

Recently Proposed Amendments

The controversial Georgia Right to Farm Act of 2020, likely the most heavily lobbied bill of the session, passed the Georgia Senate but failed to reach the House floor.[18] The sweeping bill sought to change the law so that courts automatically awarded attorney fees to agricultural operations that successfully defended themselves, but not the other way around (when plaintiffs won). The bill also sought to strike RTF stipulations that operations are protected only relative to when they start and when they have not changed their conditions. Further, the RTF bill sought to limit the filing of nuisance suits to only two years after the alleged nuisance occurred. Current law allows suits to be filed for up to four years.[19] The proposed bill, which is expected to be reconsidered in the future, also sought to allow only those

Table 2.10 Georgia's Key RTF Provisions and National Comparison

Georgia's key RTF provisions		% U.S. states with similar RTF provisions
Operations are immune from lawsuits . . .	if boundaries or size of operations change.	34%
	if there is a change in locality.	46%
	if they use a new technology.	30%
	once in operation for a year.	48%
Operations are not immune from lawsuits . . .	if they are negligent.	46%
Other important details	RTF protects processing.	48%

who own the property and live within five miles of the source of the activity to file suit. In practice, this could limit the filing of lawsuits by those who live downstream and by those affected who are not direct owners, like family members, renters, or those without clear titles on their property (heir property owners).[20]

NOTES

1. Ga. Code § 41-1-7 (2021).
2. U.S. Department of Agriculture, *USDA Quick Stats Tool: June 1980 Survey, Georgia*, distributed by National Agricultural Statistics Service, accessed December 13, 2020, https://quickstats.nass.usda.gov/results/8616824F-050A-3B06-BA3E-51D9E71DA571; "2021 State Agriculture Overview: Georgia," U.S. Department of Agriculture, National Agricultural Statistics Service, accessed October 21, 2022, https://www.nass.usda.gov/Quick_Stats/Ag_Overview/stateOverview.php?state=GEORGIA.
3. Ga. Code § 41-1-1 (2021).
4. Ga. Code § 41-1-2 (2021).
5. Ga. Code § 41-1-2 (2021).
6. Ga. Code § 41-1-7(b)(3)(A)–(K) (2021).
7. Ga. Code § 41-1-7(b)(2) (2021).
8. *Condon v. Vickery*, 606 S.E.2d 336 (Ga. Ct. App. 2004).
9. Ga. Code § 41-1-7(b)(1) (2021).
10. Ga. Code § 41-1-7(b)(3.1) (2021).
11. *Alexander v. Hulsey Envtl. Servs., Inc.*, 702 S.E.2d 435 (Ga. Ct. App. 2011).
12. *Roberts v. S. Wood Piedmont Co.*, 328 S.E.2d 391 (Ga. Ct. App. 1985).
13. *Georgia-Pacific Consumer Products, LP v. Ratner*, 812 S.E.2d 120 (Ga. Ct. App. 2018).
14. Ga. Code § 41-1-7(b)(4.2) (2021).
15. *Herrin v. Opatut*, 281 S.E.2d 575 (Ga. 1981).
16. Ga. Code § 41-1-7(b)(5) (2021).

17. *Georgia-Pacific Consumer Prods.*, 812 S.E.2d 120.
18. Dave Williams, "Right to Farm Act Narrowly Clears Georgia Senate," *Moultrie (Ga.) Observer*, June 18, 2020; Jim Galloway, "AJC Exclusive—Behind Stalled Agriculture Bill Is Farmer vs. Farmer," *Atlanta Journal-Constitution*, February 26, 2020.
19. Ga. Code § 9-3-32 (2021).
20. Dave Williams, "Right to Farm Debate Likely to Return to General Assembly," *Moultrie (Ga.) Observer*, November 29, 2020; Jim Galloway, "AJC Exclusive—Behind Stalled Agriculture Bill Is Farmer vs. Farmer."

Hawaii

Hawaii's legislature passed its right-to-farm law with the stated intention of stopping "the premature removal of lands from agricultural use" and ensuring future investment in agriculture. Related statutes declare the preservation and promotion of farming to be part of the public purpose.[1] However, since Hawaii first enacted its RTF law in 1982, the number of operations has grown by 59 percent while the number of acres in farmland has dropped by 44 percent.[2] So what does this law do in practice?

Hawaii's RTF Law at a Glance

Hawaii's Right to Farm Act provides no explicit protection for farmland. Like those present in the other forty-nine states, the state's law centers on protecting certain types of farming operations from nuisance suits when they impact neighboring property, for example through noise or pollution.[3] Hawaii has a lengthy definition of farming operations, which includes commercial agricultural operations that pertain to silviculture, aquaculture, livestock production, and planting, cultivating, harvesting, and processing of crops; apiary products; plant and animal production for nonfood uses; and the farming or ranching of any plant or animal species in a controlled salt, brackish, or freshwater environment. The definition also specifically includes noises, odors, dust, and fumes emanating from commercial agricultural or aquaculture facilities; the operation of machinery and irrigation pumps; ground and aerial seeding and spraying; and the application of chemical fertilizers and pesticides. Roadside stands, food establishments, farmers' markets, food hubs, and commercial kitchens selling value-added and agricultural goods grown in Hawaii also receive protections.[4] Hawaii is only one of a handful of states that also includes employment and the use of labor as part of the definition of farming operations.

Conditions and Activities

Hawaii's original RTF law required farm operations to meet a series of conditions to receive protection from nuisance suits: (1) the farming operation could not have been a nuisance when it began; (2) the conditions surrounding the farm changed after it was established; (3) the farm lawfully operated at least a year prior to the nuisance claim; and (4) the farm operation was not operating negligently or improperly.

The current law in Hawaii has removed these requirements for protection. Hawaii now defines nuisance expansively, meaning RTF protections apply in a variety of legal contexts. Amendments define "nuisance" as any claim that meets the definition in the statute, regardless of whether the suit calls it nuisance, negligence, trespass, or any other similar cause of action. Nuisance defense also applies to interference with reasonable use and enjoyment of land (smoke, odors, dust, noise, or vibration). However, the definition does not protect an alleged nuisance that involves water pollution or flooding.[5]

The law stipulates that farm operations cannot be declared a public nuisance in Hawaii if they use generally accepted agricultural and management practices. When they use such practices, the law provides a rebuttable presumption that a farming operation does not constitute a nuisance.[6] In practice, this means farm activities are assumed to be acceptable unless proved otherwise. In light of Hawaii's broad protection of farm operations from nuisance suits, the meaning of accepted agricultural and management practices has proved important in court. In one case, with various rulings appealed six times, the court made an operation's awareness about practices key to liability. In the case, neighbors sued the owners of the land, who leased it to Pioneer Hi-Bred International Inc., for negligence, nuisance, and trespass in regard to its genetically modified organism test fields. Before leasing to Pioneer, the landlords conducted sugarcane farming on the property and neighbors complained then of dust drifting into their homes. The landlords responded by paying cleaning costs. The plaintiffs argued that because of this history, the landlords should have been aware of the risks when they rented the land to Pioneer. The court ruled that there was no evidence to support that the landowners knew about or consented to activities on the property that would create a nuisance.[7] In a related case, the court also ruled against neighbors in favor of Pioneer, stating that "farming is not inherently a nuisance."[8]

82 HAWAII

Table 2.11 Hawaii's Key RTF Provisions and National Comparison

Hawaii's key RTF provisions		% U.S. states with similar RTF provisions
Operations are immune from lawsuits . . .	if they pollute water.	36%
Other important details	RTF protects processing	48%

Local Governance

Hawaii's RTF law prevents courts, public servants, and public employees (including any local government actor) from declaring farming operations nuisances, relative to the aforementioned criteria. However, the statute also contains a clause that preserves the rights of the state to protect the public's health, safety, and welfare. It is unclear how these two provisions interact, as they have yet to play out in court.[9]

County zoning laws are limited relative to agricultural districts and their contiguous lands. Zoning laws restrict counties' capacity to pass ordinances/regulations that interfere with or restrain farming operations. These zoning laws use the same definition for farming operations as the RTF law but also include many other protected operations and activities.[10]

For example, Pioneer Hi-Bred, Syngenta Seeds, and several genetics corporations sued the County of Kauai for an ordinance that was designed to regulate the application of restricted-use pesticides and the planting of modified crops. The ordinance would have required corporate agricultural entities to report the use of restricted-use pesticides and the possession of GMOs to nearby neighbors; create pesticide buffer zones; mandate a county environmental and public health study related to large-scale commercial agricultural entities; and require anyone who violated the ordinance to pay a civil fine of at least $10,000. The court ruled that the ordinance was invalid because the RTF law preempted it.[11]

NOTES

1. Haw. Rev. Stat. § 165-3 (2021).
2. U.S. Department of Commerce, "Table 1. Farms, Land in Farms, and Land Use: 1982 and Earlier Census Years," in *1982 Census of Agriculture, Volume 1: Geographic Area Series, Part 11: Hawaii State and County Data, Chapter 1: State Data* (Washington, D.C.: U.S. Bureau of the Census, 1984), https://agcensus.library.cornell.edu/wp-content/uploads/1982-Hawaii -CHAPTER_1_State_Data-121-Table-01.pdf; "2021 State Agriculture Overview: Hawaii," U.S. Department of Agriculture, National Agricultural Statistics Service, accessed October 21, 2022, https://www.nass.usda.gov/Quick_Stats/Ag_Overview/stateOverview.php ?state=HAWAII.
3. Haw. Rev. Stat. § 165-2 (2021).
4. Haw. Rev. Stat. § 205-2 (2021).
5. Haw. Rev. Stat. § 165-2 (2021).
6. Haw. Rev. Stat. § 165-4 (2021).
7. *Aana v. Pioneer Hi-Bred Int'l, Inc.*, 965 F. Supp. 2d 1157 (D. Haw. 2013).
8. *Casey v. Pioneer Hi-Bred Int'l, Inc.*, No. 12-00655 LEK-BMK, 2013 WL 1701873 (D. Haw. Apr. 17, 2013).
9. Haw. Rev. Stat. § 165-4 (2021).
10. Haw. Rev. Stat. §§ 165-4, 205-3.5 (2021).
11. Haw. Rev. Stat. § 165-2 (2021).

Idaho

When enacting its right-to-farm law, Idaho legislators called farming "a natural right" that was threatened by urbanization. They advocated the RTF law as a tool to stop the "premature removal of the lands from agricultural uses."[1] Since first passed in 1981, the number of farm operators in the state has grown by just over 1 percent, while the acres of land farmed have dropped by 23 percent.[2] So what does this legislation do in practice?

Idaho's RTF Law at a Glance

Idaho's state law provides no explicit protection for farmland. Rather, Idaho's RTF law, like those present in the other forty-nine states, centers on protecting agricultural and farming operations from nuisance suits when they impact neighboring property, for example through noise or pollution. In a 2002 case, landowners neighboring a proposed subdivision attempted to use the RTF law to stop the conversion of land into residential lots. While future owners in the subdivision would have RTF deed restrictions, the plaintiffs alleged that surrounding dairies and feedlots still could be subject to nuisance suits. However, the court ruled that this was speculation.[3] Thus, the RTF law provided no such land use protections.

Idaho's RTF protections apply to either private nuisance suits (those brought by people, like neighbors) or public nuisance suits (those brought by the government on behalf of the general public). Prior to 2011, only agricultural operations—but not facilities and expansions—were protected in the law. For example, the Idaho Supreme Court ruled in 2000 that the expansion of a farrow-to-finish hog operation qualified as a nuisance.[4] Likewise, in a 1995 case, the court ruled that a feedlot could not expand from approximately 1,000–2,500 cattle to 4,900 cattle and still receive RTF

85

protections.[5] In a 1983 case, the court similarly did not apply RTF protections to another cattle feedlot that expanded.[6]

However, controversial 2011 amendments advocated by farm industry lobbyists made these operations consequently protected by adding "expansion" to the law.[7] In addition, the amendments provide explicit protections for facilities, defining them as buildings, structures, ponds, and machinery (among other things) used in an agricultural operation.[8] Protected agricultural operations include the production of animal and crop products, application of chemicals, and the production and processing of agricultural products and by-products.[9]

Conditions and Activities

Idaho's law protects agricultural operations, facilities, and their expansion from nuisance suits once they have been in operation for one year.[10] The law also protects agricultural activities from nuisance lawsuits if the area around them changes.[11] But if the area around them remains unchanged, agricultural operations may not receive RTF protections. For example, a riding arena built adjacent to a neighboring property did not predate its neighbors. Thus, the court ruled that the Bar Double Dot Quarter Horses LLC and the couple running it were not entitled to RTF protections.[12] In another case, families and their children with preexisting health conditions filed a class action suit for damages, future costs of exposure, expenses of medical monitoring, and other relief related to the burning of grass seed.[13] The North Idaho Farmers Association and affiliated farmers alleged that the RTF law protected them from such claims. The Idaho Supreme Court ruled that the children and their families predated the nuisance and were not part of any urbanization. Thus, the RTF protections did not apply. Directly after, the Idaho Farm Bureau Federation introduced a bill to immunize farmers from lawsuits based on smoke and odor in the context of trespass laws.[14] The law passed but was later repealed in 2008.[15]

Agricultural operations are protected so long as they use generally recognized agricultural practices or if they comply with state or federally issued permits. In 2011, however, a controversial bill proposed transferring some confined animal feeding operations processes from the Department of Environmental Quality to the Idaho Department of Agriculture.[16] Today, the Department of Environmental Quality and the Idaho Department of Agriculture split responsibilities when it comes to CAFOs.[17] Relatedly, the

Table 2.12 Idaho's Key RTF Provisions and National Comparison

Idaho's key RTF provisions		% U.S. states with similar RTF provisions
Operations are immune from lawsuits . . .	once in operation for a year.	48%
	if there is a change in locality.	46%
	if boundaries or size of operations change.	34%
Operations are not immune from lawsuits . . .	if they do not comply with other laws.	50%
	if they are a nuisance from the start.	38%
	if they are negligent.	46%
	if they do not comply with federal laws.	62%
	if they do not comply with state laws.	68%
Other important details	RTF supersedes local ordinances and laws.	62%
	RTF protects processing.	48%

RTF law does not define what "generally recognized agricultural practices" means.

Operations also must conform with federal, state, and local laws and regulations and not adversely affect the public's health and safety.[18] For example, one court found in 2020 that a composting facility had to comply with the Department of Environmental Quality solid waste management rules, even though the facility tried to claim RTF immunity.[19] It is not clear how the RTF law interacts with the Department of Environmental Quality's standards for odor.[20]

Local Government

In 1994, an amendment to Idaho's RTF law drastically reduced the power of cities, counties, taxing districts, and other political subdivisions to regulate agricultural operations using generally accepted agricultural practices.[21] In addition to stating that these different levels of local government had no such power, the amendment also removed a sentence that made an exception, which formerly allowed local governments to act when operations were negligent (failure to take proper care) or improper (wrongful acts, like violence or trespass). Another amendment in 1997 gave local governments the capacity to require "nuisance waivers"—regarding such things as flies, odors, animal noises, and other operations found annoying, unpleasant,

IDAHO 87

or obnoxious—when people bought properties.[22] Then in 2011, yet another amendment further extended the policing power of the state over local government, stating, "Any such ordinance or resolution shall be void and shall have no force or effect."[23]

As noted earlier, the RTF law does not prevent political subdivisions from granting land use permits that transform agricultural land into residential uses.[24]

NOTES

1. Idaho Code § 22-4501 (2021).
2. U.S. Department of Agriculture, *USDA Quick Stats Tool: June 1981 Survey, Idaho*, distributed by National Agricultural Statistics Service, accessed December 13, 2020, https://quickstats .nass.usda.gov/results/B4A3C39B-9AFD-3C4A-8B8D-5248961C9922; "2021 State Agriculture Overview: Idaho," U.S. Department of Agriculture, National Agricultural Statistics Service, accessed October 21, 2022, https://www.nass.usda.gov/Quick_Stats/Ag_Overview /stateOverview.php?state=IDAHO.
3. *Proesch v. Canyon Cty. Bd. of Comm'rs*, 44 P.3d 1173 (Idaho 2002).
4. *Crea v. Crea*, 16 P.3d 922 (Idaho 2000).
5. *Payne v. Skaar*, 900 P.2d 1352 (Idaho 1995).
6. *Carpenter v. Double R Cattle Co., Inc.*, 669 P.2d 643 (Idaho Ct. App. 1983).
7. Laura Lundquist, "Lawmaker Will Introduce Bill to Protect Confined Animal Feeding Operations in Idaho," *Twin Falls (Idaho) Times-News*, February 21, 2011; "Speaker Denney, Right-to-Farm and the Arrogance of Power," *Twin Falls Times-News*, February 24, 2013; Jon Norstog, "Ag Bill," *Idaho State Journal* (Pocatello), March 13, 2011; "Panel Backs Changes in Right to Farm Act," *Lewiston (Idaho) Morning Tribune*, March 23, 2011.
8. Idaho Code § 22-4502(1) (2021).
9. Idaho Code § 22-4502(2) (2021).
10. Idaho Code § 22-4503 (2021).
11. Idaho Code § 22-4503 (2021).
12. *McVicars v. Christensen*, 320 P.3d 948 (Idaho 2014); *Crea*, 16 P.3d 922.
13. *Moon v. N. Idaho Farmers Ass'n*, No. CV 2002 3890, 2002 WL 32102995 (Idaho Dist. Nov. 19, 2002).
14. "Idaho Legislature 2003. Attorney: Laws May Be Unconstitutional," *Twin Falls (Idaho) Times-News*, March 13, 2003.
15. See Idaho Code §§ 22-4801 to 22-4804, which were repealed by 2008 Idaho Sess. Laws ch. 71, § 4 (H.B. 557). See also *Moon v. N. Idaho Farmers Ass'n*, 140 Idaho 536, 539 (Idaho 2004) ("HB 391, which was passed as an emergency measure, amended the Smoke Management and Crop Residue Disposal Act of 1999, I.C. § 22-4801 et seq., and effectively extinguished liability for all North Idaho grass farmers that burn in compliance with its provisions. Of particular significance, HB 391 amended portions of I.C. § 22-4803 and added a new statute, I.C. § 22-4803A").
16. "New CAFO Bills Carry a Stench," *Idaho State Journal* (Pocatello), March 15, 2011.
17. See "Concentrated Animal Feeding Operations," Idaho Department of Environmental Quality, accessed December 16, 2020, https://www.deq.idaho.gov/water-quality/waste water/cafos/. Also see "Rules Governing Beef Cattle Animal Feeding Operations," Idaho Department of Agriculture, accessed December 16, 2020, https://adminrules.idaho.gov /rules/current/02/020415.pdf.
18. See Idaho Code § 22-4503 (2021).
19. *Department of Environmental Quality v. Gibson*, 461 P.3d 706 (Idaho 2020).

20. N. S. Nokkentved, "State: Odors Can Close Dairies. Difficulty Lies in What Constitutes a Problem, Office States," *Twin Falls (Idaho) Times-News*, November 4, 2000.
21. 1994 Idaho Sess. Laws ch. 107 (H.B. 695) (repealing and then adding Idaho Code § 22-4504).
22. 1997 Idaho Sess. Laws ch. 341 (H.B. 1145) (amending Idaho Code § 22-4504). See also Betsy Z. Russell, "Bill Protects Farm Practices from Lawsuits: New Neighbors Would Waive Right to Sue Over 'Nuisances,'" *Idaho Spokesman-Review* (Spokane, Wash.), February 7, 1997.
23. 2011 Idaho Sess. Laws ch. 229 (H.B. 210) (amending Idaho Code § 22-4504).
24. *Proesch*, 44 P.3d 1173.

Illinois

Legislators justified Illinois's 1981 right-to-farm law and subsequent amendments as tools to prevent the loss of farmland.[1] Since that time, the number of farms in the state has dropped by 28 percent, with 6 percent fewer acres of farmland.[2] So what does this legislation do in practice?

Illinois's RTF Law at a Glance

Although "land" is used in its definition of "farming," Illinois's Farm Nuisance Suit Act provides no explicit protection for land or for family farmers. Rather, Illinois's RTF law, like those present in the other forty-nine states, centers on protecting certain types of operations from nuisance suits when they impact neighboring property, for example through noise or pollution. In 2018, the law expanded its definition of farming to add horses to an expansive list that includes crops, livestock, and "any other agricultural or horticultural use or combination."[3] Following a 1995 amendment to Illinois's RTF law, the burden of litigation fees falls on the plaintiffs (typically the local government and neighboring property owners) in the event they lose in court and the defendant takes no corrective action.[4] In contrast, defendants (typically agricultural operations) are not required to pay such fees in the event they lose. This fee-shifting provision was upheld by an Illinois court in 2020. Local property owners sued corporate hog farm operators, arguing that the provision was a violation of the special legislation clause within Illinois's state constitution.[5] The court held in favor of the corporate concentrated animal feeding operation, determining that the fee-shifting provision was not a violation of the state constitution.[6]

90

Conditions and Activities

Once in operation for one year, farms and their related properties cannot be declared a nuisance as long as the operation was not a nuisance at the time it began.[7] Even if conditions change in the surrounding area, ownership changes, or the type of agricultural use changes, the one-year time clock for immunity does not restart so long as land use remains agricultural.[8] Courts have treated new or changed ordinances as a "changed condition," in effect barring lawsuits that come after any agricultural use.[9] Any agricultural use can be treated as the same agricultural use, meaning the clock does not restart when a farm changes, for example, from a corn field to a CAFO.

What constitutes a change in the surrounding area plays an important role in RTF outcomes. In a 2012 case, the Illinois Supreme Court ruled that a new cattle operation was not a nuisance, because the owners of the adjacent land and farmhouse had changed. A father had willed his century-old farmhouse, which was on 160 acres of farmland, to his son, who was one of the plaintiffs. While the father had farmed the land long prior to the cattle operation's arrival, the court considered a family exchange of landownership a "changed condition" for the old farmhouse. However, it did not apply the same level of scrutiny to the new cattle operation.[10]

To receive RTF protection, farms must not be operating improperly or negligently. The law still allows persons to recover damages for injuries caused by (1) pollution of water; (2) any changed conditions in the waters of any stream; or (3) harm caused by the overflow of water onto land.[11] While air pollution is not similarly referred to, courts have held that the Farm Nuisance Suit Act does not provide a defense against air pollution violations under the state's Environmental Protection Act.[12]

Local Government

Illinois's Farm Nuisance Suit Act does not address the power of local government but still has an impact on the validity of ordinances. In 2015, a court used the RTF law as a basis for denying a village's enforcement of a nuisance ordinance against a farm.[13] One month prior to the transition of a tree and grass nursery to a commercial corn and soybean growing operation, the village amended an existing ordinance prohibiting farm animals to also prohibit other types of commercial farming. The court ruled the ordinance was invalid, stating, "It is well established that municipalities may not adopt ordinances which infringe upon the spirit of the state law or are repugnant

Table 2.13 Illinois's Key RTF Provisions and National Comparison

Illinois's key RTF provisions		% U.S. states with similar RTF provisions
Operations are immune from lawsuits . . .	once in operation for a year.	48%
	if there is a change in locality.	46%
Operations are not immune from lawsuits . . .	if they are a nuisance from the start.	38%
	if they are negligent.	46%
	if they pollute water.	36%
Other important details	Attorney fees are awarded to prevailing defendant.	34%

to the general policy of the state. . . . A local ordinance which infringes upon the legislative intent of a state statute is preempted." In addition, the Illinois Counties Code and the Illinois Livestock Management Facilities Act explicitly limit the power of counties to regulate nuisances when the land is not zoned or is zoned as agricultural.[14]

Attorney Fees

A farming operation that is a prevailing defendant can recover costs and expenses, including attorney fees, "reasonably incurred" in its defense. Prevailing defendants are those with the final court order or judgment in their favor, which does not include a negotiated settlement or taking any corrective action.[15] Notably, the reverse is not true: prevailing plaintiffs are not automatically awarded attorney fees, which may have a chilling effect on the filing of nuisance litigation.

NOTES

1. 740 Ill. Comp. Stat. 70/0.01 (1981); "Farm Bureau Adopts Land Policy," *Farmers' Weekly Review* 59, no. 47 (May 7, 1981): 1.
2. U.S. Department of Commerce, "Table 1. Farms, Land in Farms, and Land Use: 1982 and Earlier Census Years," in *1982 Census of Agriculture, Volume 1: Geographic Area Series, Part 13: Illinois State and County Data, Chapter 1: State Data* (Washington, D.C.: U.S. Bureau of the Census, 1984), https://agcensus.library.cornell.edu/wp-content/uploads/1982-Illinois -CHAPTER_1_State_Data-121-Table-01.pdf; "2021 State Agriculture Overview: Illinois," U.S. Department of Agriculture, National Agricultural Statistics Service, accessed October 21, 2022, https://www.nass.usda.gov/Quick_Stats/Ag_Overview/stateOverview.php ?state=ILLINOIS.

3. 740 Ill. Comp. Stat. 70/2 (2021). Effective January 1, 2018, the law was amended to add horse boarding and horse keeping. See 2017 Ill. Laws ch. 447 (S.B. 1529) (amending 740 Ill. Comp. Stat. 70/2).
4. 1995 Ill. Laws ch. 256 (H.B. 1940) (adding 740 Ill. Comp. Stat 70/4.5).
5. *Marsh v. Sandstone N., LLC*, 179 N.E.3d 402 (Ill. App. Ct. 2020).
6. *Marsh*, 179 N.E.3d 402.
7. 740 Ill. Comp. Stat. 70/0.01, et seq. (2021).
8. *Vill. of Chadwick v. Nelson*, 95 N.E.3d 1230 (Ill. App. Ct. 2017).
9. *Vill. of LaFayette v. Brown*, 27 N.E.3d 687 (Ill. App. Ct. 2015).
10. *Toftoy v. Rosenwinkel*, 983 N.E.2d 463 (Ill. 2012).
11. 740 Ill. Comp. Stat. 70/4 (2021).
12. *Donetta Gott, Lyndell Chaplin, Gary Wells, Ernest L. Ellison v. M'orr Pork, Inc.*, No. PCB#96-68, 1997 WL 85191 (Ill. Pol. Control. Bd. Feb. 20, 1997) (noting that the Illinois Supreme Court has held that actions under the Environmental Protection Act "alleging air pollution are distinct from common law nuisance claims" and quoting *Incinerator, Inc. v. Pollution Control Bd.*, 319 N.E.2d 794, 799 (Ill. 1974) ("violations of the Act here in question are not defined in terms of nuisances")).
13. *Vill. of LaFayette*, 27 N.E.3d 687.
14. 55 Ill. Comp. Stat. 5/5-12001 (2021); 510 Ill. Comp. Stat. 77/12 (2021).
15. 740 Ill. Comp. Stat. 70/4.5 (2021).

Indiana

Indiana declares in its right-to-farm law the conservation, protection, development, and improvement of agricultural land for production as its state policy.[1] But since the law first passed in 1981, the number of farms has dropped by 36 percent and the acres of farmland by 11 percent.[2] So what does the state's RTF legislation do in practice?

Indiana's RTF Law at a Glance

Indiana's law provides no protection tailored to farmland. Rather, Indiana's RTF law, like those present in the other forty-nine states, protects operations spanning agriculture, forestry, and industry at large from nuisance suits when their activities impact neighboring property, for example through noise or pollution.[3] The law defines agricultural operations as any facility that is used for the production of crops, livestock, poultry, or the growing of timber.[4] Agricultural operations also include facilities used for the production of livestock, poultry, or horticultural products. Forestry operations include facilities, activities, and equipment related to raising, managing, harvesting, and removing trees. Industrial operations include facilities used for the manufacture of a product from other products; the transformation of a material from one form to another; the mining of material and related mine activities; and the storage or disposition of a product or material.[5] Despite the RTF law's protection of industries well beyond agriculture, the Indiana courts contend that the law, "by its plain terms, was intended to prohibit nonagricultural land uses from being the basis of a nuisance suit against an established agricultural operation."[6]

RTF Conditions and Protections

In the original 1981 version of the law, agricultural operations that had operated continuously at their location for more than one year were protected from nuisance suits in the event of a significant change, with the exception of a significant change to the operation's hours or type.[7] Amendments in 2005 made a series of major clarifications regarding what is considered a protected significant change.[8] Changes protected from nuisance suits include (1) the conversion from one type of agricultural operation to another type of agricultural operation; (2) a change in the ownership or size of the agricultural operation; (3) enrollment, reduction, or cessation of participation in a government program; or (4) the adoption of new technology. Indiana courts have interpreted these provisions to protect operations that change from crop and smaller-scale livestock production to industrial-scale CAFOs. For example, the Indiana Court of Appeals held that a farm that converted from cropland with 100 dairy cows to a 760-head dairy CAFO did not constitute a significant change.[9] The court stated, "The Act removes claims against existing farm operations that later undergo a transition from one type of agriculture to another." The court of appeals similarly ruled, in a later case, that the transition from being a row-crop farm to an 8,000-hog CAFO did not constitute a significant change under the 2005 amendments, even though it would have prior to that time.[10]

Under Indiana's law, agricultural operations receive RTF protections only if they have been operating continuously on the same area of land for more than one year.[11] An operation can experience an interruption that lasts for one year or less and still be considered to have operated continuously.[12] In addition, an agricultural operation will be protected only if it would not have been a nuisance at the time it began operating at its present location.[13]

Indiana's RTF law stipulates that it will not protect an agricultural operation from a nuisance lawsuit in the case of negligence.[14] Recently, neighbors that predated the construction of a hog CAFO filed a nuisance suit alleging, in part, that the facility was negligently operated.[15] However, the court ruled that there was no evidence it was negligently operated or that the CAFO violated Indiana Department of Environmental Management regulations. The court stated that the siting of a CAFO at a particular location, in and of itself, cannot constitute a negligent operation under the state's RTF law. The court thus ruled that the negligence exception under the RTF act did not apply. The plaintiffs then attempted to appeal the matter to the Supreme Court of the United States, arguing that the Indiana RTF law violates the

Table 2.14 Indiana's Key RTF Provisions and National Comparison

Indiana's key RTF provisions		% U.S. states with similar RTF provisions
Operations are immune from lawsuits . . .	if boundaries or size of operations change.	34%
	if there is a change in locality.	46%
	if they use a new technology.	30%
	if they produce a different product.	26%
	once in operation for a year.	48%
	if there is an ownership change.	26%
Operations are not immune from lawsuits . . .	if they are a nuisance from the start.	38%
	if they are negligent.	46%
Other important details	Attorney fees are awarded to prevailing defendant.	34%
	Attorney fees are awarded to prevailing party.	14%
	RTF protects processing.	48%
	RTF protects mining operations.	4%

Takings Clause of the U.S. Constitution. Specifically, they argued that the law provides complete immunity from nuisance and trespass liability, even when neighbors predate the construction of an agricultural operation that causes noxious substances to invade their homes and remove their ability to use and enjoy their property.[16] The case, however, was recently denied review by the U.S. Supreme Court.[17]

Local Government

The RTF act does not explicitly address how local governments may or may not regulate agriculture. Another law, however, stipulates that the Department of Agriculture "shall promote the growth of agricultural business" by assisting such businesses in the permitting process.[18] Other statutes limit county zoning and regulations of agricultural land.[19]

Attorney Fees

Indiana's RTF law stands apart from other states when it comes to costs and attorney fees. This is because the law allows fees and costs to be awarded not only to the prevailing defendant (typically the agricultural operation) but also to the prevailing plaintiff, under certain circumstances.[20] A 2012 amendment clarifies that if a nuisance case brought under the RTF law is deemed frivolous, the successful defendant or plaintiff is awarded costs and reasonable attorney fees.[21] While not defined in the state's law, "frivolous" typically means that a party involved (either defendant or plaintiff) takes action even when that party knows the claim does not have sufficient merit to win. The law clarifies that simply not prevailing in a lawsuit is not enough to conclude that the action was frivolous.[22] In addition, if a county, city, or town brings a successful nuisance action under Indiana's RTF law, it can recover reasonable attorney fees incurred.[23] A governmental body has yet to be a party in an Indiana RTF case, while CAFOs and/or business firms are winning more cases in Indiana than anywhere else in the nation.[24]

NOTES

1. Ind. Code § 32-30-6-9 (2021).
2. U.S. Department of Agriculture, *USDA Quick Stats Tool: June 1981 Survey, Indiana*, distributed by National Agricultural Statistics Service, accessed October 14, 2020, https://quickstats.nass.usda.gov/results/5C5D88A1-28E2-3007-90EF-A426767F3940; "2021 State Agriculture Overview: Indiana," U.S. Department of Agriculture, National Agricultural Statistics Service, accessed October 21, 2022, https://www.nass.usda.gov/Quick_Stats/Ag_Overview/stateOverview.php?state=INDIANA.
3. Ind. Code § 32-30-6-9 (2021). See also *Himsel v. Himsel*, 122 N.E.3d 935 (Ind. Ct. App. 2019) (quoting Ind. Code Ann. § 15-11-2-6, also known as "The Agricultural Canon," enacted in 2014, which provides, "The general assembly declares that it is the policy of the state to conserve, protect, and encourage the development and improvement of agriculture, agricultural businesses, and agricultural land for the production of food, fuel, fiber, and other agricultural products. The Indiana Code shall be construed to protect the rights of farmers to choose among all generally accepted farming and livestock production practices, including the use of ever changing technology.").
4. Ind. Code § 32-30-6-1 (2021).
5. Ind. Code § 32-30-6-9 (2021) stipulates a "policy toward agricultural and industrial operation." Industrial operations are defined in Ind. Code § 32-30-6-2.
6. *Himsel*, 122 N.E.3d 935 (quoting *TDM Farms, Inc. v. Wilhoite Family Farm, LLC*, 969 N.E.2d 97 (Ind. Ct. App. 2012)).
7. 1981 Ind. Acts 288 (adding Ind. Code § 34-1-52-4(e) (1981)) (now codified at Ind. Code § 32-30-6-9).
8. See 2005 Ind. Acts 23 (S. Enrolled Acts 267) (amending Ind. Code § 32-30-6-9).
9. *Parker v. Obert's Legacy Dairy, LLC*, 988 N.E.2d 319 (Ind. Ct. App. 2013).
10. *Himsel*, 122 N.E.3d 935.
11. Ind. Code §§ 32-30-6-3, 32-30-6-9 (2021).
12. Ind. Code § 32-30-6-9 (2021).
13. Ind. Code § 32-30-6-9 (2021).
14. Ind. Code § 32-30-6-9 (2021).
15. *Himsel*, 122 N.E.3d 935.
16. Petition for Writ of Certiorari in *Himsel v. Himsel*, 122 N.E.3d 935 (Ind. Ct. App. 2019), *cert. denied*, 141 S. Ct. 364 (U.S. Oct. 5, 2020) (No. 20-72); Sarah Bowman, "Does Right to Farm

Act Violate Constitution? Hog Farm's Neighbors Say It Decimates Their Property Value," *Evansville (Ind.) Courier and Press,* July 27, 2020.

17. *Himsel v. 4/9 Livestock, LLC,* 141 S. Ct. 364 (2020).
18. Ind. Code § 15-11-2-6 (2021).
19. Ind. Code § 36-7-4-616 (2021).
20. Ind. Code § 32-30-6-9.5 (2021).
21. See 2012 Ind. Acts 73 (H.E.A. 1091) (adding Ind. Code § 32-30-6-9.5).
22. Ind. Code § 32-30-6-9.5 (2021).
23. Ind. Code § 32-30-6-7 (2021).
24. See the introduction for more details on outcomes of Indiana cases compared to those in the rest of the nation.

Iowa

Legislators justified Iowa's suite of right-to-farm laws as a tool to preserve "private property rights" and "the availability and use of agricultural land for agricultural production."[1] Yet since such legislation was first enacted by name in 1982, the number of farm operations in Iowa has dropped by 33 percent and the number of acres farmed by 10 percent.[2] So how do Iowa's RTF laws work in practice?

Iowa's RTF Laws at a Glance

Iowa's RTF laws do not protect land from urban sprawl, nor do they protect private property rights broadly. Like those present in the other forty-nine states, Iowa's RTF laws protect animal feeding operations (AFOs) and farming operations from nuisance suits when their activities impact neighboring property, for example through noise or pollution.[3] Iowa specifically defines nuisances as the construction of buildings that emit noxious odors and offensive smells that interfere with the health, comfort, or property of individuals or the public; water pollution; and the collection of offal or filthy or noisome substances.[4] Iowa defines farming operations broadly and includes any condition or activity that occurs on a farm in connection with the production of farm products and crop raising and storage; the care or feeding of livestock; the disposal of related wastes; the marketing of products; the creation of noise, odor, dust, or fumes; the application of chemical fertilizers, conditioners, insecticides, pesticides, or herbicides; and the employment and use of labor.[5]

In addition to protecting farming operations at large, Iowa also safeguards from nuisance suits those areas zoned as agricultural, understood as a designated parcel of land (generally greater than 300 acres) that encourages agricultural activities related to farm operations.[6] According to statutory law, farming operations located in agricultural areas automatically receive protection from nuisance claims regardless of when the farm began operating or whether it has expanded.[7] These agricultural areas are designated through county zoning.

Initially, the Iowa Supreme Court in 1998 ruled that these agricultural areas constitute an unjust taking, violating the constitutional protections of private property ownership. In fact, Iowa—the state with the most hogs in the nation—was the only state where portions of the RTF law were found unconstitutional. In *Bormann v. Board of Supervisors*, the Iowa Supreme Court ruled in 1998 that the state's RTF law created an easement without just compensation for activities that would have been considered a nuisance if the land had not been designated an agricultural area.[8] The Iowa Supreme Court cited the state constitution, noting that it provides for the protection of private property from takings without just compensation.[9] The Iowa Farm Bureau openly expressed its disappointment with the court ruling.[10] In a consequent 2004 case, *Gacke v. Pork Xtra, LLC*, property owners sued neighboring hog confinement operators for nuisance. The Iowa Supreme Court upheld a lower court's ruling, confirming that the RTF statute violated Iowa's constitutional protections against excessive state exercises of power.[11] In a 2006 letter, Jeff Vonk—then director for Iowa's Department of Natural Resources—concurred, calling large-scale concentrated animal feeding operations uncompensated takings by "corporate neighbors."[12] For many years, Iowa courts continued to affirm that the RTF law was in part unconstitutional and thus not a defense if certain conditions were met.[13] In 2016, a statewide coalition called for a moratorium on hog confinements, which a spokesperson for then governor Terry Branstad called "extreme."[14]

However, these constitutional limits on RTF laws no longer hold. In 2022, the Iowa Supreme Court heard a nuisance case pertaining to a limited liability partnership hog operation and overturned *Gacke*. The court argued that the three-pronged test for unconstitutionality was an outlier in Iowa law when compared with RTF laws in other states.[15] Additionally, the court held that the RTF statutes do not constitute an unconstitutional use of state police power. However, the court ruled that nuisance claims are not entirely barred by the RTF laws, as they provide only partial immunity from nuisance claims.[16]

Conditions and Activities

Iowa's RTF laws protect farming operations, AFOs, and feedlots from both private nuisance suits (filed by individuals) and public nuisance suits (filed on behalf of the public by the government). Since a 1993 amendment, the plaintiff must first go through the state's farm mediation service prior to bringing a nuisance lawsuit in court. Farming operations lose nuisance suit protections if they violate federal or state laws; if they are operated negligently; if they pollute waterways or adjacent land; or if they contribute to soil erosion.[17]

Outside of agricultural areas, RTF protections still exist at large for AFOs and feedlots, which include areas where animals are "totally roofed" and areas used for the confined feeding and growth of animals prior to slaughter.[18] RTF protections for livestock feedlots have existed in Iowa since 1976 and apply if the feedlot adheres to both regulatory provisions set forth by Iowa's Department of Environmental Quality and local zoning ordinances.[19] RTF protections for AFOs were enacted in 1995 and apply regardless of when the AFO began or whether it has undergone an expansion. Activities protected include the care or transport of animals; the treatment, disposal, or application of manure; and the creation of noise, odor, dust, or fumes.[20] However, nuisance claims can be brought against AFOs if those suing can prove the operation does not use "prudent generally accepted management practices" and that the AFO interferes with the plaintiffs' reasonable use and enjoyment of their life or property for a substantial period of time.[21] In 1996, Iowa's RTF law was amended to strip protections for AFOs that repeatedly violate state regulations.[22] Operations are deemed chronic violators if they incur three or more violations relating to the improper storage and disposal of manure. Penalties assessed for these operations may include a civil penalty greater than $3,000.[23]

Local Government

Iowa's RTF laws authorize counties to designate agricultural areas and create agricultural land preservation areas by passing ordinances to preserve land for agricultural use.[24] In addition to allowing for agricultural areas, Iowa's RTF laws exempt farming operations and land used for soil and water conservation from local zoning ordinances otherwise.[25] Attempts to reinstate local control over livestock feeding operations have failed to make their way past the Iowa legislature.[26]

In effect, Iowa creates two-way zoning for agricultural exceptionalism: establishing agricultural areas with nuisance protections for farming operations and then excluding farming operations from any zoning that would curtail their operations. Animal feedlots, however, can still be subject to local zoning in Iowa if the feedlot's start date occurs after the enactment date of the local ordinance.[27] This exception is only slight, as counties do not have the authority to enact any legislation that regulates the conditions or practices of animal operations unless explicitly allowed by state law.[28]

The interplay between Iowa's RTF laws and the power of local government underlies several lawsuits. In 1995, the Iowa Supreme Court affirmed a lower court ruling that a hog confinement facility was exempt from zoning ordinances.[29] Similarly, in 1996, the Iowa Supreme Court reversed a lower court ruling, finding that a hog facility was exempt from county zoning ordinances as it was an agricultural facility.[30] In another case, the Iowa Supreme Court used Iowa's RTF laws to invalidate four county ordinances, ruling that local governments do not have the authority to regulate agricultural operations and activities or to regulate air pollution.[31]

Attorney Fees and Limits on Damages

Those filing nuisance lawsuits against farming operations are responsible for attorney fees and damages if the suit is deemed frivolous, meaning that the lawsuit lacks legal substance or merit. This applies to lawsuits against farms in agricultural areas as well as AFOs.[32] The opposite, however, is not true, meaning that the defendants (typically agricultural operations) do not have to pay attorney fees and damages if the plaintiff prevails. This and similar language may have a chilling effect on the filing of nuisance suits in favor of industrial operators.[33] For example, the Iowa Supreme Court held in a 2020 case that because those suing an AFO had voluntarily dismissed the suit and had no material interest in the property under consideration, they were responsible for attorney fees.[34]

In a recent addition to Iowa's RTF laws, there are now specific types of damages that a plaintiff who prevails in a nuisance lawsuit against an AFO may receive.[35] If the plaintiff in such a lawsuit wins and the AFO is found to be a nuisance, the plaintiff can receive monetary damages for any diminution in the fair market value of the plaintiff's property, as well as damages for the plaintiff's past, present, and future adverse health conditions.[36] However, this law on damages applies only to causes of action that arose after March 29, 2017.[37]

Table 2.15 Iowa's Key RTF Provisions and National Comparison

Iowa's key RTF provisions		% U.S. states with similar RTF provisions
Operations are immune from lawsuits . . .	if they are there first.[†]	44%
Operations are not immune from lawsuits . . .	if they do not comply with state laws.	68%
	if they do not comply with federal laws.	62%
	if they pollute water.	36%
	if they do not comply with other laws.	50%
	if they are negligent.	46%
	if they do not comply with environmental laws.	26%
Other important details	RTF supersedes local ordinances and laws.[††]	62%
	Attorney fees are awarded to prevailing defendant.	34%

[†] Applies only to feedlots, Iowa Code § 172D.4 (2020).
[††] Feedlots are required to adhere to local zoning ordinances, Iowa Code § 172D.4 (2020).

The Iowa Supreme Court has awarded damages to plaintiffs, holding that protections provided by the RTF laws did not disallow collection of past, present, and future damages for the plaintiffs given that the operation began prior to designation of the land as an agricultural area.[38] In one closely watched case, the Iowa Farm Bureau and Iowa Pork Producers Association backed a hog confinement sued by a family raising alternative livestock, which predated the confinement.[39] To the disappointment of the commodity association and the Farm Bureau, the Iowa Supreme Court ruled that the hog confinement could be considered a permanent nuisance rather than a temporary one. Damages awarded could then include future ones, like the diminished value of their property.[40]

Other Related Agricultural Laws

With amendments in 1998 and 2002, Iowa established a commission to regulate construction, expansion, and operation of AFOs and feedlots to protect air and water quality.[41] The commission requires AFOs and feedlots to submit plans for manure management, initial construction, and operation expansion, among other things.[42] The laws regulating AFO and feedlot pollution have been challenged in court; however, the Iowa Supreme Court has held that the state legislature has the authority to regulate pollution more stringently than what is spelled out in federal laws.[43]

NOTES

1. 1982 Iowa Acts 1245, § 12; *Bormann v. Bd. of Supervisors*, 584 N.W.2d 309 (Iowa 1998). Iowa first extended nuisance protections to livestock feedlots during 1976 and later enacted a suite of nuisance protections referred to as right-to-farm laws during 1982.

2. U.S. Department of Agriculture, *USDA Quick Stats Tool: June 1976 Survey, Iowa*, distributed by National Agricultural Statistics Service, accessed February 5, 2021, https://quickstats .nass.usda.gov/results/968363F4-53D8-3F00-9D8C-B5FA8730AD67; "2021 State Agriculture Overview: Iowa," U.S. Department of Agriculture, National Agricultural Statistics Service, accessed October 21, 2022, https://www.nass.usda.gov/Quick_Stats/Ag_Overview /stateOverview.php?state=IOWA.

3. Some Iowa statutes have distinct provisions for AFOs versus general farm operations.

4. Iowa Code § 657.2 (2021).

5. Iowa Code § 352.2(6) (2021).

6. Iowa Code § 352.6(1) (2021).

7. Iowa Code § 352.11(1)(a) (2021).

8. *Bormann*, 584 N.W.2d 309.

9. Iowa Const. art. I, §§ 1, 18.

10. "Court Shuts Door on 'Right to Farm' Law," *Dubuque (Iowa) Telegraph Herald*, February 23, 1999.

11. *Gacke v. Pork Xtra, LLC*, 684 N.W.2d 168 (Iowa 2004).

12. Jeff Vonk, "DNR Director Concerned with Property Rights Issues," *Clinton (Iowa) Herald*, August 4, 2006.

13. *McIlrath v. Prestage Farms of Iowa, LLC*, 889 N.W.2d 700 (Iowa Ct. App. 2016); *Honomichl v. Valley View Swine, LLC*, 914 N.W.2d 223 (Iowa 2018).

14. Rod Boshart, "Iowa Statewide Alliance Calls for Moratorium on Large-Scale Livestock Operations—Halt Sought until Iowa's Water Quality Improves," *Cedar Rapids (Iowa) Gazette*, September 21, 2016.

15. *Garrison v. New Fashion Pork, LLP*, 977 N.W.2d 67 (Iowa 2022). This case is not included in the statistical analysis presented in part 1 of the book because it happened after we closed our search with the end of the calendar year in 2021.

16. *Garrison*, 977 N.W.2d 67.

17. Iowa Code § 352.11(1)(b) (2021).

18. Iowa Code §§ 172D.1, 657.11(3)(a) (2021).

19. Iowa Code §§ 172D.2, 172D.3, 172D.4 (2021).

20. Iowa Code § 657.11(4) (2021).

21. Iowa Code § 657.11(2)(b) (2021).

22. 1996 Iowa Acts 1118 (S.F. 2375) (amending Iowa Code § 657.11).

23. Iowa Code § 657.11(3)(b) (2021); Rod Boshart, "Senate to Debate Hog-Lot Reform," *Cedar Rapids (Iowa) Gazette*, March 5, 1996.

24. Iowa Code § 335.27 (2021).

25. Iowa Code §§ 335.2, 335.3 (2021).

26. Rod Boshart, "Local Hog-Lot Rules Rejected—Iowa House Approves Livestock Bill, 51–48," *Cedar Rapids (Iowa) Gazette*, March 13, 1998; Kristin Guess, "Legislature Denies 14 Bills on Changing the Master Matrix Provisions for CAFOs," *Waterloo–Cedar Falls (Iowa) Courier*, July 29, 2018.

27. Iowa Code § 172D.4(2)(a)–(e) (2021).
28. Iowa Code § 331.304A (2021).
29. *Thompson v. Hancock Co.*, 539 N.W.2d 181 (Iowa 1995).
30. *Kuehl v. Cass Co.*, 555 N.W.2d 686 (Iowa 1996).
31. *Goodell v. Humboldt Co.*, 575 N.W.2d 486 (Iowa 1998).
32. Iowa Code § 352.11(1)(d) (2021). See also *Merrill v. Valley View Swine, LLC*, 941 N.W.2d 10 (Iowa 2020).
33. Cordon M. Smart, "The 'Right to Commit Nuisance' in North Carolina: A Historical Analysis of the Right-to-Farm Act," *North Carolina Law Review* 94, no. 6 (2016): 2097–154. For more on the chilling effect of such statutes, see the section "Geopolitical Extraction" in the introduction.
34. *Merrill*, 941 N.W.2d 10.
35. Iowa Code § 657.11A (2021).
36. Iowa Code § 657.11A(3) (2021).
37. Iowa Code § 657.11A(7) (2021).
38. *Weinhold v. Wolff*, 555 N.W.2d 454 (Iowa 1996).
39. "Court: Hog Lot Permanent Nuisance," *Dubuque (Iowa) Telegraph Herald*, October 24, 1996.
40. *Weinhold*, 555 N.W.2d 454.
41. 1998 Iowa Acts 1209 (H.F. 2494) (adding Iowa Code § 455B.200, now codified at Iowa Code § 459.103); 2002 Iowa Acts 1137 (S.F. 2293) (amending Iowa Code § 455B.200, now codified at Iowa Code § 459.103).
42. Iowa Code § 459.312 (2021).
43. *Freeman v. Grain Processing Corp.*, 848 N.W.2d 58 (Iowa 2014).

Kansas

Legislators advocated Kansas's right-to-farm law in 1982 as a tool to prevent the loss of farmland.[1] Since that time, the number of farms in the state has dropped by 20 percent, with 3 percent fewer acres of farmland.[2] So what does this legislation do in practice?

Kansas's RTF Law at a Glance

Kansas's RTF law does not explicitly protect farmland from development. Rather, Kansas's RTF law, like those present in the other forty-nine states, centers on protecting certain activities on farmland from nuisance suits when they impact neighboring property, for example through noise or pollution. The statute defines farmland as "land devoted primarily to an agricultural activity." Agricultural activities protected from nuisance suits range from growing horticultural and agricultural crops to raising livestock, as well as handling, storage, and transportation of agricultural commodities.[3]

Conditions and Activities

To receive protection from nuisance suits, the law stipulates that agricultural activities be "good agricultural practices" but does not specify what this means. Agricultural activities must comply with applicable local, state, and federal laws and not substantially harm public health and safety. However, some state and federal environmental rules and regulations exempt agricultural operations from standards required of other industries.[4] Air pollution, like odor, is not mentioned.

Kansas courts have held that RTF protections apply only to agricultural activities established prior to surrounding agricultural or nonagricultural activities.[5] In accordance with this, a court ruled in 1993 that because a cattle

Table 2.16 Kansas's Key RTF Provisions and National Comparison

Kansas's key RTF provisions		% U.S. states with similar RTF provisions
Operations are immune from lawsuits . . .	if boundaries or size of operations change.	34%
	if they produce a different product.	26%
	if there is an ownership change.	26%
	if there is a cessation or interruption in farming.	26%
	when they are there first.	44%
Operations are not immune from lawsuits . . .	if they do not comply with county laws.	42%
	if they do not comply with federal laws.	62%
	if they do not comply with other laws.	50%
	if they do not comply with environmental laws.	26%
	if they do not comply with state laws.	68%
Other important details	Attorney fees are awarded to prevailing defendant.	34%

feeding operation did not predate a family's use of a farmhouse on their agricultural land, RTF protections did not apply.[6] However, a 2013 series of amendments markedly altered this previously understood meaning. Now, an operation can (1) expand in scope by adding more animals or acreage; (2) alter its activities or cease them temporarily; (3) or change owners—and still qualify as existing before surrounding owners.

Local Government

Generally, counties cannot apply state regulatory laws to land or buildings used for agricultural purposes, except in floodplain areas.[7] In one case, a court ruled that a political subdivision can enforce ordinances related to nuisances when an agricultural operation does not meet the required conditions mentioned in the prior section.[8]

Other Important Aspects

Only owners can file nuisance suits, and if they win, their awards are limited. In one 1998 ruling, a couple was awarded $15,000 in punitive (intended to punish) damages against a cattle feedlot for pollution, odors, and flies.

However, the statute now prevents such awards.[9] Further, more recent amendments limit permanent (not possible to lessen) nuisance awards to the fair market value reduction of the owner's property. If a nuisance is determined to be temporary (possible to lessen), the owner can receive only the lesser value of (1) the decrease in fair rental value; (2) the value of the loss of the use and enjoyment of the property; or (3) the reasonable cost to repair or mitigate any injury. If the defendant tries to mitigate the nuisance and cannot, damages are limited to the permanent category.[10]

For agricultural chemicals, Kansas's RTF law has a special provision for when a court orders an activity to cease—what is known as an injunction. Defendants can sometimes claim attorney fees alongside other retrospective costs if they can prove they used chemicals properly, no damages were sustained by the plaintiff, and they sustained losses as a result of the injunction.[11]

NOTES

1. Kan. Stat. § 2-3201 (2021).
2. U.S. Department of Commerce, "Table 1. Farms, Land in Farms, and Land Use: 1982 and Earlier Census Years," in *1982 Census of Agriculture, Volume 1: Geographic Area Series, Part 16: Kansas State and County Data, Chapter 1: State Data* (Washington, D.C.: U.S. Bureau of the Census, 1984), https://agcensus.library.cornell.edu/wp-content/uploads/1982-Kansas -CHAPTER_1_State_Data-121-Table-01.pdf; "2021 State Agriculture Overview: Kansas," U.S. Department of Agriculture, National Agricultural Statistics Service, accessed October 21, 2022, https://www.nass.usda.gov/Quick_Stats/Ag_Overview/stateOverview.php ?state=KANSAS.
3. Kan. Stat. § 2-3203 (2021).
4. Danielle Diamond, Loka Ashwood, Allen Franco, Aimee Imlay, Lindsay Kuehn, and Crystal Boutwell, "Farm Fiction: Agricultural Exceptionalism, Environmental Injustice and U.S. Right-to-Farm Law," *Environmental Law Reporter* 52 (Sept. 2022): 10727–48.
5. Kan. Stat. § 2-3202 (2021); *Desaire v. Solomon Valley Co-Op, Inc.*, No. 94-1271-PFK, 1995 WL 580064 (D. Kan. Sept. 14, 1995).
6. *Finlay v. Finlay*, 856 P.2d 183 (Kan. Ct. App. 1993).
7. Kan. Stat. § 19-2921 (2021).
8. *Weber v. Board of County Comm'rs of Franklin Co.*, 884 P.2d 1159 (Kan. Ct. App. 1994).
9. J. Hays, "Jury Punishes Feedlot Owner for Making Neighbors' Lives Miserable," *Wichita (Kans.) Eagle*, May 27, 1998
10. Kan. Stat. § 2-3205 (2021).
11. Kan. Stat. § 2-3204 (2021).

Kentucky

Legislators passed Kentucky's initial right-to-farm law with the stated intention of conserving and protecting but simultaneously developing and improving agricultural land.[1] Since the law was first passed in 1980, the number of farms in the state has dropped by 27 percent and the number of acres in farmland by 12 percent.[2] So what does the state's RTF law do in practice?

Kentucky's RTF Law at a Glance

Kentucky's RTF law provides no explicit protection for farmland. Rather, Kentucky's RTF law, like those present in the other forty-nine states, centers on protecting certain types of operations from nuisance suits when they impact neighboring property, for example through noise or pollution. Initially, Kentucky defined protected agricultural operations as "without limitation, any facility for the production of crops, livestock, poultry, livestock products, or poultry products including horticultural and growing of timber."[3] However, in 1996 the law was amended to include equine, the application of pesticides and herbicides approved by a "public authority," and the construction of buildings and other associated activities. That same year, silviculture gained its own protected section, inclusive of timber harvest, site preparation, slash disposal, controlled burning, and insect and disease control, among other things required for "monetary profit."[4] Further, the amendment expanded the definition of agricultural operations to include "any generally accepted, reasonable, and prudent method for the operation of a farm to produce monetary profit."[5]

Unique to Kentucky, a 2010 amendment introduced protections for sustainable agricultural operations, defined as "science-based practices that are supported by research and the use of technology, demonstrated to lead to broad outcomes-based performance improvements that meet the needs of the present, and that improve the ability of future generations to meet their needs while advancing progress toward environmental, social, and economic goals."[6] The law stipulates that best management practices related to sustainable agriculture may be used to qualify for protection from nuisance suits. However, sustainable agricultural operations or agricultural operations more generally still receive RTF protection from nuisance suits even if they do not use best management practices.[7] Rather, the RTF definition of agricultural operations includes those that use "any generally accepted, reasonable, and prudent methods."[8]

Conditions and Activities

Originally, in 1980, Kentucky stipulated that agricultural operations could not become public or private nuisances if (1) local conditions changed around the operation after it had been operating for over a year and (2) the operation was not a nuisance at the time it began.

However, in 1996 the law changed to substantially broaden protections for agricultural operations. Since then, operations are protected once they are up and running for over a year regardless of any changed conditions in their locality. A federal court interpreted this in 2013 to mean that the RTF law protects only agricultural operations that were in place before the neighbors filed suit.[9] In the 2013 case, the neighbors' residences predated the installation of intensive hog confinements, and they filed suit after hogs were brought to the site.[10] Relatedly, the court stated that parent companies or livestock producers that control aspects of hog-raising operations could be liable for the actions of the producers that they contract with.[11]

The 1996 amendments also changed the law to protect agricultural operations that have been in existence for at least a year regardless of any later changes in ownership.[12] Further, such operations do not lose their protected status if they cease operations for five years or less or for one year after a state or national contract expires. The 1996 amendment also ensured protections for operations that change crops or methods of production due to the introduction and use of new and generally accepted technologies.[13]

Kentucky explicitly identifies corporations as protected by the RTF law.[14]

Table 2.17 Kentucky's Key RTF Provisions and National Comparison

Kentucky's key RTF provisions		% U.S. states with similar RTF provisions
Operations are immune from lawsuits ...	if there is a change in locality.	46%
	if they use a new technology.	30%
	if they produce a different product.	26%
	if there is an ownership change.	26%
	if there is a cessation or interruption in farming.	26%
	once in operation for a year.	48%
Operations are not immune from lawsuits ...	if they are negligent.	46%
	if they are a nuisance from the start.	38%
	if they do not comply with other laws.	50%
	if they pollute water.	36%
Other important details	RTF supersedes local ordinances and laws.	62%

Local Governance

Kentucky's RTF law prohibits local governments from using zoning or other ordinances that restrict the use of "normal" and "accepted" practices by silvicultural and agricultural operations.[15] The Kentucky Court of Appeals has interpreted the law to apply only in areas zoned for agriculture but not residentially zoned areas.[16]

In response, some counties have passed their own ordinances with RTF language.[17] In one case, a county attempted to require a conditional use permit for a fish-farming operation in an area that was zoned as low-density residential, which allowed for agricultural uses. The court held that the county's own RTF ordinance prohibited it from restricting such agricultural use.[18] The court also noted that farmers were afforded broad protections through the "agricultural supremacy clause," meaning that conditional use permits or building permits for outbuildings could not be required.[19]

Courts have described the agricultural supremacy clause as exempting agriculture from the jurisdiction of local zoning ordinances and subdivision regulations but not from county land use or comprehensive planning.[20] Typically, to qualify as an "agricultural use," a parcel of land must consist of at least five contiguous acres.[21]

NOTES

1. 1980 Ky. Acts 214 (H.B. 909).
2. U.S. Department of Agriculture, *USDA Quick Stats Tool: June 1980 Survey, Kentucky*, distributed by National Agricultural Statistics Service, accessed October 28, 2020, https://quickstats.nass.usda.gov/results/A3A519CF-F11D-3C57-B8D3-1232C37EC4FB; "2021 State Agriculture Overview: Kentucky," U.S. Department of Agriculture, National Agricultural Statistics Service, accessed October 21, 2022, https://www.nass.usda.gov/Quick_Stats/Ag_Overview/stateOverview.php?state=KENTUCKY.
3. 1980 Ky. Acts 214 (H.B. 909).
4. 1996 Ky. Acts 91 (H.B. 335) (amending Ky. Rev. Stat. § 413.072).
5. 1996 Ky. Acts 91 (H.B. 335) (amending, in relevant part, Ky. Rev. Stat. § 413.072(3)).
6. 2010 Ky. Acts 100 (H.B. 486) (amending, in relevant part, Ky. Rev. Stat. § 413.072(3)).
7. Ky. Rev. Stat. § 413.072(3) (2021). See also Ky. Rev. Stat. §§ 224.71-100 to 224.71-140 (2021).
8. Ky. Rev. Stat. § 413.072(3) (2021).
9. *Powell v. Tosh*, 929 F.Supp.2d 691 (W.D. Ky. 2013).
10. *Powell*, 929 F.Supp.2d 691.
11. *Powell*, 929 F.Supp.2d 691.
12. 1996 Ky. Acts 91 (H.B. 335) (amending, in relevant part, Ky. Rev. Stat. § 413.072(5)).
13. 1996 Ky. Acts 91 (H.B. 335) (amending, in relevant part, Ky. Rev. Stat. § 413.072(5)).
14. 1996 Ky. Acts 91 (H.B. 335) (amending, in relevant part, Ky. Rev. Stat. § 413.072(5)).
15. Ky. Rev. Stat. § 413.072(2) (2021).
16. *Price v. Johnson*, No. 2011-CA-000011-MR, 2013 WL 2359728 (Ky. Ct. App. May 31, 2013).
17. See Doug Waters, "Allen County Drafting Farm Ordinance," *Bowling Green (Ky.) Daily News*, February 3, 2007; Crystal Harden, "'Right to Farm' Push On—Boone Farmers Fear Encroachment," *Kentucky Post* (Cincinnati, Ohio), February 13, 1996; and Associated Press, "Forewarned: Country Has Its Smells, Sounds," *Kentucky Post*, September 4, 1998.
18. *Oldham Co. Bd. of Adjustments and Appeals v. Davis*, No. 2003-CA-001492-MR, 2004 WL 1857309 (Ky. Ct. App. Aug. 20, 2004) (citing Ky. Rev. Stat. §§ 100.203, 413.072).
19. *Davis*, 2004 WL 1857309.
20. According to *21st Century Develop. Co., LLC v. Watts*, 958 S.W.2d 25 (Ky. Ct. App. 1997), even if the property or use is exempt from zoning under the "agricultural supremacy clause" or through case law, the comprehensive plan must still consider future changes and make recommendations. Therefore, in *Nash v. Campbell Cty. Fiscal Court*, 345 S.W.3d 811 (Ky. 2011), land used for agricultural purposes is exempt from most regulations.
21. Ky. Rev. Stat. § 100.111(2) (2021). See also *Nash*, 345 S.W.3d 811; and *Watts*, 958 S.W.2d 25.

Louisiana

When legislators passed and amended Louisiana's right-to-farm law, they declared it a tool that protected the value of agricultural land and reduced the loss of it.[1] But since the law was enacted in 1983, the number of farm operations in the state has dropped by 23 percent and the number of acres farmed by 20 percent.[2] So what does this legislation do in practice?

Louisiana's RTF Law at a Glance

Louisiana's RTF law provides no explicit protection for farmland. Like those present in the other forty-nine states, the law centers on protecting certain types of operations and processing facilities from nuisance suits when they impact neighboring property, for example through noise or pollution. The law explicitly protects "persons" engaged in agricultural operations or production.[3] In 2008, the law was amended to expand the definition of protected agricultural operations to include any agricultural facility or land used for production or processing, including crops, livestock, farm-raised fish and fish products, wood, timber and forest products, and poultry. Protected operations also include the use of farm machinery, equipment, chemicals, and structures.[4] The RTF protection of agricultural processing includes the slaughtering and processing of livestock and poultry as well as the elevation and drying of grain, among other things.[5] Agricultural production refers to the planting of crops, leaving land idle, participating in government programs, using support services, or crop and livestock rotations.[6] In 1995, the law was also amended to include a right to forest.[7]

113

Conditions and Activities

Once up and running for a year, agricultural operations cannot be sued for nuisance. Since a set of sweeping amendments in 2008, in addition to being protected from private nuisance suits (those brought by people like neighbors), agricultural operations are also protected from public nuisance suits (those brought by the government on behalf of the general public).

Louisiana's RTF law creates a presumption that agricultural operations utilize traditional or generally accepted agricultural practices, which the law explicitly protects from nuisance suits. This presumption places the burden of proof on any litigant trying to contend otherwise.[8] For example, one court ruled that even though a ConAgra Foods Inc.'s Peavey grain elevator had been cited for violations by the Louisiana Department of Environmental Quality, its agricultural practices still qualified as generally accepted. The court faulted the residents who brought the suit for not providing sufficient evidence that the elevator's practices were not generally accepted.[9]

However, on appeal, the same court clarified that some residents were eligible to proceed with the nuisance suit because their homeownership or landownership predated the facility. Louisiana's RTF law explicitly protects agricultural operations from "persons who subsequently acquire an interest in any land in the vicinity."[10] Operations cannot constantly change themselves to receive protection and must be established prior to substantive changes nearby.[11] For example, an Archer-Daniels-Midland Co. facility was ordered to pay a judgment of $280,000 (an award of $500 to $1,500 per over 200 residents) for penetrating dust from its River Road grain elevator.[12]

Initially, Louisiana's RTF law protected only generally accepted agricultural practices, defining them as consistent with accepted and customary standards by similar agricultural operations.[13] However, a 2008 amendment expanded what qualified as protected practices by adding "traditional" ones, which can include best management practices. Best management practices for animal feeding operations and confined animal feeding operations are determined by the Louisiana Department of Agriculture and Forestry and the Louisiana State University AgCenter.[14] They suggest best management practices for specific commodities, stating their intent is to control the transmission of pollutants from agricultural resources to the state.[15]

The definition of what qualifies as an agricultural operation often intersects with what are acceptable practices. For example, a resident sued a produce business for nuisance. Initially, the trial court used the RTF law to rule that the business was an agricultural operation and thus shielded

Table 2.18 Louisiana's Key RTF Provisions and National Comparison

Louisiana's key RTF provisions		% U.S. states with similar RTF provisions
Operations are immune from lawsuits ...	if there is a change in locality.	46%
	if any type of agricultural production predated operation.	4%
	once in operation for a year.	48%
	when they are there first.	44%
Operations are not immune from lawsuits ...	if they are negligent.	46%
	if they do not comply with federal laws.	62%
	if they do not comply with state laws.	68%
Other important details	Attorney fees are awarded to prevailing defendant.	34%
	Attorney fees are awarded to prevailing party.	14%
	RTF supersedes local ordinances and laws.	62%
	RTF protects processing.	48%

from nuisance suits.[16] However, the state appellate court reversed the ruling, saying it was up to a court to determine not just whether the business was an agricultural operation but also whether it utilized generally accepted agricultural practices. In a separate 2020 case, the court ruled that a series of companies could claim an RTF defense as it pertained to timber production. However, the court had a split ruling, where it allowed the residents to proceed with suing for damages in regard to alleged chemical exposure to formaldehyde. But the court did not allow the plaintiffs to seek injunctive relief—meaning stopping the chemical spraying immediately—as the RTF law barred such action.[17]

Agricultural operations do not qualify for RTF protections if they are negligent (that is, fail to take proper care), intentionally cause injury (that is, harm purposefully directed), or violate state or federal laws or rules.[18] However, some state and federal environmental rules and regulations exempt agricultural operations from standards applicable to other industries.[19]

LOUISIANA 115

Local Government

Louisiana's RTF law prevails over local ordinances that governments try to enforce, as long as the agricultural operation is not negligent and uses generally accepted or traditional practices.[20] Municipal zoning and nuisance ordinances do not apply to operations established outside the corporate limits of the town and later incorporated.[21]

More generally, as of 1995, any governmental entity must provide an extensive written assessment of any action that potentially diminishes the value of private agricultural property.[22] A private owner of an agricultural property can sue the government to determine whether its action has diminished the value of the property at hand.[23] If the owner prevails, the government not only is required to pay the owner's litigation fees but can rescind or repeal the regulation. When such happens, the government is also liable for damages sustained by the property owner.[24] Importantly, actions by government entities charged with the promotion, protection, and advancement of agriculture cannot be held liable for the diminution of the value of agricultural property.

Attorney Fees

Those who file nuisance suits and their attorneys can be required to pay attorney fees and costs if the court determines there was not substantial justification for the suit.[25] This and similar language may have a chilling effect on the filing of nuisance suits in favor of industrial operators.[26]

NOTES

1. La. Stat. § 3:3601 (2021).
2. U.S. Department of Agriculture, *USDA Quick Stats Tool: June 1983 Survey, Louisiana*, distributed by National Agricultural Statistics Service, accessed December 14, 2020, https://quickstats.nass.usda.gov/results/CB69E29B-7097-38A1-A18E-73F45CAF3523; "2021 State Agriculture Overview: Louisiana," U.S. Department of Agriculture, National Agricultural Statistics Service, accessed October 21, 2022, https://www.nass.usda.gov/Quick_Stats/Ag_Overview/stateOverview.php?state=LOUISIANA.
3. La. Stat. § 3:3603(A).
4. La. Stat. § 3:3602(5) (2021).
5. La. Stat. § 3:3602(6) (2021).
6. La. Stat. § 3:3602(8) (2021).
7. La. Stat. § 3:3621 (2021).
8. La. Stat. § 3:3604 (2021).
9. *Albert v. Peavey Co.*, No. 04-1611, 2009 WL 321934 (E.D. La. Feb. 6, 2009); *Trosclair v. Matrana's Produce, Inc.*, 717 So. 2d 1257 (La. Ct. App. 1998).
10. La. Stat. § 3:3603(A) (2021).

11. La. Stat. § 3:3603(B) (2021).
12. Gordon Russell, "Residents Win Grain Elevator Suit," *New Orleans Times-Picayune*, December 30, 1999.
13. La. Stat. § 3:3602(12) (2021).
14. La. Stat. § 3:3602(18) (2021).
15. Ron E. Sheffield, Karl Harborth, Guillermo Scaglia, Brian D. LeBlanc, Karen Nix, and Kim Pope, *Sustainable Best Management Practices for Beef Production*, Louisiana State University Agricultural Center Publication 2884, 2012, accessed December 14, 2020, https://www.lsuagcenter.com/~/media/system/c/f/1/6/cf1624fa7391138c9a9fa5ff206ee88f/pub2884beefbmppublowres.pdf.
16. *Trosclair*, 717 So. 2d 1257.
17. *Collett v. Weyerhaeuser Company*, No. 19-11144, 2020 WL 6828613 (E.D. La. Nov. 19, 2020).
18. La. Stat. § 3:3606 (2021).
19. Danielle Diamond, Loka Ashwood, Allen Franco, Aimee Imlay, Lindsay Kuehn, and Crystal Boutwell, "Farm Fiction: Agricultural Exceptionalism, Environmental Injustice and U.S. Right-to-Farm Law," *Environmental Law Reporter* 52 (Sept. 2022): 10727–48.
20. La. Stat. § 3:3607(A), (C) (2021).
21. La. Stat. § 3:3607(B) (2021).
22. 1995 La. Acts 302 (H.B. 2199) (adding, in relevant part, La. Stat. § 3:3609).
23. La. Stat. § 3:3610(A) (2021).
24. La. Stat. § 3:3610(F) (2021).
25. La. Stat. § 3:3605 (2021).
26. Cordon M. Smart, "The 'Right to Commit Nuisance' in North Carolina: A Historical Analysis of the Right-to-Farm Act," *North Carolina Law Review* 94, no. 6 (2016): 2097–154. For more on the chilling effect of such statutes, see the section "Geopolitical Extraction" in the introduction.

Maine

Maine legislators passed the state's original right-to-farm law in 1981, later altering the law's preamble in 2008 to protect agricultural land more explicitly.[1] Since 1981, the number of farms in the state has dropped by 6 percent and the land in farms by 19 percent.[2] So what does the state's RTF legislation do in practice?

Maine's RTF Law at a Glance

Despite changes to the 2008 preamble, Maine's law provides no explicit protection of farmland from development in its RTF statutes. Rather, Maine's RTF law, similar to other such statutes nationally, centers on protecting farms and agricultural operations from nuisance lawsuits over matters like pollution. Maine's law specifically protects farms, farm operations, and composting that takes place on a farm, known as agricultural composting operations, from nuisance suits. Farms are defined as "the land, plants, animals, buildings, structures, ponds and machinery used in the commercial production of agricultural products." A farm operation is "a condition or activity that occurs on a farm in connection with the commercial production of agricultural products and includes, but is not limited to, operations giving rise to noise, odors, dust, insects and fumes; operation of machinery and irrigation pumps; disposal of manure; agricultural support services; and the employment and use of labor."[3] Maine is among only a handful of states that reference labor in their RTF statutes, part of its unique history of enacting legislation that seeks to protect underpaid workers in industrial-scale agricultural production.[4]

Conditions and Activities

Initially, Maine's RTF law required that farms adhere to generally accepted agricultural practices but heightened farms' standards to compliance with best management practices (BMPs) in 2008. Today, any protected farm or operation must meet one of three conditions: (1) it must conform to BMPs;[5] (2) it must be consistent with the Maine Nutrient Management Act;[6] or (3) it must have existed before a change in the land use or occupancy of land within one mile of the boundaries of the operation as long as the operation was not a nuisance before the change in land use or occupancy. This condition does not apply to operations that materially change their conditions or nature after a use or occupancy change within one mile of its boundaries.[7]

Oversight

In 2008, the state enacted a unique procedure for nuisance complaints where the commissioner of the Department of Agriculture, Conservation, and Forestry investigates. If operations fail to adopt BMPs, the commissioner of agriculture is required to send a written report to the appropriate agency. In addition, the commissioner will send a letter to the attorney general for the state of Maine if a federal or state law has been violated. The attorney general may file a legal action to stop the nuisance or enforce applicable laws. Failure to apply BMPs is a separate civil violation carrying a fine of up to $1,000, with an additional fine of up to $250 per day for every day the violation continues.[8]

Maine's RTF law includes more general administrative procedures that explain complaint procedures regarding farms and operations. The commissioner can use a fund to investigate complaints involving an operation. If the commissioner finds that operation is using BMPs, the operation and complainant will be notified. If, however, the commissioner finds the problem is caused by not using BMPs, the commissioner shall (1) determine the changes needed to comply with BMPs and prescribe site-specific BMPs for that operation; (2) advise those responsible of the changes necessary to conform with BMPs and then determine if those changes are implemented; and (3) provide any related findings to the complainant and person responsible.[9]

Table 2.19 Maine's Key RTF Provisions and National Comparison

Maine's key RTF provisions		% U.S. states with similar RTF provisions
Operations are immune from lawsuits . . .	if there is a change in locality.	46%
	when they are there first.	44%
Operations are not immune from lawsuits . . .	if they do not comply with federal laws.	62%
	if they do not comply with other laws.	50%
	if they do not comply with state laws.	68%
	if they are a nuisance from the start.	38%
	if they pollute water.	36%
Other important details	RTF supersedes local ordinances and laws.	62%
	RTF supersedes local ordinances and laws in agricultural zones.	12%
	RTF protects processing.	48%

Local Governance

Maine's RTF law prevails over local ordinances if (1) the operation is located in an area that permits agricultural activities and (2) if the operation conforms to BMPs as determined by the commissioner. In addition, municipalities are required to provide the commissioner with a copy of any proposed ordinance that affects farm operations or agricultural composting operations.[10] State and federal laws apply, regardless.

In the case of *Dubois Livestock, Inc. v. Town of Arundel,* the livestock operation claimed it was a farm, but the court disagreed. Dubois imported thousands of tons of material, including fish waste from sea processors, horse manure and bedding from Scarborough Downs, and cow manure and other materials from various off-site locations to create compost. The court ruled in 2014 that these activities did not constitute a farm and thus could not be considered an agricultural composting operation. Further, the court clarified that even if the operation could be considered a farm, agricultural composting operations could be regulated by municipalities.[11]

Other Important Aspects

Maine's RTF law broadens the scope of the state's Rules of Civil Procedure, Rule 11. A court may award attorney fees and reasonable expenses to the defendant farm operation if the court determines that a nuisance action was not brought in good faith and was frivolous or was intended for harassment only.[12] However, plaintiffs can also be entitled independently of the state's RTF law for compensation under Rule 11.

Maine has a creative stipulation that requires the commissioner of agriculture to conduct an educational outreach program to increase awareness about the RTF law.[13]

NOTES

1. 2008 Me. Laws 649 (S.P. 591).
2. U.S. Department of Agriculture, *USDA Quick Stats Tool: June 1981 Survey, Maine*, distributed by National Agricultural Statistics Service, accessed October 14, 2020, https://quickstats .nass.usda.gov/results/A78ECEC4-E0DB-3E54-9469-9C70193B6C74; "2021 State Agriculture Overview: Maine," U.S. Department of Agriculture, National Agricultural Statistics Service, accessed October 21, 2022, https://www.nass.usda.gov/Quick_Stats/Ag_Overview /stateOverview.php?state=MAINE.
3. Me. Stat. tit. 7, § 152 (2021).
4. Avery Yale, "Pass Law That Helps Egg Farm? Consider History First," *Portland (Maine) Press Herald*, May 4, 2011.
5. Best management practices are determined by the state of Maine's commissioner of the Department of Agriculture, Conservation and Forestry ("commissioner"). Maine Stat. tit. 7, § 158 (2021).
6. For complaints regarding the storage or use of farm nutrients at a concentrated animal feeding operation, the operation must be consistent with the nutrient management plan approved under the Maine Nutrient Management Act. The Nutrient Management Act is found at Maine Stat. tit. 7, §§ 4201–4214 (2021).
7. Me. Stat. tit. 7, § 153(1)–(3) (2021).
8. Me. Stat. tit. 7, § 158 (2021).
9. Me. Stat. tit. 7, § 156 (2021).
10. Me. Stat. tit. 7, §§ 154–155 (2021).
11. *Dubois Livestock, Inc. v. Town of Arundel*, 103 A.3d 556 (Maine 2014).
12. Me. Stat. tit. 7, § 157 (2021).
13. Me. Stat. tit. 7, §§ 159–160 (2021).

Maryland

· ·

Legislators proposed and amended Maryland's right-to-farm law, calling it a tool to combat the threat of urban encroachment.[1] Yet since becoming law in 1981, Maryland has lost 32 percent of its farm operations and 29 percent of its acreage in farms.[2] So what does this legislation do in practice?

Maryland's RTF Law at a Glance

Maryland's law provides no protection tailored to farmland or farms by size (for example, family or small operations). Rather, Maryland's RTF law, like those present in the other forty-nine states, protects certain types of farm operations from nuisance suits when their activities impact neighboring property, for example through noise or pollution. Maryland generally defines nuisance as a "condition that is dangerous to health or safety," which includes "a foul pigpen."[3] Simultaneously, though, the state's nuisance law explicitly exempts farms as well as commercial fishing or seafood operations from its definition of nuisances so long as they follow generally accepted practices that do not endanger health or safety.[4]

Maryland extends RTF protections to agricultural operations, defined as the processing of agricultural crops or on-farm production, harvesting, or marketing of any agricultural, horticultural, silvicultural, aquacultural, or apicultural product that has been grown, raised, or cultivated by a farmer.[5] Since a 2009 amendment, RTF nuisance suit protections also extend to silvicultural operations, defined as those involved in the establishment, composition, growth, and harvesting of trees.[6] Since 2014, the state's RTF law also protects commercial fishing and seafood operations from nuisance suits, encompassing harvesting, storage, processing, marketing, sale, purchase, trade, or transport of any seafood product.[7] From that time, "commercial watermen" gained the same protections as agricultural operations from nuisance suits.[8]

Conditions and Activities

Maryland's RTF law protects agricultural operations that have been underway for at least one year from being deemed either a public nuisance (interfering with public rights generally) or a private nuisance (interfering with individual property rights).[9]

This protection remains subject to a few conditions. Operators must comply with applicable federal, state, and local permits.[10] If such operations are negligent, meaning they fail to take proper care, they lose RTF protections. Additionally, agricultural operations must implement a nutrient plan for nitrogen and phosphorus if required by law.

As long as operations meet these conditions, they gain immunity from nuisance suits related to sight, noises, odors, dust, or insects.[11] A 1986 amendment further stipulated that if these conditions are met, no private action can be taken that accuses an operation of interfering with the use or enjoyment of another's property.[12]

Mediation

Since 1996, Maryland requires that any complaints against agricultural operations use mediation before proceeding to litigation. Before a nuisance suit can be filed, the complaint must be considered by a local agency. No person can file a nuisance suit until the local agency hears the complaint and makes a decision or recommendation. Local agencies' decisions can be appealed to a circuit court.

When no local agency is available, the State Agricultural Mediation Program considers the complaint. Only once the mediation concludes can a nuisance suit be filed against an agricultural operation.[13] Agricultural mediation, according to the law, is a process whereby "a mediator helps private parties or government agencies resolve agriculturally related disputes in a confidential and non-adversarial setting."[14] The mediation process remains confidential, except to meet reporting requirements of the U.S. Department of Agriculture.[15]

The prominent role of local agencies and the state's mediation program may have kept nuisance suits out of Maryland's courts.[16]

Table 2.20 Maryland's Key RTF Provisions and National Comparison

Maryland's key RTF provisions		% U.S. states with similar RTF provisions
Operations are immune from lawsuits . . .	once in operation for a year.	48%
Operations are not immune from lawsuits . . .	if they do not comply with county laws.	42%
	if they do not comply with environmental laws.	26%
	if they do not comply with federal laws.	62%
	if they do not comply with other laws.	50%
	if they do not comply with state laws.	68%
	if they are negligent.	46%
Other important details	RTF protects processing.	48%

Local Government

Maryland's RTF law does not prohibit federal, state, or local government from enforcing health, environmental, zoning, or any other applicable laws.[17] This includes the right to prevent and remove nuisances, including keeping contagious diseases out of counties.[18] More specifically, counties may approve the location for soap manufacturing, fertilizer manufacturing, slaughterhouses, packinghouses, or "any other facility that may involve conditions that are unsanitary or detrimental to health."[19]

Before passing an ordinance, counties must hold a public hearing.[20] County commissioners are required to publish notice of the public hearing and a summary of the proposed act, ordinance, or resolution in at least one newspaper of general circulation in the county once each week for two successive weeks.[21] County commissioners may not adopt an act, an ordinance, or a resolution until ten days after a public hearing has been held on it.[22] As a result, much debate about the extent of permitting and special exemptions for agriculture plays out at the county level.[23] The Carroll County Farm Bureau, for example, played a central role in introducing regulations that expanded RTF protections for operations and reduced neighbors' capacity to make claims. Simultaneously, the county provides some of the most far-reaching protections for agricultural operations in the state.[24]

While counties can adopt ordinances, resolutions, and regulations pertaining to seafood businesses, they must be approved by the secretary of natural resources.[25]

NOTES

1. "Farms' Right to Smell Draws Complaints—Neighbors Opposed to Glendening's Plan to Strengthen Law," *Baltimore Sun*, March 25, 1997.
2. U.S. Department of Agriculture, *USDA Quick Stats Tool: June 1981 Survey, Maryland*, distributed by National Agricultural Statistics Service, accessed December 13, 2020, https:// quickstats.nass.usda.gov/results/5CEED3D9-288E-317C-B751-0291B5DD01A1; "2021 State Agriculture Overview: Maryland," U.S. Department of Agriculture, National Agricultural Statistics Service, accessed October 21, 2022, https://www.nass.usda.gov/Quick_Stats /Ag_Overview/stateOverview.php?state=MARYLAND.
3. Md. Code, Health-Gen. § 20-301(a) (2021).
4. Md. Code, Health-Gen. § 20-301(b)(1)–(2) (2021).
5. Md. Code, Cts. & Jud. Proc. § 5-403(a)(2) (2021).
6. Md. Code, Cts. & Jud. Proc. § 5-403(a)(4) (2021).
7. Md. Code, Cts. & Jud. Proc. § 5-403(a)(3)(i) (2021).
8. Craig O'Donnell, "'Right to Fish' Lawsuit Immunity Moves Forward," *Easton (Md.) Sunday Star*, April 6, 2014.
9. Md. Code, Cts. & Jud. Proc. § 5-403(c) (2021)
10. Md. Code, Cts. & Jud. Proc. § 5-403(b)(1)(iii) (2021).
11. Md. Code, Cts. & Jud. Proc. § 5-403(c)(1) (2021).
12. Md. Code, Cts. & Jud. Proc. § 5-403(c)(2) (2021).
13. Md. Code, Cts. & Jud. Proc. § 5-403(c)(3)–(4) (2021).
14. Md. Code, Agric. § 1-1A-01(b) (2021).
15. Md. Code, Agric. § 1-1A-04 (2021).
16. Our research did not uncover any published court opinions pertaining to nuisance suits in Maryland, but see George Dorsey, "Judge Dismisses Hog Farm Lawsuit," *Frederick (Md.) News-Post*, December 3, 1999.
17. Md. Code, Cts. & Jud. Proc. § 5-403(b)(1) (2021).
18. Md. Code, Local Gov't § 13-401(c)(2) (2021).
19. Md. Code, Local Gov't § 13-401(d)(5) (2021).
20. For more details on the specific definitions of counties, see Md. Code, Local Gov't § 13-401 (2021).
21. Md. Code, Local Gov't § 9-105(c)(2) (2021).
22. Md. Code, Local Gov't § 9-105(c)(1) (2021).
23. Jake Owens, "CAFO Committee Debates Purpose, Mitigation Factors," *Cecil (Md.) Whig*, August 23, 2017; Chris Knauss, "Commissioners Place Property Nuisance Law on Hold," *Easton (Md.) Times Record*, November 23, 2011; David Abrams, "Lawmaker's Bill Asserts Farmers' Rights," *Maryland Gazette* (Annapolis), August 18, 2004.
24. Carrie Ann Knauer, "Carroll's Right to Farm Ordinance One of Maryland's Toughest," *Carroll County Times* (Westminster, Md.), July 26, 2009; Christian Alexandersen, "Bills Going to General Assembly," *Carroll County Times*, January 2, 2011.
25. Md. Code, Local Gov't § 13-601(b)(2) (2021).

Massachusetts

Advocates proposed the right-to-farm law in Massachusetts as a tool to prevent the loss of farmland and to protect farmers.[1] Since enacting its RTF law in 1990, Massachusetts's farm operations have grown by 12 percent while the state has lost 22 percent of its acreage in farms.[2] So what does this legislation do in practice?

Massachusetts's RTF Law at a Glance

Massachusetts's RTF law provides no explicit protection for farmland. Neither does the law tailor protection to certain farm sizes or forms, such as small or family farms. Rather, Massachusetts's RTF law, like those present in all other states, centers on protecting agriculture and farming at large from nuisance suits over matters that impact neighboring property, like noise or pollution. The statute's definition of farming and agriculture ranges from cultivation and tillage to dairying, aquaculture, livestock, horses, lumbering, and forestry operations. The act also explicitly defines a farmer "as one engaged in agriculture or farming as herein defined, or on a farm as an incident to or in conjunction with such farming operations," which also includes transportation to markets.[3]

Conditions and Activities

Massachusetts's RTF law protects people and entities as well as their related and subsidiary forms from nuisance lawsuits so long as they are (1) an "ordinary aspect of said farming operation or ancillary or related activity" and (2) in operation for more than one year. RTF protection from nuisance suits does not apply if the conduct is negligent (failing to take proper care) or inconsistent with generally accepted agricultural practices.[4]

The practical meaning of "generally accepted agricultural practices" has been subject to litigation. For example, a county board of health ordered a cranberry bog farm to abate an alleged nuisance consisting of sand piles that blew onto neighboring property. The farm subsequently claimed that the sand piles constituted an ordinary aspect of farming and was thus protected by the RTF law. The court disagreed, ruling that the RTF law did not apply and the county board of health could issue an abatement of the nuisance.[5] In a 2013 case, homeowners claimed certain farm activities interfered with the enjoyment of their property. Grievous actions included deliberately dumping snow on the homeowners' driveway, operating tractors in early mornings and late at night, and deliberately spraying dirt and manure onto the homeowners' property during their outdoor activities. The court found that none of these activities constituted "generally acceptable agricultural practices," and thus the RTF law did not protect the farm activities.[6]

Local Government

Local governments through their boards of health retain some authority to determine that a farm or operation is a nuisance. Still, if odors or noises are part of "normal maintenance" or generally acceptable farming practices, these boards cannot declare the operations nuisances.[7]

When boards determine an operation is a nuisance, they can order the activity be abated within ten days. Although operations have the right to petition review of such decisions, if no petition is filed by the farm or upon final order of the court, the board may proceed in the manner it deems appropriate. However, petitions filed for review by farms suspend a board's order until courts decide whether the RTF law applies.

Even before the enactment of its RTF law, Massachusetts's zoning law barred ordinances or bylaws that "prohibit, unreasonably regulate, or require a special permit for the use of land" that is used primarily for farming and agriculture.[8] Since 1985, the meaning of "farming" and "agriculture" has consequently been subject to conflict in court. In 1986, the town of Mansfield ordered a farm with sixty pigs on seventeen acres in an agricultural zone to desist. When the farmer refused, the inspector brought action seeking an injunction (an order to stop activities) and monetary relief. However, the court ruled that the town's zoning attempt was void, and thus the agricultural operation was shielded from zoning laws. In a 2016 case, a mulching business owner claimed his agricultural operation was exempt from special permit requirements. Nonetheless, the court affirmed the zon-

Table 2.21 Massachusetts's Key RTF Provisions and National Comparison

Massachusetts's key RTF provisions		% U.S. states with similar RTF provisions
Operations are immune from lawsuits . . .	once in operation for a year.	48%
Operations are not immune from lawsuits . . .	if they are negligent.	46%

ing board's decision that the mulching business was not an agricultural operation because the activity "does not involve growing or harvesting any forest products."[9] Likewise, Massachusetts courts have ruled that waste and recycling services do not qualify as farming or agriculture and thus remain subject to local zoning laws.[10]

Other pertinent lawsuits in Massachusetts include a realty trust that owned a grocery store where food, produce, and sundry items were sold. The trust attempted to use the RTF law's agricultural exemption to defend its grocery store's sign. The town government alleged that the sign violated its ordinance regulating how much a sign could flash or use neon light. The court ruled that the store did not qualify as using land primarily for commercial agriculture, and thus the agricultural exemption did not apply.[11]

Local governments can also choose to pass laws that provide additional protections to operations deemed agricultural.[12] Governmental bodies in Massachusetts win more RTF cases than in any other state in the nation.[13]

NOTES

1. Ralph Gordon, "Farmland Losses Are Deplored," *Springfield (Mass.) Union-News*, June 16, 1988; Ralph Gordon, "Public, Private Recommendations Advised for Saving County Farms," *Springfield Union-News*, June 27, 1988.

2. U.S. Department of Agriculture, *USDA Quick Stats Tool: June 1990 Survey, Massachusetts*, distributed by National Agricultural Statistics Service, accessed January 6, 2021, https://quickstats.nass.usda.gov/results/8064ABF8-9BAE-38CA-8B0E-146652A23C90; "2021 State Agriculture Overview: Massachusetts," U.S. Department of Agriculture, National Agricultural Statistics Service, accessed October 21, 2022, https://www.nass.usda.gov/Quick_Stats/Ag_Overview/stateOverview.php?state=MASSACHUSETTS.

3. Mass. Gen. Laws ch. 111, § 1 (2021).

4. Mass. Gen. Laws ch. 243, § 6 (2021).

5. *Francisco Cranberries LLC v. Gibney*, 1999 Mass. App. Div. 223.

6. *Smith v. Wright*, 2013 Mass. App. Div. 24.

7. Mass. Gen. Laws ch. 111, § 122 (2021).

8. Mass. Gen. Laws ch. 40A, § 3 (2021).

9. *Cotton Tree Services Inc. v. Zoning Bd. of Appeals of Westhampton*, 89 Mass. App. Ct. 1136 (2016).

10. *A Plus Waste & Recycling Servs., LLC v. Stewart*, 2018 Mass. App. Div. 132.

11. *Bruni v. Gambale*, No. MISC 313482, 2008 WL 2955388 (Land Ct. Aug. 4, 2008).

12. Rita Savard, "Right to Farm Passes Muster," *Lowell (Mass.) Sun*, May 9, 2006; Bonnie Chandler, "Moving Ahead on 'Right to Farm' Bylaw," *Bolton (Mass.) Common*, April 7, 2006.

13. See the section "Geopolitical Extraction" in the introduction for more about the prevalence of governmental body wins in Massachusetts RTF case law.

Michigan

Supporters of right-to-farm legislation in Michigan, first passed in 1981, have argued it protects farmland and family farmers, while critics have suggested it favors industrial-scale operations to the detriment of communities.[1] Since the law was enacted, the number of farms in the state has dropped by 22 percent, with 11 percent fewer acres of farmland.[2] So what does this legislation do in practice?

Michigan's RTF Law at a Glance

Michigan's RTF law provides no specific protections for family farmers or means to stop suburban sprawl. Rather, Michigan's RTF law, like those present in the other forty-nine states, protects certain types of operations from nuisance suits when their activities impact neighboring property, for example through noise or pollution. In 1995, legislators amended the act to broaden what qualifies as protected activities, which include animal or plant production processes, structures and equipment used in commercial-scale production, and harvesting and storage, as well as the generation of noise, odors, dust, fumes, and other associated conditions.[3]

Conditions and Activities

To receive special RTF protections, farms and operations must be of commercial scale. In 1995, legislators passed amendments that substantially expanded the protection provided to farms and operations to also include (1) a change in ownership or size; (2) temporarily ceasing operations; (3) enrollment in government operations; (4) adopting new technology; or (5) a change in the type of farm product being produced.[4] Operations also receive protections if they existed before a change in land use or occupancy

130

within a mile of their boundaries and if, before the change in land use, an operation would not have been a nuisance.

To receive nuisance suit protection, farms or operations must adhere to generally accepted agricultural and management practices. In 1995, the meaning of "generally accepted agricultural practices" became subject to determination by the Michigan Department of Agriculture and Rural Development and the Michigan Commission of Agriculture and Rural Development.[5] The public can propose revisions to the department through comments, but they are not necessarily binding and thus are subject to controversy.[6] In 2019, the Michigan Department of Environmental Quality tried to change the generally accepted agricultural practices to limit concentrated animal feeding operations' waste application on frozen and snow-covered ground but was sued by agricultural industry groups.[7] The proposed criteria were never imposed.

Residents can file grievances, but they remain subject to verification by the Department of Environmental Quality's interpretation of generally accepted agricultural and management practices.[8] If someone "brings more than 3 unverified complaints against the same farm or operation within 3 years," that person may be ordered to pay the full costs of investigation of any fourth or subsequent unverified complaints. Since generally accepted agricultural and management practices can be vague or voluntary, it can be difficult to verify complaints in accordance with prevailing protocol. Residents rarely resort to nuisance lawsuits, but when they do and win, the farming operation is not responsible for paying their litigation costs. However, in accordance with a 1995 amendment to the RTF law, when the outcomes reverse and the farming operation wins, it is automatically awarded costs, expenses, and reasonable attorney fees.[9]

Courts also have ruled that CAFO activities must meet the RTF law's definition or conform to accepted management practices.[10] In one case, the court ruled that even though the homeowners lived on their property before a hog facility began operating on the neighboring land, the facility warranted RTF protection because the overall land use in the surrounding one-mile area had not changed from primarily agricultural to residential.[11] Further, the RTF law leaves its mark directly on property, providing language that encourages sellers to disclose RTF protections and generally accepted agricultural practices on land deeds.[12]

Local Government

Local governments are barred from enacting, maintaining, or enforcing an ordinance, regulation, or resolution that conflicts in any manner with the RTF law or with any generally accepted agricultural and management practices developed under the law.[13] However, if the local government anticipates negative environmental or public health impacts, the Department of Agriculture and Rural Development will review a proposed ordinance that suggests different standards and make a recommendation to the Commission of Agriculture and Rural Development on whether the ordinance should be approved. In some cases, political subdivisions were able to uphold their ordinances, even when defendants tried to use the RTF law to claim otherwise. Cases have included these rulings:

- The RTF law does not prevent political subdivisions from regulating noncommercial farms.[14]
- The RTF law does not prevent political subdivisions from regulating activities that do not meet the statutory definition of "farm" or are not necessary for the production, harvesting, or storage of "farm products," such as composting, construction of buildings for an unrelated use, or auctions.[15]
- The RTF law does not apply to farming practices for which there are no generally accepted agricultural management practices.[16]
- RTF protections do not extend to a farming operation established after a change in zoning.[17]
- The RTF law does not exempt farms from violations of the Natural Resources and Environmental Protection Act.[18]

Other Related Agricultural Laws

In 1998, the Michigan Agricultural Processing Act was enacted, offering a suite of nuisance protections to operations engaged in processing of agricultural products, including food for human consumption and animal feed.[19] The act offers immunity to processing operations regardless of change in locality within one mile of the operation, a change in ownership or size, or a temporary cessation or interruption of processing or if the operation adopts a new technology or produces a new or different product.[20] The act also requires that nuisance complaints be handled by Michigan's Department of Environmental Quality prior to bringing suit in court and discourages

Table 2.22 Michigan's Key RTF Provisions and National Comparison

Michigan's key RTF provisions		% U.S. states with similar RTF provisions
Operations are immune from lawsuits . . .	if there is a change in locality.	46%
	if they use a new technology.	30%
	if they produce a different product.	26%
	if there is an ownership change.	26%
	if there is a cessation or interruption in farming.	26%
	if they are there first.	44%
Operations are not immune from lawsuits . . .	if they are a nuisance from the start.	38%
Other important details	RTF protects processing.	48%
	Attorney fees are awarded to prevailing defendant.	34%
	RTF supersedes local ordinances and laws.	62%

repeat complaints. The law stipulates that a complainant who brings more than three "unverified nuisance complaints" within three years to Michigan's Department of Agriculture will be responsible for the costs associated with the investigation.[21] An "unverified nuisance complaint" is defined as "a nuisance complaint in which the director of the department of agriculture or his or her designee determines that the processing operation is using generally accepted fruit, vegetable, dairy product, meat, and grain processing practices."[22]

In a 2021 class action suit, a Michigan court upheld a lower court opinion involving nuisance and negligence claims against an operation involved in sugar beet processing. The defendants claimed that the noxious odors produced by the operation constituted a nuisance. Upon appeal, the court held that the defendants were protected by Michigan's Agricultural Processing Act as they were engaged in generally accepted practices.[23] Additionally, the court held that the plaintiffs did not fully utilize the required administrative procedures stipulated in the act.[24]

NOTES

1. Kevin Braciszeski, "Issue to Be Looked at [by] State Legislature—Hog Farming," *Ludington (Mich.) Daily News*, October 16, 1998; Erin Skene, "Townships, Farmers at Odds of Act—Right to Farm," *Ludington Daily News*, November 4, 2019; Jeremy Wahr, "Proposed Farm Practice Has Critics—Some Say the New Rules Would Allow Farmers to Ignore Local Zoning Regulations," *Ionia (Mich.) Sentinel-Standard*, November 15, 2018.

2. U.S. Department of Commerce, "Table 1. Farms, Land in Farms, and Land Use: 1982 and Earlier Census Years," in *1982 Census of Agriculture, Volume 1: Geographic Area Series, Part 22: Michigan State and County Data, Chapter 1: State Data* (Washington, D.C.: U.S. Bureau of the Census, 1984), https://agcensus.library.cornell.edu/wp-content/uploads/1982-Michigan-CHAPTER_1_State_Data-121-Table-01.pdf; "2021 State Agriculture Overview: Michigan," U.S. Department of Agriculture, National Agricultural Statistics Service, accessed October 21, 2022, https://www.nass.usda.gov/Quick_Stats/Ag_Overview/stateOverview.php?state=MICHIGAN.

3. See 1995 Mich. Pub. Acts 94 (H.B. 4300); Mich. Comp. Laws § 286.472 (2021).

4. 1995 Mich. Pub. Acts 94 (H.B. 4300) (amending, in relevant part, Mich. Comp. Laws § 286.473).

5. 1995 Mich. Pub. Acts 94 (H.B. 4300) (amending, in relevant part, Mich. Comp. Laws § 286.472).

6. Edward Hoogterp, "'Right-to-Farm' Rules Go before State Panel," *Muskegon (Mich.) Chronicle*, May 9, 2000.

7. See Ashley Davenport, "Michigan Ag Organizations, Farmers File CAFO Permit Appeal," *Michigan Ag Today*, June 3, 2020.

8. Mich. Comp. Laws § 286.474 (2021).

9. Mich. Comp. Laws § 286.473 (2021).

10. *Milan Tp. v. Jaworski*, No. 240444, 2003 WL 22872141 (Mich. Ct. App. Dec. 4, 2003).

11. *Steffens v. Keeler*, 503 N.W.2d 675 (Mich. Ct. App. 1993).

12. Mich. Comp. Laws § 286.473 (2021).

13. Mich. Comp. Laws § 286.474 (2021).

14. *Brown v. Summerfield Twp.*, No. 304979, 2012 WL 3640330 (Mich. Ct. App. Aug. 23, 2012); *Shelby Twp. v. Papesh*, 704 N.W.2d 92 (Mich. Ct. App. 2005).

15. *Charter Twp. of White Lake v. Ciurlik Enterprises*, No. 326514, 2016 WL 2772160 (Mich. Ct. App. May 12, 2016); *Cty. of Mason v. Indian Summer Co-Op Inc.*, No. 301952, 2012 WL 3536789 (Mich. Ct. App. Aug. 16, 2012).

16. *Claybanks Twp. v. Feorene*, No. 322043, 2015 WL 8277773 (Mich. Ct. App. Dec. 8, 2015).

17. *Jerome Twp. v. Melchi*, 457 N.W.2d 52 (Mich. Ct. App. 1990).

18. *King of the Wind Farms Inc. v. Michigan Comm'n of Ag.* No. 257097, 2005 WL 3556150 (Mich. Ct. App. Dec. 29, 2005).

19. Mich. Comp. Laws § 289.821–289.825 (2022).

20. Mich. Comp. Laws § 289.823 (2022).

21. Mich. Comp. Laws § 289.284 (2022).

22. Mich. Comp. Laws § 289.824(5) (2022).

23. *Morley v. Michigan Sugar Co.*, No. 354085, 2021 WL 5405867 (Mich. Ct. App. Nov. 18, 2021).

24. *Morley*, 2021 WL 5405867.

Minnesota

Since Minnesota enacted its first right-to-farm law in 1982, the number of farmers in the state has dropped by 28 percent, with 8 percent fewer acres of farmland.[1] Advocates of RTF laws promoted Minnesota's RTF legislation in 1982 as a tool to protect farmland from encroachment.[2] But what does this legislation now do in practice, particularly after a series of significant amendments?

Minnesota's RTF Law at a Glance

Minnesota's original RTF law protected agricultural operations that were part of family farms so long as they had been in existence for at least six years and were not nuisances at the time they began. However, the law was amended in 1994, 2001, and 2004, reducing the number of years in existence to receive protection (from six years to two years) and no longer requiring the operation to be part of a "family farm."[3] The law does not safeguard farmland but rather protects operations that are engaged in the production of crops, livestock, poultry, dairy products, or poultry products (with the exception of processing).[4]

Conditions and Activities

Like other states across the nation, Minnesota's RTF statute stipulates time- and activity-specific protections for operations. Once up and running for two years, operations cannot be declared a general nuisance to the public or a private nuisance to neighboring owners.[5] The operation must be located in an area zoned for agriculture, use agricultural practices common to the area, and meet other applicable laws. Even if entities have been in operation less than two years but meet other conditions, they also are somewhat protected.

135

Table 2.23 Minnesota's Key RTF Provisions and National Comparison

Minnesota's key RTF provisions		% U.S. states with similar RTF provisions
Operations are immune from lawsuits . . .	once in operation for two years.	6%
	if they use a new technology.	30%
	if they produce a different product.	26%
	if there is an ownership change.	26%
	if there is a cessation or interruption in farming.	26%
Operations are not immune from lawsuits . . .	if they do not comply with county laws.	42%
	if they do not comply with federal laws.	62%
	if they do not comply with other laws.	50%
	if they do not comply with state laws.	68%
Other important details	RTF protects processing.	48%

Operations in Minnesota can change without restarting their two-year clock required for nuisance immunity.[6] Accepted changes include changes in ownership, use of new technologies, changes to the type of crops being produced, or a gap in time when production stops. There are two additional criteria that are unique to Minnesota, as no other state has the same language. If a facility expands the number of animals or livestock by 25 percent or more, the clock starts over. Further, the RTF protections do not apply to feedlots with a swine capacity of 1,000 animal units or more, defined by the Pollution Control Agency, or a cattle capacity of 2,500 animals or more.

Local Government

The state of Minnesota has a unique history of enforcing nuisance claims against operations, such as a corporate dairy farm violating emission standards.[7] In addition, local governments, like townships, can enact zoning ordinances, like setback requirements, against agricultural operations as long as they do not conflict with the RTF law or other state laws.[8]

NOTES

1. U.S. Department of Commerce, "Table 1. Farms, Land in Farms, and Land Use: 1982 and Earlier Census Years," in *1982 Census of Agriculture, Volume 1: Geographic Area Series, Part 23: Minnesota State and County Data, Chapter 1: State Data* (Washington, D.C.: U.S. Bureau of the Census, 1984), https://agcensus.library.cornell.edu/wp-content/uploads/1982-Minnesota-CHAPTER_1_State_Data-121-Table-01.pdf; "2021 State Agriculture Overview: Minnesota," U.S. Department of Agriculture, National Agricultural Statistics Service, accessed October 21, 2022, https://www.nass.usda.gov/Quick_Stats/Ag_Overview/stateOverview.php?state=MINNESOTA.

2. See Darry Elwood Owens, "Where City and Country Collide—'Right to Farm' Law Protects Smell, Sound of Agriculture," *Star Tribune: Newspaper of the Twin Cities* (Minneapolis–St. Paul, Minn.), June 26, 1989.

3. See 2004 Minn. Laws 254 (S.F. 2428); 2001 Minn. Laws 128 (S.F. 1659); and 1994 Minn. Laws 619 (H.F. 2493) (each amending Minn. Stat. § 561.19).

4. Minn. Stat. § 561.19 (2021).

5. Minn. Stat. § 561.19 (2021).

6. Minn. Stat. § 561.19 (2021).

7. Tom Meersman, "Dairy Calls State Lawsuit on Odors 'Publicity Driven,'" *Star Tribune: Newspaper of the Twin Cities* (Minneapolis–St. Paul, Minn.), June 24, 2008.

8. *Canadian Connection v. New Prairie Twp.*, 581 N.W.2d 391 (Minn. Ct. App. 1998). See also Minn. Stat. § 561.19(c) (2021), which states that the RTF law does not apply to large animal confinement operations of a certain size, to nuisance actions brought by governmental entities under the state's criminal code, or when a county or municipality brings an action under a valid local zoning law or ordinance.

Mississippi

With little public controversy or advocacy by legislators, the Mississippi right-to-farm law has existed since 1980. Since it was first enacted, the number of farm operations in the state has dropped by 37 percent and the acreage farmed by 29 percent.[1] So what does this legislation do in practice?

Mississippi's RTF Law at a Glance

Mississippi's RTF law provides no explicit protection for farmland or family farms. Rather, its RTF law, like those present in the other forty-nine states, centers on protecting certain types of agricultural operations and forestry activities from nuisance suits when they impact neighboring property, for example through noise or pollution. Mississippi's RTF protections apply to either private nuisance suits (those brought by people, like neighbors) or public nuisance suits (those brought by the government on behalf of the general public).

The state's RTF law protects agricultural operations, defined as a facility or production and processing sites related to livestock, farm-raised fish and products, timber and wood-related products, and poultry for industrial or commercial purposes, among other things.[2] In a 1986 case, a court initially ruled that a cotton gin did not qualify as an agricultural operation and thus did not warrant RTF protections.[3] The court ordered the abatement of the nuisance and awarded damages to one of the plaintiffs, a man with chronic asthma who lived around 400 feet away from the gin. However, the ruling was appealed to and reversed by the Supreme Court of Mississippi in 1992. The court ruled that the facility constituted an agricultural activity that had not expanded, even though the plaintiffs struggled, in the words of the court, "mightily to convince us" otherwise.

138

Mississippi's RTF law was amended in 1994 to extend nuisance suit protections to forestry activities, which includes reforesting, growing, managing, and harvesting timber, wood, and forest products.[4] In a 1995 case, the Mississippi Supreme Court classified timber as a crop that warranted RTF protections when eleven citizens filed suit against operators of the Leaf River Mill, which included Leaf River Forest Products Inc., Great Northern Nekoosa Corporation, and Georgia-Pacific Corporation.[5]

Conditions and Activities

Once up and running for one year or more, agricultural operations and forestry activities receive absolute defense from nuisance action if the operation is in compliance with all applicable state and federal permits.[6] An "absolute defense" means an operation has immunity from liability for wrongdoing associated with nuisances.

The RTF defense of operations once up and running for a year proved central in a 2002 case concerning Prestage Farms Inc., a partner of Smithfield Foods Inc., largely owned and operated by investors in China.[7] Prestage Farms and its seven associated debtors/defendants, including limited liability companies, sought to defend themselves from sixty-eight plaintiffs who sued for nuisance. The associated cases played out in bankruptcy court, as swine operations increasingly use a folding corporate structure to limit their liability for wrongdoing.[8] The companies sought to dismiss the suit, saying that their operations had been ongoing for over a year. However, the plaintiffs countered that the operations had substantially changed, because an incinerator that burned dead animal carcasses was more recently installed. The court responded that a new activity, in this case the incinerator, restarted the operations' clock relative to when the burning started.[9]

However, the bankruptcy court ruled and affirmed on appeal that only the incinerators were eligible for nuisance suits, as the rest of the operations' activities—such as waste lagoons and associated runoff—had been ongoing for over a year. In a final appeal with the state's district court, the court was "sympathetic to the plight of the plaintiff landowners . . . [and was] of the opinion that plaintiffs whose property is adversely affected by an air polluting operation deserve some remedy; but, because . . . plaintiffs failed to bring their claims within the statutory period and because there has been no evidence presented that the hog farms substantially changed after operations began, the court's hands [were] tied."[10] Since all of the defendant farms were in operation more than a year before the lawsuit was filed and there was no dispute regarding whether or not the farms remained substantially unchanged, the plaintiffs' action was barred.[11] In Mississippi, hog CAFOs tend to be located in areas with high percentages of African Americans and persons in poverty.[12]

To receive RTF protection, Mississippi's RTF law also stipulates that such operations and activities must be in compliance with all applicable state and federal permits, including the Mississippi Air and Water Pollution Control Law.[13] In 1995, the Supreme Court of Mississippi reviewed a lower court ruling where the jury awarded over $3 million to residents for alleged damages from exposure to 2,3,7,8-Tetrachlorodibenzo-P-dioxin ("dioxin"), a toxic substance detected in mill sludge.[14] The state supreme court determined that the Leaf River Mill qualified for absolute defense from nuisance suits, as the paper mill was a "crop" that had existed for at least one year. However, the court also ruled that even though the paper mill qualified for RTF protections, it still could face nuisance litigation via the pollution control laws. Based on this, the opposite also became true, where the RTF law still could protect an operation from liability, even in cases when the state's pollution control laws were violated.[15] After reviewing the case, the state supreme court reversed the earlier $3 million verdict, determining that there was not enough evidence to demonstrate that Leaf River Mill owed damages for alleged exposure.

However, not all agricultural operations must comply with the Mississippi Air and Water Pollution Control Act. The law exempts concentrated animal feeding operations, but not those housing swine.[16] Swine CAFOs must be permitted. Those applying after 1998 must demonstrate that their animal waste management system reduces the "effects of the operation on the public health, welfare or the environment." No more than five such permits can be issued to swine CAFOs in any given year.[17] Those who violate this law can be subject to a civil penalty of up to $25,000 for each violation and/ or be subject to temporarily or permanently ending their operations and activities.[18] However, the law does not allow private actions to be brought against hog facilities for violating the act. The court treats the act as a regulatory scheme to oversee and abate air and water pollution.[19]

More generally, the public retains the right "to initiate a request with the [Mississippi Department of Environmental Quality]" to take action for violations of the Air and Water Pollution Control Act.[20] However, it remains up to the state whether or not to take action on reported violations.

Table 2.24 Mississippi's Key RTF Provisions and National Comparison

Mississippi's key RTF provisions		% U.S. states with similar RTF provisions
Operations are immune from lawsuits . . .	once in operation for a year.	48%
Operations are not immune from lawsuits . . .	if they do not comply with state laws.	68%
	if they do not comply with federal laws.	62%
Other important details	RTF protects processing.	48%

Local Government

The RTF law does not allow local governments to require permits for any buildings, structures, or uses that pertain to agriculture, including forestry activities.[21] In addition, the RTF law takes away municipal or county authority to adopt or impose ordinances, regulations, rules, or policies that prohibit or restrict agricultural operations, forestry activities, or traditional farm practices, the latter of which are defined as those that adhere to accepted customs or standards used by similar operations in similar circumstances.[22] This applies to agricultural land or land otherwise unclassified, unless it creates an obstruction to navigable airspace.[23]

County and municipal governments retain their ability to reclassify property from one zone to another.[24] The appellate court affirmed that a county board could enforce zoning regulations, as pertained to a nonprofit horse-riding arena.[25] In another case, the court ruled that the building of a home on twenty-five acres did not qualify for RTF protection, and thus exemption, from a zoning ordinance.[26]

NOTES

1. U.S. Department of Agriculture, *USDA Quick Stats Tool: June 1980 Survey, Mississippi*, distributed by National Agricultural Statistics Service, accessed December 13, 2020, https://quickstats.nass.usda.gov/results/276191E8-01B3-30EE-9232-126794DC5995; "2021 State Agriculture Overview: Mississippi," U.S. Department of Agriculture, National Agricultural Statistics Service, accessed October 21, 2022, https://www.nass.usda.gov/Quick_Stats /Ag_Overview/stateOverview.php?state=MISSISSIPPI.
2. Miss. Code § 95-3-29(2)(a) (2021).

3. *Bowen v. Flaherty*, 601 So. 2d 860 (Miss. 1992).
4. 1994 Miss. Laws 647 (S.B. 2464) (amending, in relevant part, Miss. Code § 95-3-29).
5. *Leaf River Forest Prods. v. Ferguson*, 662 So. 2d 648 (Miss. 1995).
6. Miss. Code § 95-3-29(1) (2021).
7. Prestage Farms Inc. has many interfirm ties with Smithfield Foods. For example, Prestage uses Smithfield's processing plant, in addition to operating two of its own: Prestage Foods of Iowa and Prestage Foods of North Carolina (for poultry). For more information, see Loka Ashwood, Andy Pilny, John Canfield, Mariyam Jamila, and Ryan Thompson, "From Big Ag to Big Finance: A Market Network Approach to Power in Agriculture," *Agriculture and Human Values* 39, no. 4 (2022): 1421–34.
8. Loka Ashwood, Danielle Diamond, and Kendall Thu, "Where's the Farmer? Limiting Liability in Midwestern Industrial Hog Production," *Rural Sociology* 79, no.1 (2014): 2–27.
9. *Moore v. Prestage Farms, Inc.* (In re *Moore*), 306 B.R. 849 (Bankr. N.D. Miss. 2004).
10. *Norman v. Prestage Farms, Inc.*, No. 3:05CV64, 2007 WL 1031371 (N.D. Miss. Mar. 30, 2007).
11. *Norman*, 2007 WL 1031371; Miss. Code § 49-17-35 (2021).
12. Sacoby M. Wilson, Frank Howell, Steve Wing, and Mark Sobsey, "Environmental Injustice and the Mississippi Hog Industry," *Environmental Health Perspectives* 110, no. suppl. 2 (2002): 195–201.
13. Miss. Code § 95-3-29(1), (4) (2021).
14. *Leaf River Forest Products*, 662 So. 2d 648.
15. *Norman*, 2007 WL 1031371.
16. Miss. Code § 49-17-29(1)(b), 2(a) (2021), which states that "concentrated animal feeding operations may be a source or a category of sources exempted under this paragraph. However, no new or existing applications relating to swine concentrated animal feeding operations within a county shall be exempted from regulations and ordinances which have been duly passed by the county's board of supervisors and which are in force on June 1, 1998."
17. Miss. Code § 49-17-29(3)(f) (2021).
18. Miss. Code § 49-17-43(1)–(2) (2021).
19. *Norman v. Prestage Farms, Inc.* (In re *Moore*), 310 B.R. 795 (Bankr. N.D. Miss. 2004).
20. Miss. Code § 49-17-35; *Norman*, 2007 WL 1031371.
21. Miss. Code § 17-1-3(1) (2021).
22. Miss. Code § 95-3-29 2(c) (2021).
23. Miss Code § 17-1-21(2)(a)–(b) (2021).
24. Miss Code § 95-3-29 2(c) (2021).
25. *Hinds Co. Bd. of Supervisors v. Leggette*, 833 So. 2d 586 (Miss. Ct. App. 2002).
26. *Ladner v. Hancock Co.*, 899 So. 2d 899 (Miss. Ct. App. 2004).

Missouri

Ample controversy has surrounded a series of right-to-farm amendments in Missouri, including a constitutional one in 2014. Proponents advocated the law to keep agriculture thriving, while opponents countered that it drives out family farms.[1] Since RTF first became law in 1982, the number of Missouri farms has dropped by 15 percent, with 6 percent fewer acres of farmland.[2] So what does this legislation do in practice?

Missouri's RTF Law at a Glance

Missouri's RTF law, like those present in the other forty-nine states, centers on protecting certain types of facilities from nuisance suits when they impact neighboring property, for example through noise or pollution. Missouri's RTF law protects any commercial facility used in the production or processing of crops, livestock, swine, poultry, livestock products, swine products, or poultry products.[3]

Missouri codified the RTF law in the state constitution (one of only two states to do so) after a controversial amendment passed by fewer than 3,000 votes in 2014. The amendment guarantees "the right of farmers and ranchers to engage in farming and ranching practices."[4] However, this is subject to the definition of "farming and ranching practices." For example, when a defendant tried to use the constitutional amendment to defend against charges of animal cruelty, the court would not allow it. The jury consequently found that the defendant had committed a purposefully abusive act and was not engaging in a legitimate farming practice.[5] Further, a court ruled that the Christian County Health Department in 2016 could halt the sale and distribution of raw milk, superseding the farmer's constitutional claim of RTF defense.[6]

Conditions and Activities

Missouri's original law protected commercial facilities once they were in operation for a year. In 1990, legislators repealed the 1982 law and replaced it with a version that dramatically expanded protections for commercial facilities. From that point forward, an operation was protected from nuisance lawsuits if (1) the area around it changed after it began operating; (2) the operation expanded in acres or animal units, as long as it did not violate existing laws; and (3) that operation temporarily halted or downsized its production.[7]

If a court determines that the operation constituted a nuisance at the time it began or that it was negligent (that is, operating improperly), RTF protections do not apply. They also do not apply if the operation's expansion has a substantially adverse effect on the environment or public health and safety or otherwise increases environmental pressures on surrounding neighbors due to increased pollution.[8] The law also does not protect animal operations that fail to use waste handling standards set by the University of Missouri's Agriculture Extension Service.[9]

Local Government

Missouri's right-to-farm law does not specifically address how local governments can regulate agricultural operations. Rather, a suite of other laws contextualize the power of the RTF law. Prior to 2019, local governments had some latitude to pass their own ordinances. For example, the Missouri Supreme Court held in 1997 that counties could pursue equitable relief under certain circumstances to abate public nuisances, along with cities, towns, and villages.[10] However, townships had no such authority. In 1999, the Linn County government successfully defended its ordinance through a statute that authorizes local governments to enact legislation "[tending] to enhance the public health and prevent the entrance of infectious, contagious, communicable or dangerous diseases into such a county."[11] The court agreed that the standards the county placed on hog facilities enhanced public health and prevented disease.[12] Other counties likewise enacted health ordinances to curtail concentrated animal feeding operations.

However, as of 2019, a recent amendment limits the ability of counties and local health boards to enact ordinances that regulate agricultural operations.[13] Other restrictions separately limit townships and counties from regulating farm buildings or farm structures.[14]

Table 2.25 Missouri's Key RTF Provisions and National Comparison

Missouri's key RTF provisions		% U.S. states with similar RTF provisions
Operations are immune from lawsuits . . .	if boundaries or size of operations change.	34%
	if there is a change in locality.	46%
	if there is a cessation or interruption in farming.	26%
	once in operation for a year.	48%
Operations are not immune from lawsuits . . .	if they are a nuisance from the start.	38%
	if they are negligent.	46%
	if they do not comply with county laws.	42%
	if they do not comply with environmental laws.	26%
	if they do not comply with federal laws.	62%
	if they do not comply with state laws.	68%
	if they pollute water.	36%
Other important details	Attorney fees are awarded to prevailing defendant.	34%
	RTF supersedes local ordinances and laws.	62%
	RTF protects processing.	48%

Attorney Fees and Limits on Damages

In 2009, legislators passed amendments that placed limits on the recovery of damages for those who sue agricultural operations. The 2009 amendment followed a case, initially filed in 2002, where the jury awarded over $11 million to residents and farmers living near a Premium Standard Farms hog operation, later absorbed by WH Group's Smithfield Foods Inc. The verdict was issued in 2008 and was subsequently upheld on appeal in 2011. It was the largest monetary award ever issued against a hog farm in an odor nuisance case, according to a press release issued by the plaintiffs' attorneys.[15]

The 2009 amendment limited possible monetary compensation for permanent nuisances (ones that cannot be stopped through altering practices) to the reduction in property value, capped at the overall assessed value. Those suing could no longer claim awards based on use and enjoyment.[16] For example, neighbors of an industrial hog operation sued Cargill Pork LLC and its host for nuisance in 2015, but the court ruled that statute 537.296 prohibits noneconomic damages such as the loss of use (like future earnings from raising cattle or collecting rent) and enjoyment of property (like sitting on the back porch).[17] In the case of temporary nuisances (ones that can be stopped through altering practices), damages are limited to current fair rent value. Once damages are awarded, the ruling becomes codified on the property deed. If the property is sold in the future and someone later wants to bring a nuisance suit against the same operator, that individual's damages are limited to those allowed for permanent nuisances.

These limitations on awards have been challenged as unconstitutional because they violate private property rights. However, a court determined that promoting agricultural activity is to the public's benefit. The court thus ruled that this authorizes the taking of private property by limiting damages.[18]

Missouri's RTF law also allows for qualified operations to recover the expenses and attorney fees they incur while defending against frivolous nuisance lawsuits.[19]

NOTES

1. Tim Hoover, "Missouri Bill Divides Rural Communities," *Kansas City (Mo.) Star*, March 8, 2007; Karen Dalton, "Bill to Limit Factory Farms' Liability Faces Possible Veto," *Kansas City Star*, May 2, 2011.
2. U.S. Department of Commerce, "Table 4. Farms, Land in Farms, and Land Use, by Size of Farm: 1982 and 1978," in *1982 Census of Agriculture, Volume 1: Geographic Area Series, Part 25: Missouri State and County Data, Chapter 1: State Data* (Washington, D.C.: U.S. Bureau of the Census, 1984), https://agcensus.library.cornell.edu/wp-content/uploads/1982 -Missouri-CHAPTER_1_State_Data-121-Table-04.pdf; "2021 State Agriculture Overview: Missouri," U.S. Department of Agriculture, National Agricultural Statistics Service, accessed October 21, 2022, https://www.nass.usda.gov/Quick_Stats/Ag_Overview/stateOverview .php?state=MISSOURI.
3. Mo. Rev. Stat. § 537.295(2) (2021).
4. Mo. Const. art. 1, § 35 (2021).
5. *State v. Hammond*, 569 S.W.3d 21 (Mo. Ct. App. 2018).
6. *Vimont v. Christian Cty. Health Dep't*, 502 S.W.3d 718, 719–20 (Mo. Ct. App. 2016) ("Constitutional farming rights, whatever they may be, are subject to local-government powers duly authorized and conferred by article VI of Missouri's constitution. . . . As relevant here, article VI directs that county commissions 'shall manage all county business prescribed by law' (§ 7) and for county powers to be defined by 'general laws' (§ 8)").
7. 1990 Mo. Laws (S.B. 686) (enacting what is now Mo. Rev. Stat. § 537.295).
8. Mo. Rev. Stat. § 537.295 (2021).
9. Mo. Rev. Stat. § 537.295 (2021).
10. *Premium Standard Farms v. Lincoln Twp.*, 946 S.W.2d 234, 240 (Mo. 1997) (stating that "counties have been granted the power to pursue equitable relief under certain circumstances to abate a public nuisance, sections 67.410, 263.262, [Mo. Rev. Stat.] 1994, as have cities, towns and villages, sections 71.285, 77.530, 77.560, 79.370, 79.380, 79.383, 80.090, [Mo. Rev. Stat.] 1994").
11. *Borron v. Farrenkopf*, 5 S.W.3d 618, 621 (Mo. Ct. App. 1999).

12. *Borron,* 5 S.W.3d at 621–22 (noting that "the purpose of the ordinance was to regulate for health concerns rather than for a uniform development of real estate").

13. See 2019 Mo. Laws (S.B. 391) (amending Mo. Rev. Stat. § 192.300, subd. 1(2), to state that counties shall not "[2] impose standards or requirements on an agricultural operation and its appurtenances, as such term is defined in section 537.295, that are inconsistent with or more stringent than any provision of this chapter or chapters 260, 640, 643, and 644, or any rule or regulation promulgated under such chapters").

14. See, e.g., Mo. Rev. Stat. § 65.677 (2021). See also *Premium Standard Farms,* 946 S.W.2d 234.

15. See the Speer Law Firm, "Missouri Jury Awards Residents Eleven Million in Damages from Living under Cloud of Stench Caused by Industrial Hog Farms," PR Newswire, March 5, 2010. See also *Owens v. ContiGroup Companies, Inc.,* 344 S.W.3d 717 (Mo. Ct. App. 2011); 2009 Mo. Laws (H.B. 481) (adding what is now Mo. Rev. Stat. § 537.296(7), which allows parties to request that the court or jury visit the location of an alleged private nuisance if the amount at issue in the case exceeds $1 million).

16. Mo. Rev. Stat. § 537.296(2)(1) (2021).

17. Mo. Rev. Stat. § 537.296 (2021); *Labrayere v. Bohr Farms, LLC,* 458 S.W.3d 319 (Mo. 2015).

18. *Labrayere,* 458 S.W.3d 319.

19. Mo. Rev. Stat. § 537.295(5) (2021).

Montana

Since 1973, Montana's constitution commits to protecting, enhancing, and developing agriculture.[1] The legislature later justified the state's right-to-farm statutes as crucial for sustaining the "farm economy and land bases associated with it," particularly in the face of nuisance claims by newcomers.[2] Since the state first enacted RTF provisions in 1981, the number of farm operations in the state has grown by 13 percent, while the number of acres in farmland has dropped 6 percent.[3] So what do these laws do in practice?

Montana's RTF Laws at a Glance

Montana's RTF laws provide no explicit protection for land. Rather, Montana's RTF laws, like those present in the other forty-nine states, center on protecting certain types of operations from nuisance suits when they impact neighboring property, for example through noise or pollution. Montana's statutes protect most agricultural activities and operations commonly associated with farming. Montana's civil and criminal code protects from nuisance suits an agricultural or farming operation, a place, or a facility, none of which is defined.[4] However, in 1995 the state passed amendments that expanded and clarified protected activities in its land use, planning, and zoning code. Since then, agricultural activities are defined as those that provide a gross income of $1,500 or more or that occur on land taxed as agricultural or forest land.[5]

Nonetheless, Montana's laws regulating nuisance remain subject to its unique protection of private property rights. As part of its emphasis on open range doctrine, Montana allows persons to remedy an injury to their property more forcefully and directly if a neighbor causes a public nuisance so long as the property owner does not commit a "breach of the peace" or do "unnecessary injury."[6] This unique provision stands apart nationally.

If owners' right to use and enjoy their property is infringed upon, an authorized person can remedy the nuisance, without regard to any argument concerning competing land uses. The law does not define what constitutes an authorized person.

Conditions and Activities

The agricultural activities protected in Montana's RTF statutes in some ways mirror those in other states, including noise, odors, dust, and fumes. However, other protected activities in Montana stand apart, for example the protection from wildlife damage; employment and use of labor; and prevention of trespass. Protected activities can also include the conversion from "one agricultural activity to another, provided that the conversion does not adversely impact adjacent property owners."[7]

Agricultural operations are not protected under Montana's law if they fall under one of two conditions. In the first, if the operation conducts an activity outside of its normal course of operation, it can lose RTF protections. The statute does not, however, define what "normal" consists of. In the second, if the operation creates a nuisance for a neighboring resident or business that owned its land before the agricultural operation began production, that operation can lose its RTF protection.[8] For example, landowners and residents brought a nuisance lawsuit against a neighboring family that raised cattle and crops as well as against the corporation the family hired to help with hay-grinding. The plaintiffs alleged that the hay-grinding activities produced dust and particulate matter that damaged their property value, led to the loss of enjoyment of property, and created cleanup expenses and respiratory problems. The neighbors also claimed that the farming operation had changed over time by increasing in intensity. However, the court ruled that the RTF laws apply whether the operation changes over time or uses new technology so long as the agricultural operation existed before the plaintiffs owned their property. The court stated that "the interest that has been in existence longer wins." In this case, that was the farming operation.[9]

Local Governance

Montana states in its legislative finding and purpose that it is "the intent of the legislature to protect agricultural activities from governmental zoning and nuisance ordinances."[10] Ordinances or resolutions cannot prohibit any existing agricultural activities or force the termination of any existing agri-

Table 2.26 Montana's Key RTF Provisions and National Comparison

Montana's key RTF provisions		% U.S. states with similar RTF provisions
Operations are immune from lawsuits . . .	if there is a change in locality.	46%
	if they are there first.	44%
Other important details	RTF supersedes local ordinances and laws.	62%

cultural activities outside the boundaries of an incorporated city or town. Zoning and nuisance ordinances may not prohibit agricultural activities that were established outside the corporate limits of a municipality and then incorporated into that municipality by annexation.[11]

If within a district, 40 percent of the owners of land and buildings have their names on the last assessment roll or 50 percent of the building owners or landowners are taxed for agricultural purposes (for example, brick and mortar businesses), they can protest the establishment of a district or regulations. If they do so, the board of county commissioners is not allowed to adopt the existing resolution or propose another one for a year.[12] However, this provision was found to be an unconstitutional delegation of legislative power in *Williams v. Board of County Commissioners of Missoula County*.[13] Now, Montana law provides that the board of county commissioners may, at its discretion, adopt resolutions that create zoning districts or regulations, regardless of whether landowners or building owners protest the zoning.

Open Range Livestock

In 1984 the state of Montana brought a case against the Finleys, alleging that their loose livestock constituted a public nuisance because the livestock interfered with the plaintiffs' free use and enjoyment of their property and the livestock ran at large upon public roads, causing hazardous road and driving conditions.[14] The Supreme Court of Montana ruled that Montana's public nuisance abatement statutes "should not be utilized to require a livestock owner to prevent his or her stock from running free on county roads in an open range area."[15] Even though the livestock posed potential hazards, the court concluded that the state could not prevent the stockowners from running their livestock at large. However, the Finleys had to demonstrate that their livestock met the requirements of the state's open range law (that is, purebred in accordance with pertinent laws).[16] The case was remanded for the lower court to determine if the Finleys met this requirement.

NOTES

1. Mont. Const. art. XII, § 1.
2. Mont. Code § 76-2-901 (2021). See also Charles S. Johnson, "Candidates for Governor Weigh in on 'Right to Farm' Legislation," *Independent Record* (Helena, Mont.), April 27, 2004.
3. U.S. Department of Agriculture, *USDA Quick Stats Tool: June 1981 Survey, Montana*, distributed by National Agricultural Statistics Service, accessed October 27, 2020, https://quickstats.nass.usda.gov/results/EC493E6F-1EC6-3AE4-B6D0-0208B1FF53B6; "2021 State Agriculture Overview: Montana," U.S. Department of Agriculture, National Agricultural Statistics Service, accessed October 21, 2022, https://www.nass.usda.gov/Quick_Stats/Ag_Overview/stateOverview.php?state=MONTANA.
4. Mont. Code §§ 27-30-101, 27-30-204, 45-8-111 (2021).
5. Mont. Code § 76-2-902(1) (2021).
6. Mont. Code § 27-30-204 (2021).
7. Mont. Code § 76-2-902 (2021).
8. Mont. Code § 45-8-111 (2021).
9. *Dreeszen v. Dan Swartz, Inc.*, No. DV-09-579, 2010 WL 8747752 (Mont. Dist. July 12, 2010).
10. Mont. Code § 76-2-901 (2021).
11. Mont. Code § 76-2-903 (2021).
12. Mont. Code § 76-2-205(6) (2013).
13. *Williams v. Bd. of Co. Comm'rs of Missoula Co.*, 308 P.3d 88 (Mont. 2013).
14. See Mont. Code § 45-8-111 (2021).
15. *State ex rel. Martin v. Finley*, 738 P.2d 497 (Mont. 1987) (emphasis added).
16. Mont. Code §§ 81-4-210 to 81-4-211 (2021).

Nebraska

· ·

Proponents of Nebraska's right-to-farm law, first enacted in 1982, argued it would stop sprawl and protect family farmers. Others countered that the law would cripple smaller farmers and violated constitutional rights to private property.[1] Yet since the RTF law first passed, the number of Nebraska farms has dropped by 26 percent, with less than a percentage point in loss of farmland.[2] So what does this legislation do in practice?

Nebraska's RTF Law at a Glance

Nebraska's law provides no explicit protection for farmland or family farmers. Rather, Nebraska's RTF law, like those present in the other forty-nine states, centers on protecting certain types of operations from nuisance suits when their activities impact neighboring property, for example through activities like noise or pollution.

Conditions and Activities

To receive special RTF protections in Nebraska, operations must be engaged in the commercial production of farm products on over ten acres of land.[3] As long as the operation existed before a change in the surrounding land or occupancy and as long as it was not a nuisance before the change, it is protected.[4]

Nebraska has a long-standing history of nuisance suits. In two cases decided in 1985, neighboring farmers and homeowners sued hog facilities (which in one case was a corporation) for nuisance. In both cases, the courts found the operation to be a nuisance, required the operation to cease the nuisance activity, and declared that the RTF law did not apply, as there had been no proximate change in land use or occupancy.[5]

Table 2.27 Nebraska's Key RTF Provisions and National Comparison

Nebraska's key RTF provisions		% U.S. states with similar RTF provisions
Operations are immune from lawsuits . . .	if there is a change in locality.	46%
	if they are there first.	44%
Operations are not immune from lawsuits . . .	if they are a nuisance from the start.	38%

In 1998, the RTF law was amended to include protections for grain warehouses and operations.[6] Even though a business owner first brought a nuisance case against a grain elevator in 1997, the original court, when eventually hearing the case, considered whether the 1998 amendment nonetheless applied. The court ruled that the amendment to protect grain elevators from nuisance suits applied, even retroactively. On appeal, however, the Nebraska Supreme Court overturned this decision in 2002, holding that the legislature did not intend a retrospective application; thus the grain warehouse was not shielded from the 1997 nuisance action.[7]

NOTES

1. See David Hendee, "Court Action Raises Fears of Neighbors' Suits against Farmers," *Omaha (Neb.) World-Herald*, February 23, 1999; Paul Hammel and Martha Stoddard, "Proposed Expansion of Nebraska's Right to Farm Act Runs into Opposition," *Grand Island (Neb.) Independent*, April 10, 2019.
2. U.S. Department of Commerce, "Table 1. Farms, Land in Farms, and Land Use: 1982 and 1978," in *1982 Census of Agriculture, Volume 1: Geographic Area Series, Part 27: Nebraska State and County Data, Chapter 2: County Data* (Washington, D.C.: U.S. Bureau of the Census, 1984), https://agcensus.library.cornell.edu/wp-content/uploads/1982-Nebraska -CHAPTER_2_County_Data-122-Table-01.pdf; "2021 State Agriculture Overview: Nebraska," U.S. Department of Agriculture, National Agricultural Statistics Service, accessed October 21, 2022, https://www.nass.usda.gov/Quick_Stats/Ag_Overview/stateOverview.php ?state=NEBRASKA.
3. Neb. Rev. Stat. § 2-4402 (2021).
4. Neb. Rev. Stat. § 2-4403 (2021).
5. *Flansburgh v. Coffey*, 370 N.W.2d 127 (Neb. 1985); *Cline v. Franklin Pork, Inc.*, 361 N.W.2d 566 (Neb. 1985).
6. 1998 Neb. Laws 1193, § 6 (amending, in relevant part, Neb. Rev. Stat. § 2-4402).
7. *Soukop v. Conagra, Inc.*, 653 N.W.2d 655 (Neb. 2002).

Nevada

Nevada's right-to-farm law has attracted little controversy or general fanfare in the state. It exists alongside more general nuisance statutes that pertain to property at large, setting it apart nationally. The statutes have remained largely unamended since originally passed in 1985, except to extend protections to shooting ranges. Since Nevada passed its right-to-farm law during 1985, the number of farms has increased by 26 percent, while the number of acres used for farmland has decreased by 31 percent.[1] So what does this law do in practice?

Nevada's RTF Law at a Glance

Nevada's RTF law protects certain agricultural activities from nuisance suits when they impact neighboring property, for example through activities like noise or pollution. Nevada's statute protects any agricultural activity conducted on farmland that does not violate a federal, state, or local law.[2] Nevada's law requires that protected operations use good agricultural practices, defined as those that do not violate any laws or regulations.

Conditions and Activities

Nevada's statute protects agricultural operations if the area around a facility changes after it begins operating.[3] Agricultural activities on farmland are protected when they are established before surrounding nonagricultural activities. Nevada's statute does not protect any activity that has a substantial adverse effect on public health or safety. Further, the activities cannot be injurious to health or offensive to the senses. The state law utilizes some unique language, protecting the "free use of property" from interference

Table 2.28 Nevada's Key RTF Provisions and National Comparison

Nevada's key RTF provisions		% U.S. states with similar RTF provisions
Operations are immune from lawsuits . . .	if they are there first.	44%
Operations are not immune from lawsuits . . .	if they do not comply with county laws.	42%
	if they do not comply with federal laws.	62%
	if they do not comply with state laws.	68%
	if they do not comply with other laws.	50%

with the personal or comfortable enjoyment "of life."[4] The overall ambiguity of Nevada's statute likely means agricultural operations cannot claim the same broad protections afforded in other states, although the full implications of the law have yet to play out in court.

Local Government

Nevada's RTF law does not impact local government's authority. In other state statutes, counties are provided the authority to regulate nuisances without the RTF law or other laws exempting agricultural land, as many other states do. For example, one county fined a swine operation for odor and then worked with it to create a plan to reduce the odor.[5]

Attorney Fees

In a recent nuisance case filed against a large-scale corporate dairy operation, the court considered whether to award attorney fees and costs to the operation.[6] The Smith Valley Dairy argued that since the plaintiffs did not receive a preliminary or permanent injunction, damages, or any other relief requested in their complaint, the dairy was the prevailing party for the purposes of recovering litigation costs. However, the dairy had also made counterclaims against the plaintiffs in the litigation proceedings for abuse of process and civil conspiracy—contending that the plaintiffs conspired together to file a malicious nuisance claim. The court rejected these claims.

It was therefore held that since the jury did not award either party a monetary judgment, there was no prevailing party entitled to cost recovery. Notably, the residents who sued the dairy had to defend themselves from paying attorney costs and fees.

NOTES

1. U.S. Department of Agriculture, *USDA Quick Stats Tool: June 1985 Survey, Nevada*, distributed by National Agricultural Statistics Service, accessed October 7, 2020, https://quickstats.nass.usda.gov/results/5C5D88A1-28E2-3007-90EF-A426767F3940; "2021 State Agriculture Overview: Nevada," U.S. Department of Agriculture, National Agricultural Statistics Service, accessed October 21, 2022, https://www.nass.usda.gov/Quick_Stats/Ag_Overview/stateOverview.php?state=NEVADA.
2. Nev. Stat. § 40.140(2) (2021).
3. Nev. Stat. § 40.140(2) (2021).
4. Nev. Stat. § 40.140 (2021).
5. J. V. Casey, "Pact Resolves Odor Issues for Pig Farm, County," *Las Vegas Review-Journal*, February 13, 2003.
6. *McLeod v. Smith Valley Dairy, Corp.*, No. 79010-COA, 2020 WL 4236879 (Nev. App. July 23, 2020). See also Nev. Stat. § 18.020 (2021) (discussing attorney fees and cost awards).

New Hampshire

Since enacting its right-to-farm law in 1985, New Hampshire has lost 20 percent of its acres of farmland while its number of farm operations has grown by 20 percent.[1] Other pieces of legislation, like the state's Granite State Farm to Plate Food Policy passed in 2014, explicitly help support small-scale producers.[2] But what does New Hampshire's RTF law do in practice?

New Hampshire's RTF Law at a Glance

New Hampshire's RTF law provides no explicit protection of farmland or farms by size (for example, small) or organization (for example, family). New Hampshire's RTF law, like those present in the other forty-nine states, centers on protecting certain types of agricultural operations from nuisance suits when they impact neighboring property (for example, through noise or pollution). New Hampshire defines "protected agricultural operations" as any farm, agricultural, or farming activity.[3] The law defines farms as any land, buildings, or structures where farming operations or activities are carried out, as well as the residences of any owners, occupants, or employees on the land.[4]

The types of activities that fall within the definition of "agriculture" and "farming" are very broad, encompassing practically every dimension of production, ranging from general growing and cultivation of crops to the application of chemicals; the spreading of compost, septage, and manure (as permitted by municipal and state rules); the husbandry of livestock and fur-bearing animals; forestry; aquaculture; and transportation related to marketing.[5] The law also includes the transportation of farmworkers as part of farming operations and activities that are shielded from nuisance suits.[6] In addition, the definition of "farming" and "agriculture" covers any management practices that involve technologies that are recommended

157

"from time to time" by the University of New Hampshire or other pertinent state and federal agencies.[7]

Following a 2016 amendment to state law, agritourism also now falls within the definition of agriculture and can therefore be protected from nuisance lawsuits under the RTF law.[8] Prior to this amendment, a court concluded in 2015 that agritourism was not part of the state's definition of agriculture. The court then upheld that local zoning regulations could prohibit certain agritourism activities on land that was zoned rural residential and that allowed agriculture as a permitted use, in this case the hosting of a wedding on a Christmas tree farm.[9] The legislature responded by amending the law to include agritourism in the definition of agriculture.[10]

New Hampshire also protects dog breeding as a "farm" use under its definition of agriculture. In a 2017 case involving a dispute on land zoned both residential and agricultural, a court ruled that breeding dogs on-site and selling them would fall within the meaning of "farming" because dogs could be considered livestock or fur-bearing animals.[11] The court, however, clarified that the sale of animals alone (without breeding on-site) is not a customary farm occupation and therefore was not an allowed use under the town's zoning ordinances.

Conditions and Activities

New Hampshire's RTF law protects agricultural operations from public nuisance suits (those brought by the government on behalf of the general public) and private nuisance suits (those brought by people, like neighbors) when the local conditions in or around them change, as long as a series of conditions are met.[12] First, agricultural operations are required to be in operation one year, but no more, meaning they do not have to predate neighboring property owners. Second, agricultural operations cannot be injurious to public health or safety. Third, such operations cannot have been a nuisance at the time they began. Fourth, they cannot act in negligent (failing to use prudent care) or improper ways.[13] However, agricultural operations cannot be found negligent or improper when they conform to federal, state, and local laws, rules, and regulations.

Additionally, the RTF law stipulates that it does not "modify or limit" the duties and authorities of the Department of Environmental Services as pertains to the Safe Drinking Water Act and the Water Pollution and Waste Disposal Program.[14] However, the existing laws in the state may not safeguard rural groundwater. While New Hampshire's Safe Drinking Water Act regulates public water supplies, it is not clear that it protects private rural wells.[15] The Water Pollution and Waste Disposal Program has established a National Pollutant Discharge Elimination System. This program seeks to abate all sources of water pollution by making them compliant with state or federal law, whichever is more stringent.[16]

Local Government

New Hampshire's RTF law does not protect agricultural operations when local governments make determinations that the operations are injurious to public health or safety.[17] For example, town health officers can regulate the prevention and removal of nuisances as they judge necessary for the health and safety of the people.[18] The commissioner of the Department of Health and Human Services can also adopt other rules in line with the state's Administrative Procedure Act.[19] In addition, a separate public health statute explicitly states that sties and pens for swine, as well as privies, toilets, sinks, drains, cesspools, and septic tanks, cannot be constructed if public health officials determine them or the discharges from such facilities to be a nuisance or injurious to public health.[20]

Nothing in the RTF law expressly restricts the ability of local governments to control the planning, zoning, and related regulations in their communities.[21] However, the state's zoning code stipulates that agricultural activities, agritourism, and forestry activities shall not be unreasonably limited by municipal planning and zoning.[22] The law then defines "unreasonable" as the failure of local land use authorities to recognize such activities as traditional, fundamental, and accessory uses of land.[23]

More generally, when zoning districts or locations do not explicitly address agricultural operations, they are assumed to be permitted, as long as they utilize best management practices.[24] Operations can then expand, change their technology or markets, and change uses or activities.[25] However, any such expansion, alteration, or change must comply with state and federal laws, alongside best management practices. In addition, some operations could be subject to permits, site plan reviews, or other forms of approval.

The right to fish is also protected in New Hampshire. In 1998, a movement began to create a Family Fishing Protection Act, which would have prevented local governments from enacting ordinances making commercial or recreational fishing operations nuisances.[26] Although the 1998 act failed to pass and become law, nearly two decades later—in 2015—the legislature

Table 2.29 New Hampshire's Key RTF Provisions and National Comparison

New Hampshire's key RTF provisions		% U.S. states with similar RTF provisions
Operations are immune from lawsuits . . .	if there is a change in locality.	46%
	once in operation for a year.	48%
Operations are not immune from lawsuits . . .	if they do not comply with county laws.	42%
	if they do not comply with state laws	68%
	if they are a nuisance from the start.	38%
	if they are negligent.	46%
	if they do not comply with federal laws.	62%
	if they do not comply with other laws.	50%
Other important details	RTF supersedes local ordinances and laws.	62%

enacted the Traditional Commercial and Recreational Fishing Protection Act, which prohibits local ordinances from declaring commercial or recreational fishing operations to be nuisances solely because of the nature of their business but which does allow for the local regulation of such operations, including their expansion, in order to prevent nuisance conditions from arising.[27] The act also protects commercial and recreational fishing operations from public and private nuisance suits due to a change in ownership or a change in the locality around the operation.[28]

Attorney Fees

New Hampshire's RTF law does not explicitly address the burden of paying attorney fees. However, New Hampshire law does allow the courts to award attorney fees in "any action commenced, prolonged, required or defended without any reasonable basis in the facts provable by evidence, or any reasonable claim in the law as it is, or as it might arguably be held to be."[29]

This law played out in a 1992 case in which a town and the operators of a mobile park each sued a neighboring agricultural property over the application of chicken manure, which was not plowed under for weeks. The mobile park operator sought attorney fees on the basis that the chicken manure was spread intentionally to harass the residents of the mobile park. The town, on the other hand, which had informed the agricultural operation that the manure was a public nuisance, sought attorney fees because the operation was knowingly prolonging the litigation. The town and the mobile park operator were originally awarded both injunctive relief (stopping the practice) as well as attorney fees. On appeal, the New Hampshire Supreme Court upheld the award of attorney fees.

NOTES

1. U.S. Department of Agriculture, *USDA Quick Stats Tool: June 1985 Survey, New Hampshire*, distributed by National Agricultural Statistics Service, accessed January 6, 2021, https://quickstats.nass.usda.gov/results/772E1C5B-0C8D-3650-957B-3599C9C937AC; "2021 State Agriculture Overview: New Hampshire," U.S. Department of Agriculture, National Agricultural Statistics Service, accessed October 21, 2022, https://www.nass.usda.gov/Quick_Stats/Ag_Overview/stateOverview.php?state=NEW%20HAMPSHIRE.
2. S.B. 141 established the Granite State Farm to Plate Food Policy and Principles while other legislation, H.B. 608 and 1138, established new local markets for producers. See Clara Conklin, "As State Help for Farms Grows, Local Difficulties Remain—Farmers across the State Are Facing Hurdles as Residents Seek to Keep Operations Out of Their Backyard," *New Hampshire Business Review* (Manchester), July 25, 2014.
3. N.H. Rev. Stat. § 432:32 (2021).
4. N.H. Rev. Stat. § 21:34-a (2021).
5. N.H. Rev. Stat. § 21:34-a (2021).
6. N.H. Rev. Stat. § 21:34-a (2021).
7. N.H. Rev. Stat. § 21:34-a (2021). See also *Forster v. Town of Henniker*, 118 A.3d 1016 (N.H. 2015).
8. 2016 N.H. Laws 267 (S.B. 345) (amending N.H. Rev. Stat. § 21:34-a).
9. *Forster*, 118 A.3d 1016.
10. N.H. Rev. Stat. § 21:34-a (2021).
11. *Cote v. Town of Danville*, No. 2016-0679, 2017 WL 6629166 (N.H. Nov. 8, 2017).
12. N.H. Rev. Stat. § 432:33 (2021).
13. N.H. Rev. Stat. § 432:34 (2021).
14. N.H. Rev. Stat. § 432:35 (2021).
15. N.H. Rev. Stat. § 485:1 (2021).
16. N.H. Rev. Stat. § 485-A:3 (2021).
17. N.H. Rev. Stat. § 432:33 (2021).
18. N.H. Rev. Stat. § 147:1 (2021).
19. N.H. Rev. Stat. § 147:2 (2021). The New Hampshire Administrative Procedure Act can be found at N.H. Rev. Stat. § 541-A et seq.
20. N.H. Rev. Stat. § 147:10 (2021).
21. N.H. Rev. Stat. § 672:1 (2021).
22. N.H. Rev. Stat. § 672:1 (2021).
23. N.H. Rev. Stat. § 672:1 (2021).
24. N.H. Rev. Stat. § 674:32-a (2021).
25. N.H. Rev. Stat. § 674:32-b(1) (2021).
26. John Toole, "'Veggie Libel Law' Praised, Panned before House Panel," *New Hampshire Union Leader* (Manchester), January 21, 1998.
27. 2015 N.H. Laws 236 (H.B. 464) (enacting N.H. Rev. Stat. §§ 674:67 to 674:70).
28. N.H. Rev. Stat. § 674:68 (2021).
29. *Koch v. Randall*, 618 A.2d 283 (N.H. 1992).

New Jersey

. . . .

Legislators justified New Jersey's right-to-farm law as "mitigat[ing] unnecessary constraints on essential farming practices" so long as they were "nonthreatening to the public health and safety."[1] Since the law was first enacted in 1983, the state has lost 25 percent of its farmland acres while the number of farm operations has grown by 4 percent.[2] So what does this legislation do in practice?

New Jersey's RTF Law at a Glance

New Jersey's RTF law provides no explicit protection for farmland, nor does the state tailor its protection to small or family farms. Rather, New Jersey's RTF law, like those present in the other forty-nine states, centers on broadly protecting commercial farms from nuisance suits when they impact neighboring property, for example through noise or pollution. After sweeping 1998 amendments, the state expanded its RTF protections to "farm management units" that can be a parcel or parcels of land, buildings, facilities, or other structures that may not be proximate to one another but are operated as a single enterprise.[3] The extension of RTF protections to farm management units forthwith protected consolidated and expanded farming operations where farmers no longer resided on their primary properties.[4] Such farm management units can fall into one of three defined categories. First, a unit can be five acres or more producing agricultural or horticultural products worth $2,500 or more (and meet Farmland Assessment Act eligibility criteria for property taxes). Second, a unit can be less than five acres that produces agricultural or horticultural products worth $50,000 or more (and meet Farmland Assessment Act eligibility criteria for property taxes). And third, as of a 2015 amendment, a unit can also include beekeeping or other apiary/pollination services and products worth $10,000 or more.[5] Permissible activities for commercial farm owners are extensive and include processing and packaging agricultural outputs.[6]

RTF Administrative Process: County and State Level

Since its inception, New Jersey's RTF law has shielded commercial agricultural operations from public nuisance lawsuits (filed on behalf of the people by the government) and private nuisance lawsuits (filed by individuals).[7] However, the 1998 amendments markedly expanded protections afforded to commercial farms by disallowing immediate court action and instead requiring that complaints first be filed with county agriculture development boards or the State Agriculture Development Committee.[8] Further, boards became the ultimate power determining whether an agricultural practice warranted RTF protection. The 1998 amendment and "fortifying" of the state's RTF law set forth an administrative process to achieve these ends.[9]

Under this administrative process, rather than proceeding directly to court, the local agricultural board determines whether the RTF law protects the commercial farm from being a public or private nuisance or from being deemed to otherwise invade the use or enjoyment of nearby lands.[10] There are two principal ways a commercial farm can be protected. In the first, an operation, activity, or structure is protected from nuisance suits if it meets the agricultural management practices adopted by the State Agriculture Development Committee.[11] In the second, an operation, activity, or structure will receive RTF protections if the agricultural board determines it is a generally accepted agricultural practice or operation. In both cases, an agricultural operation, activity, or structure still should meet relevant federal and state statutes, rules, and regulations.[12]

The results of the administrative process are binding unless the decision is later appealed to the appellate court.[13] In practice, however, the board's interpretation of a case can often influence a court's decision on appeal, because in many cases courts will give great weight to the board's expertise.[14] In one case, neighbors appealed the county board's and then the State Agriculture Development Committee's determination that the use of a liquid propane cannon noisemaking device was a generally acceptable practice because it protected sweet corn from pests. The superior court then upheld that the practice was allowed under the RTF law, mostly relying on the mediation process.[15]

Further, once commercial agricultural operations comply with recommendations via the administrative process, they gain an irrebuttable

NEW JERSEY 163

presumption that they are not public or private nuisances.[16] In effect, this means nuisance suits nearly become impossible for aggrieved neighbors to file in court, as the administrative process creates a binding presumption that agricultural operations are not nuisances.

However, if the commercial farm or operation poses a direct threat to public health and safety, it may lose its special protections afforded by the RTF law.[17] The State Agriculture Development Committee, in consultation with the attorney general and the Department of Health and Senior Services, determines what constitutes a direct threat to public health and safety.[18]

Local Government

New Jersey relies on local agricultural boards and the State Agriculture Development Committee not only to prevent the initial filing of nuisance lawsuits against commercial farming operations but also to prevent the use of local ordinances, zoning, and regulations that conflict with the RTF law. If a board or the committee recommends an agricultural management practice or deems it generally accepted, municipalities cannot enact laws to the contrary. In effect, this means—in the words of the Supreme Court of New Jersey—that "the Right to Farm Act preempts municipal land use authority over a commercial farming operation."[19] Once a commercial farming operation uses a board-recommended practice, it may do any of the following: (1) produce livestock, poultry, and agricultural and horticultural crops; (2) process and package agricultural products from the farm; (3) operate a farm market; (4) control pests, predators, and diseases of plants and animals; (5) conduct on-site disposal of organic agricultural wastes; (6) generate renewable energy on-farm; or (7) conduct agriculture-related educational and recreational activities.[20] This holds as long as the activities do not directly threaten public health or safety and the operation complies with federal and state laws.

If any conflicts arise between a commercial farm and a municipality, the RTF law gives local agriculture development boards the primary authority to resolve such disputes, with appeals possible to the State Agriculture Development Committee.[21] As with claims of nuisance, before a dispute between a commercial farm and a local government can be brought in court, it must first be addressed by the county board and the State Agriculture Development Committee.

New Jersey courts have ruled that the courts are improper places to initially address the following issues: (1) whether a farming operation meets the

Table 2.30 New Jersey's Key RTF Provisions and National Comparison

New Jersey's key RTF provisions		% U.S. states with similar RTF provisions
Operations are not immune from lawsuits . . .	if they do not comply with federal laws.	62%
	if they do not comply with state laws.	68%
	if they do not comply with other laws.	50%
Other important details	RTF supersedes local ordinances and laws.	62%
	RTF supersedes local ordinances and laws in agricultural zones.	12%
	RTF protects processing.	48%

definition of a "commercial farm" under the RTF act; (2) whether a specific activity constitutes a generally accepted agricultural operation or practice; and (3) whether a certain activity is a direct threat to public health and safety such that RTF protections would not apply.[22] One court opined, "We recognize that the task before the agricultural boards is complex. Agricultural activity is not always pastoral. The potential for conflict between farming interests and public health and safety exists. Nevertheless, we repose trust and discretion in the agricultural boards to decide carefully future disputes on a case-by-case basis and to balance competing interests."[23]

NOTES

1. Senate Natural Resources and Agriculture Committee Statement, 1983 N.J. Laws 31 (S. 854).
2. U.S. Department of Agriculture, *USDA Quick Stats Tool: June 1983 Survey, New Jersey*, distributed by National Agricultural Statistics Service, accessed January 6, 2021, https://quickstats.nass.usda.gov/results/BDA6256F-573F-3B75-A540-974B2EF2E806; "2021 State Agriculture Overview: New Jersey," U.S. Department of Agriculture, National Agricultural Statistics Service, accessed October 21, 2022, https://www.nass.usda.gov/Quick_Stats/Ag_Overview/stateOverview.php?state=NEW%20JERSEY.
3. 1998 N.J. Laws 48 (Assemb. No. 2014) (amending, in relevant part, N.J. Stat. § 4:1C-3).
4. Bridget Bradburn, "Farmers Seek Balance with Neighbors," *Trenton Times*, June 8, 1996.
5. 2015 N.J. Laws 75 (Assemb. No. 1294) (amending, in relevant part, N.J. Stat. § 4:1C-3).
6. N.J. Stat. § 4:1C-9 (1983).
7. N.J. Stat. § 4:1C-7 (1983).
8. 1998 N.J. Laws 48 (Assemb. No. 2014) (adding, in relevant part, N.J. Stat. § 4:1C-10.1); Harold Shelly, "State Cooking Up New Right to Farm Law," *Trenton (N.J.) Times*, June 2, 1996.
9. N.J. Stat. § 4:1C-10.1 (2021). See also Mona Moore, "Fortifying an Old Law: The Right to Farm," *Press of Atlantic City* (N.J.), June 9, 1998; *Casella v. Postorivo*, No. A-5166-14T1, 2017 WL 444315 (N.J. Super. Ct. App. Div. Feb. 27, 2017).
10. N.J. Stat. § 4:1C-10 (2021).
11. N.J. Stat. §§ 4:1C-3, "Committee," 4:1C-10, 4:1C-10.1 (2021).
12. N.J. Stat. § 4:1C-10 (2021).

13. N.J. Stat. § 4:1C-10.1 (2021).

14. N.J. Stat. § 4:1C-10.1 (2021). See also *Curzi v. Raub*, 999 A.2d 1182 (N.J. Super. Ct. App. Div. 2010); and *Borough of Closter v. Abram Demaree Homestead, Inc.*, 839 A.2d 110 (N.J. Super. Ct. App. Div. 2004).

15. *In re Samaha Farms*, No. A-2163-04T5, 2006 WL 923700 (N.J. Super. Ct. App. Div. Apr. 11, 2006).

16. 1998 N.J. Laws 48 (Assemb. No. 2014) (amending, in relevant part, N.J. Stat. § 4:1C).

17. N.J. Stat. § 4:1C-10 (2021).

18. N.J. Stat. § 4:1C-10.4 (2021).

19. *Twp. of Franklin v. Den Hollander*, 796 A.2d 874 (N.J. 2002).

20. N.J. Stat. § 4:1C-9 (2021). This aspect of the law applies only to farms that either (1) as of December 31, 1997, are located in areas that are zoned for agriculture or (2) were in operation as of July 2, 1998.

21. N.J. Stat. §§ 4:1C-10.1, 4:1C-10.2 (2021). See also *Borough of Closter*, 839 A.2d 110; *Den Hollander*, 796 A.2d 874.

22. *Abram Demaree Homestead, Inc.*, 839 A.2d 110 (citing N.J. Stat. §§ 4:1C-3, 4:1C-10.1); *Den Hollander*, 796 A.2d 874.

23. *Den Hollander*, 796 A.2d 874.

New Mexico

Advocates of the right-to-farm law in New Mexico argue it protects farms and farmland from urban newcomers.[1] Since first enacted in 1981, the number of farm operations in the state has increased by 83 percent, while the acres in farmland have decreased by 15 percent.[2] Governors cited the loss of dairy operations and urban encroachment as motivation for signing 2014 and 2016 amendments to the state's RTF law.[3] But what does this legislation do in practice?

New Mexico's RTF Law at a Glance

New Mexico's RTF law provides no explicit protection for family farms or farmland. Rather, New Mexico's law, similar to those present in the other forty-nine states, protects activities and operations from nuisance suits when they impact neighboring property, for example through noise or pollution. When first passed in 1981, New Mexico's RTF law limited its protections to agricultural operations, meaning the use of land for the production of plants, crops, trees, livestock, poultry, fish, forest products, and orchard crops.[4] A 1991 amendment expanded the law's protections markedly by extending them to agricultural facilities, including any land, building, structure, pond, machinery, or equipment that is used for the commercial production of crops, livestock, or honey.[5] The 1991 amendment also greatly broadened the types of activities that fall within the definition of a protected agricultural operation. Protected activities now include most activities commonly associated with farming, as well as pesticide and herbicide application; animal production, such as breeding, hatching, feeding, slaughtering, and processing; the manufacturing of feed for poultry or livestock; the operation of a roadside market; and the application of changed or new technology, practices, processes, or products.[6] Unlike agricultural facilities, agricul-

167

tural operations do not have to be "commercial" to receive RTF protections, though they can be.[7]

Conditions and Activities

Once in existence for more than one year, agricultural operations and facilities are protected from nuisance suits arising out of changed conditions in or around the location of the operation or facility.[8] The date of establishment for an agricultural operation is the day it commenced, and for an agricultural facility it is when it was originally constructed. This date remains unaltered even if the operation or facility subsequently expands or adopts new technologies. In 2016, the law was amended to include a provision that anyone who purchases, rents, leases, or occupies land near a previously established operation or facility may not sue for nuisance unless the operation or facility has substantially changed in nature and scope.[9] In other words, if an operation or facility substantially changes, only existing neighbors can bring a nuisance lawsuit at any point after the substantial change occurs. The law does not define what "substantial change" means.

New Mexico's RTF protections apply only if the operation or facility was not a nuisance when it began and was not operated negligently or illegally.[10] In 2014, an amendment broadened the protections afforded to agricultural operations and facilities by removing the requirement that they also be operated properly.[11]

As of 1991, none of the provisions in New Mexico's RTF law prevent persons from recovering damages for injuries resulting from polluted stream water or water overflows onto their land.[12]

Local Government

No unit of local government can impose local nuisance regulations on agricultural operations or facilities or require that they stop certain activities as a result of being found to be a nuisance under the state's RTF law if the operations or facilities were located within the corporate limits of a municipality as of April 8, 1981.[13]

Table 2.31 New Mexico's Key RTF Provisions and National Comparison

New Mexico's key RTF provisions		% U.S. states with similar RTF provisions
Operations are immune from lawsuits . . .	if there is a change in locality.	46%
	if any type of agricultural production predated operation.	4%
	once in operation for a year.	48%
Operations are not immune from lawsuits . . .	if they are a nuisance from the start.	38%
	if they are negligent.	46%
	if they pollute water.	36%
Other important details	Attorney fees are awarded to prevailing defendant.	34%
	RTF supersedes local ordinances and laws.	62%
	RTF protects processing.	48%

Attorney Fees

As of a 1991 amendment, an agricultural operation can recover the money it spent defending itself if a court determines that the nuisance lawsuit was frivolous.[14] This and similar language may have a chilling effect on the filing of nuisance suits in favor of industrial operators.[15]

NOTES

1. John J. Lumpkin, "Corrales Life a Rude Awakening for Some," *Albuquerque (N.M.) Journal*, June 7, 1997.
2. U.S. Department of Commerce, "Table 1. Farms, Land in Farms, and Land Use: 1982 and Earlier Census Years," in *1982 Census of Agriculture, Volume 1: Geographic Area Series, Part 31: New Mexico State and County Data, Chapter 1: State Data* (Washington, D.C.: U.S. Bureau of the Census, 1984), https://agcensus.library.cornell.edu/wp-content/uploads/1982-New_Mexico-CHAPTER_1_State_Data-121-Table-01.pdf; "2021 State Agriculture Overview: New Mexico," U.S. Department of Agriculture, National Agricultural Statistics Service, accessed October 21, 2022, https://www.nass.usda.gov/Quick_Stats/Ag_Overview/stateOverview.php?state=NEW%20MEXICO.
3. J. Mclaughlin, "Law Expected to Give Dairy Farmers More Protections," *Roswell (N.M.) Daily Record*, March 6, 2014; Zack Ponce, "Bill Aims to Protect NM Dairies from Out-of-State Lawsuits," *Carlsbad (N.M.) Current-Argus*, January 28, 2014; Sherry Robinson, "Gov. Signs Bill to Protect Sex Assault Victims," *Gallup (N.M.) Independent*, March 4, 2014.
4. N.M. Stat. § 47-9-3 (1981).
5. 1991 N.M. Laws 129 (H.B. 310) (amending N.M. Stat. § 47-9-3 and creating N.M. Stat. § 47-9-5).
6. N.M. Stat. § 47-9-5 (2021).

7. N.M. Stat. § 47-9-5 (2021).
8. N.M. Stat. § 47-9-3 (2021).
9. 2016 N.M. Laws 44 (S.B. 72) (amending N.M. Stat. § 47-9-3); Sherry Robinson, "Bill: No Right to Complain If You Move Next to a Feedlot," *Gallup Independent*, February 13, 2016.
10. N.M. Stat. § 47-9-3 (2021).
11. The 2014 amendment removed "improperly" from the requirement that operations and facilities must not be operating "negligently, improperly or illegally" in order to receive RTF protections. See 2014 N.M. Laws 22 (H.B. 51) (amending N.M. Stat. § 47-9-3).
12. 1991 N.M. Laws 129 (H.B. 310) (creating N.M. Stat. § 47-9-6).
13. N.M. Stat. § 47-6-3 (2021). The language of this law is ambiguous. It is possible, though not certain, that a court could find that this provision means that local nuisance regulations cannot be enforced against operations or facilities that were located within a municipality anytime on or after April 8, 1981.
14. 1991 N.M. Laws 129 (H.B. 310) (creating N.M. Stat. § 47-9-7).
15. Cordon M. Smart, "The 'Right to Commit Nuisance' in North Carolina: A Historical Analysis of the Right-to-Farm Act," *North Carolina Law Review* 94, no. 6 (2016): 2097–154. For more on the chilling effect of such statutes, see the section "Geopolitical Extraction" in the introduction.

New York

New York's right-to-farm law promises to promote a strong agricultural economy, with a more recent emphasis on agritourism.[1] The state's agricultural preservation law describes agricultural lands as "irreplaceable state assets."[2] Further, New York's constitution vows to protect its scenic beauty while developing and improving agricultural land.[3] Yet since legislators first passed the initial RTF law in 1982, the number of farmers in the state has dropped by 20 percent and the amount of farmland by 25 percent.[4] So what does the state's RTF law do in practice?

New York's RTF Law at a Glance

Similar to those in other states across the nation, New York's RTF law does not afford family farms particular rights or explicitly prevent suburban sprawl, counter to common perception.[5] Rather, the state uniquely centers its law on agricultural districts. The state's RTF law uses such districts to protect those within it from nuisance suits over matters like noise or pollution. Landowners can propose the creation of an agricultural district to their county legislative body, as long as they own at least 250 acres.[6] In addition, any owners of land engaged in agricultural production outside of such districts can receive RTF protections if they used their land (both the land they own as well as any additional rented land) for selling crops, livestock, or livestock products for the preceding two years.[7] When land is located in an agricultural district, a disclosure must be made to potential buyers of the property, as well as recorded in property transfers. Such disclosures state that within the district, farming activities could cause noise, dust, and odors.[8]

Conditions and Activities

New York's RTF law pertains only to private nuisance suits (those brought by people, like neighbors), not to public nuisance suits (those brought by the government on behalf of the general public).[9] For agricultural practices to receive protection from private nuisance suits, the commissioner of agriculture and markets issues an opinion on whether the practices are "sound."[10] Any person may request that the commissioner issue such an opinion.[11] The law defines "sound" agricultural practices as those deemed necessary for on-farm production, preparation, and marketing of agricultural commodities. Examples include the operation of farm equipment, the proper use of agricultural chemicals and other crop protection methods, agricultural tourism, and direct sales to consumers of agricultural commodities. A timber operation—including the on-farm production, management, harvesting, processing, and marketing of timber grown on the farm—also can be considered a sound agricultural practice, so long as the operation encompasses at least seven acres and grosses more than $10,000 in sales.[12]

The RTF law requires that before issuing an opinion, the commissioner consult with appropriate state agencies and the state's advisory council on agriculture.[13] The commissioner is required to consider whether the practice at hand is utilized by a farm owner or operator participating in the Agricultural Environmental Management Program. The commissioner may consult with either the USDA Natural Resources Conservation Service or the New York State College of Agriculture and Life Sciences.[14] A New York court used these guidelines to rule in 2006 that sound agricultural practices should be necessary and legal; not cause bodily harm or property damage off the farm; and be reasonably effective in achieving their intended results.[15] In a 1998 case, a not-for-profit organization that represented residents proximate to a hog facility tried to challenge the opinion of the commissioner of agriculture and markets, which stated that the hog facility's agricultural practices were sound.[16] The court offered that the commissioner must balance both the promotion of agriculture and the protection of the environment, which "oftentimes conflict as new technologies and methodologies transform agriculture." A consequent investigation supported the commissioner's opinion that the hog farm's manure management practices were sound, which then barred the residents from filing a private nuisance suit.[17]

Any opinion issued by the commissioner must be published in a newspaper of general circulation in the area surrounding the property under consideration.[18] Written notice of the opinion must also be provided to the owners of the property or any adjoining property owners. While opinions generally are final, the law allows those affected to initiate a review of the opinion within thirty days after its publication.[19]

The Environmental Conservation Law has required, since 2009, concentrated animal feeding operations (industrial-scale animal facilities that meet size thresholds) to acquire a CAFO general permit. However, operators were provided a choice to adhere to the ECL or continue operating under a less restrictive version of the permit as determined by the 2004 Clean Water Act. That permit allows for discharge, whereas the ECL version does not.[20]

Local Government

New York's public health law allows local governments to investigate and examine allegations of nuisances that affect the security of life and health in any locality.[21] Under these laws, local boards of health are required to examine all complaints by inhabitants that relate to nuisances or activities that are dangerous to life or health. To investigate, local health officers may enter upon or within any place or premises where a nuisance or dangerous condition exists. After examining and then providing a written statement of their results and conclusions, they can order the suppression and removal of nuisances and conditions detrimental to life or health.[22]

However, the same law provides special protections for on-farm agricultural activities. They cannot be considered a private nuisance if (1) the farm's activities came before those surrounding it; (2) the activities have not increased substantially in magnitude or intensity; and (3) they do not cause dangerous life or health conditions, as determined by New York's commissioner of health or any local health officer or local board of health.[23] The law's definition of a farm includes stock, dairy, poultry, fur-bearing animal, fruit, and truck farms; plantations; orchards; nurseries; greenhouses; and other similar structures used primarily for the raising of agricultural or horticultural commodities.[24]

Taken together, if a local board of health determines an agricultural activity does not endanger life or health, the activities cannot be deemed a private nuisance.[25]

Table 2.32 New York's Key RTF Provisions and National Comparison

New York's key RTF provisions		% U.S. states with similar RTF provisions
Operations are immune from lawsuits . . .	if they are there first.	44%
	once in operation for two years.	6%
Other important details	Attorney fees are awarded to prevailing defendant.	34%
	RTF supersedes local ordinances and laws in agricultural zones.	12%
	RTF protects processing.	48%

Attorney Fees

If the commissioner declares an agricultural practice sound and a party still brings a nuisance lawsuit, the court must award the defendant (whose agricultural practice was deemed sound) the fees and other expenses paid in that party's defense.[26] However, courts can choose not to award such fees if they determine that the plaintiff either is substantially justified in bringing the case or there are special circumstances that make the award of fees and expenses unjust.

NOTES

1. N.Y. Agric. & Mkts. Law § 308 (2021). The inclusion of agritourism was added in 2006 upon the recognition of the legislature that agritourism was being embraced by an increasing number of farms in New York. See 2006 N.Y. Laws 600.
2. N.Y. Agric. & Mkts. Law § 321 (2021).
3. N.Y. Const. art. XIV, § 4.
4. U.S. Department of Commerce, "Table 1. Farms, Land in Farms, and Land Use: 1982 and Earlier Census Years," in *1982 Census of Agriculture, Volume 1: Geographic Area Series, Part 32: New York State and County Data, Chapter 1: State Data* (Washington, D.C.: U.S. Bureau of the Census, 1984), https://agcensus.library.cornell.edu/wp-content/uploads/1982-New _York-CHAPTER_1_State_Data-121-Table-01.pdf; "2021 State Agriculture Overview: New York," U.S. Department of Agriculture, National Agricultural Statistics Service, accessed October 21, 2022, https://www.nass.usda.gov/Quick_Stats/Ag_Overview/stateOverview .php?state=NEW%20YORK.
5. Kenneth Crowe II, "City Slickers and Country Living Law Protects Farmers from Encroaching Suburbia," *Albany (N.Y.) Times Union*, March 1, 1992.
6. N.Y. Agric. & Mkts. Law § 303 (2021).
7. N.Y. Agric. & Mkts. Law §§ 301, 306, 308 (2021).
8. N.Y. Agric. & Mkts. Law § 310 (2021).

9. N.Y. Agric. & Mkts. Law § 308 (2021).
10. N.Y. Agric. & Mkts. Law § 308 (2021). Any person may request that the commissioner issue such an opinion.
11. N.Y. Agric. & Mkts. Law § 308 (2021).
12. N.Y. Agric. & Mkts. Law §§ 301, 308 (2021).
13. N.Y. Agric. & Mkts. Law § 308 (2021).
14. N.Y. Agric. & Mkts. Law § 308 (2021).
15. *Matter of Groat v. Brennan*, 831 N.Y.S.2d 353 (Sup. Ct. 2006).
16. *Pure Air & Water, Inc. v. Davidsen*, 668 N.Y.S.2d 248 (App. Div. 1998).
17. *Pure Air & Water*, 668 N.Y.S.2d 248.
18. N.Y. Agric. & Mkts. Law § 308 (2021).
19. N.Y. Agric. & Mkts. Law § 308 (2021). For the statutes governing such a review proceeding, see N.Y. C.P.L.R. §§ 7801–06 (2021).
20. "Concentrated Animal Feeding Operations," New York State Department of Environmental Conservation, accessed February 1, 2023, https://www.dec.ny.gov/permits/6285.html.
21. N.Y. Pub. Health Law § 1300 (2021).
22. N.Y. Pub. Health Law § 1303 (2021). If a district does not have a local board of health, the local health officers and the county health commissioner have the same authority as a board of health to investigate and abate public nuisances that may affect health. See N.Y. Pub. Health Law § 1304 (2021).
23. N.Y. Pub. Health Law § 1300-c (2021).
24. N.Y. Pub. Health Law § 1300-c (2021); N.Y. Lab. Law § 671 (2021).
25. See N.Y. Pub. Health Law §§ 1300-c, 1303 (2021).
26. N.Y. Agric. & Mkts. Law § 308-a (2021).

North Carolina

Legislators proposed a right-to-farm law in North Carolina as a tool to "encourage the development and improvement of its agricultural land and forestland for the production of food, fiber, and other products."[1] Since passing its first RTF law in 1979, the state has 51 percent fewer farms and 29 percent fewer acres of farmland.[2] So what does this legislation do in practice?

North Carolina's RTF Law at a Glance

North Carolina's RTF law provides no explicit protection for farmland. Rather, North Carolina's RTF law, like those present in the other forty-nine states, centers on protecting certain types of agricultural and forestry operations from nuisance suits when they impact neighboring property, for example through noise or pollution. The state defines nuisance as actions that are "injurious to health, indecent, offensive to the senses, or an obstruction to the free use of property."[3] North Carolina's RTF law protects agricultural operations and facilities related to the commercial production of crops, livestock, poultry, livestock products, and poultry products.[4] Since an amendment in 1991, the RTF law also protects forestry operations engaged in activities related to growing, managing, and harvesting trees from nuisance suits.[5]

Before bringing an action in court for a farm nuisance dispute, North Carolina typically requires mediation.[6] This means that the court appoints a mediator to try to develop an agreement before a case proceeds to court. Upon the written agreement of all parties, however, this requirement can be waived.

Conditions and Activities

When it was first enacted in 1979, North Carolina's RTF law protected agricultural operations from nuisance lawsuits arising out of changed conditions in the area surrounding the operations. However, the protections applied only after operations had been in existence for at least one year.[7] A 1985 case, *Mayes v. Tabor*, tested the limits of the original RTF law. In *Mayes*, the North Carolina Court of Appeals concluded that if a farm came into existence after the establishment of a surrounding land use—in that case, a private camp—the farm was not protected by the RTF law because the lawsuit did not arise out of any changed circumstances in or around the location of the farm.[8] In other words, because the camp was there first, the agricultural operation in *Mayes* was not protected. In this respect, North Carolina's initial RTF protections were essentially a "coming to the nuisance" defense that allowed preexisting farms to avoid nuisance liability arising from those who might later move onto neighboring lands. Likewise, the original RTF policy stated, "When other land uses extend into agricultural and forest areas, agricultural and forestry operations often become the subject of nuisance suits. As a result, agricultural operations are sometimes forced to cease operations."[9]

In 1994, the court of appeals further interpreted the RTF law, finding that although the aim of the law was to protect "any agricultural operation, without limitation, when the operation was initially begun," the law was not intended to protect operations where the nature of the agricultural activities fundamentally changed.[10] Accordingly, the court held that when a turkey farm changed to a hog production facility, it was a fundamental change that deprived the farm of the state's RTF protections.

However, the meaning of the RTF law changed dramatically with amendments in 2013. They forthwith identified what cannot be considered a fundamental change, effectively allowing operations to substantially change while still maintaining RTF protections.[11] As a result of the amendments, courts can no longer treat the following changes as "fundamental": ownership or size changes; stopping operations for three years or less; participation in a government-sponsored program; using a new technology; or changing the type of agricultural and forestry product produced.[12]

Numerous other lawsuits and ensuing amendments furthered the protection of agricultural and forestry operations by making it harder to bring nuisance actions. Between 2014 and 2015, dozens of lawsuits were brought by neighbors of multiple hog facilities owned by Murphy-Brown LLC, a subsidiary of Smithfield Foods Inc.—a firm mostly held and run by investors and executives in China—alleging various nuisances related to the facilities.[13] These cases were consolidated, and multiple trials followed. In one of the cases, Murphy-Brown attempted to use the state's RTF law in order to bar a suit by those neighboring its facility, but the court found that the RTF law did not apply because the plaintiffs had been on their land before Murphy-Brown began its nearby swine operations.[14] As the court stated, "Here, plaintiffs' use of their properties as residences did not extend into an agricultural area. Their land use had been in existence well before the operations of the subject farms began."[15] Accordingly, the court held that the RTF law did not bar the neighbors' claims.

In a direct response to the Murphy-Brown lawsuits, the North Carolina General Assembly in 2018 once again amended the state's RTF law: "Regrettably, the General Assembly is again forced to make plain its intent that existing farms and forestry operations in North Carolina that are operating in good faith be shielded from nuisance lawsuits filed long after the operations become established."[16] Since the 2018 amendments, nuisance lawsuits may be filed against an agricultural operation only if three conditions are met.[17] First, only legal possessors of real property can now file suit. This means that while a renter or a spouse of the legal property owner could bring a nuisance lawsuit against an agricultural or forestry operation, family members (like children) who do not reside on the property would not be able to. Real property can include land, buildings, and mobile homes fixed in place.[18] Second, only those who live within one-half mile of the alleged nuisance or activity can file suit.[19] In practice, this means that those who experience air or water contamination farther away could be disqualified from filing lawsuits. Finally, any nuisance lawsuit against an agricultural or forestry operation must be filed within one year of the operation's establishment or within a year of a fundamental change.[20] These amendments have not gone without challenge. Plaintiffs sued the State of North Carolina, maintaining that the amendments constituted a legislative overreach of the state's police power and violated the Law of the Land Clause of the North Carolina Constitution.[21] North Carolina's appellate court, however, held that the amendments were constitutional.[22]

The 2018 amendments also removed the RTF law's original stipulation that operations can be protected only if there is a subsequent change in the area surrounding the operation. In other words, agricultural operations no longer need to be there first in order to be protected by the RTF law. The 2018 amendments, however, did not apply to the Murphy-Brown cases because those lawsuits were brought prior to the effective date of the amendments.[23]

The 2018 amendments also completely removed the stipulation that RTF protections did not apply when operations were negligent or improper.[24] However, the RTF law does not apply to any lawsuit for trespass, personal injury, strict liability, or other torts besides nuisance.[25] Further, if the lawsuit is not specific to nuisances, injunctive relief (meaning stopping the offending activities) remains possible for other causes of action.

In addition, agricultural and forestry operations can still be liable for nuisance damages if they pollute or change the conditions of the waters of any stream or overflow onto the lands of another person, firm, or corporation.[26] However, agricultural operations are exempt from certain pollution control laws if they meet the following conditions: the processing activities are carried out by the owner; the activities produce no more than 1,000 gallons of wastewater per day; the wastewater is disposed of by land application; no wastewater is discharged to surface waters; the disposal of the wastewater does not result in any violation of surface water or groundwater standards; and the wastewater is not generated by an animal waste management system.[27] Elsewhere, an "animal waste management system" is defined as a combination of structures and nonstructural practices serving a feedlot that provide for the collection, treatment, storage, or land application of animal waste.[28] Despite these exemptions, the operation could still be liable for nuisance under the RTF law for some instances of pollution.[29]

Local Government

North Carolina's RTF law voids local ordinances that would make agricultural or forestry operations a nuisance. However, operations that predate the RTF law's 1979 enactment are not protected if they were located within a city's limits at that time.[30]

Other North Carolina laws also limit the ability of local governments to regulate potential agricultural nuisances. For example, although one law allows counties to "remove, abate, or remedy everything that is dangerous or prejudicial to the public health or safety," the law specifically does not apply to "bona fide farms," unless the property is being used for nonfarm purposes.[31] Similarly, another law provides that "county zoning may not affect property used for bona fide farm purposes," except in cases where the farm property is being used for nonfarm purposes.[32]

With respect to swine operations specifically, courts have interpreted the state's Swine Farm Siting Act as well as its Animal Waste Management Systems rules as voiding local attempts to provide more stringent oversight of swine facilities.[33]

Caps on Payments for Damages

In 2014, as part of the consolidated Murphy-Brown lawsuits, ten neighbors of an industrial hog-feed facility owned by Murphy-Brown brought a lawsuit against the commercial hog producer alleging various nuisances related to the operation.[34] In 2018, four years after the case was filed, a jury awarded each neighbor of the hog-feed facility $75,000 in compensatory damages for the loss of the use and enjoyment of their property.[35] Between the time when the *McKiver v. Murphy-Brown* lawsuit was first filed and when the jury's verdict was issued, the North Carolina legislature responded by passing another RTF amendment that limited the damages that plaintiffs could receive when they won nuisance suits.[36] This 2017 amendment restricted compensatory damages under the RTF law by basing them exclusively on the loss of property values.[37] The amendment was a departure from a longstanding measure of recovery in nuisance suits in North Carolina, which had—for over a century—allowed plaintiffs to recover for the loss of use and enjoyment of their property, in addition to the loss of property values.[38]

Since the passing of the 2017 amendment, damages for private nuisance claims under the RTF law are now measured as follows: (1) for permanent nuisances, compensatory damages are measured by the reduction in the fair market value of the plaintiff's property caused by the nuisance, not to exceed the fair market value of the property; (2) for temporary nuisances, compensatory damages are limited to the diminution of the fair rental value of the plaintiff's property caused by the nuisance.[39]

Crucially, the 2017 amendment also added that the limitations on damages apply "to any private nuisance claim brought by any party based on that party's contractual or business relationship with an agricultural or forestry operation." In effect, this means that subsidiary corporations, like Murphy-Brown, receive the same RTF protections from paying damages as their parent corporations, like Smithfield, do. The limits on compensatory damages put in place with the 2017 amendment did not, however, affect the damages awarded in the *Murphy-Brown* case because that lawsuit was filed prior to the passing of the amendment.[40]

Table 2.33 North Carolina's Key RTF Provisions and National Comparison

North Carolina's key RTF provisions		% U.S. states with similar RTF provisions
Operations are immune from lawsuits . . .	if boundaries or size of operations change.	34%
	if they use a new technology.	30%
	if they produce a different product.	26%
	if there is an ownership change.	26%
	if there is a cessation or interruption in farming.	26%
	once in operation for a year.	48%
Operations are not immune from lawsuits . . .	if they pollute water.	36%
Other important details	Attorney fees are awarded to prevailing party.	14%
	RTF supersedes local ordinances and laws.	62%

In addition to compensatory damages, the same jury in the *McKiver* case also awarded the neighbors $5 million in punitive damages—meaning damages intended to punish a defendant for egregiously wrong acts and to deter others from committing similar acts.[41] However, because North Carolina's law caps punitive damages at $2.5 million, the jury verdict was reduced.[42] When the *McKiver* case went up on appeal, the court vacated the award of punitive damages after concluding that financial evidence of Smithfield Foods and WH Group—the legal parent entities of Murphy-Brown—should have been excluded because it could have unfairly prejudiced the jury against big businesses.[43] The case was therefore remanded back down to the lower court for a rehearing on the issue of punitive damages.

After the *McKiver* case was decided, a 2018 amendment to the state's RTF law further changed the circumstances under which punitive damages can be imposed in nuisance suits against agricultural and forestry operations.[44] Now, punitive damages are not allowed at all, unless within the previous three years the operations were subject to conviction or a civil enforcement action relating to the alleged nuisance.[45]

The impact of the RTF amendments, passed with various Murphy-Brown cases in mind, have yet to fully play out. Moving forward, however, current law will starkly reduce compensation for neighbors because property values are often lower in rural and minority communities.[46] North Carolina's hog confinement facilities are located disproportionately in communities with higher levels of poverty and numbers of nonwhite persons.[47]

Attorney Fees

North Carolina allows attorney fees to be awarded to either party in a nuisance action against an agricultural or forestry operation if the action or the defense is considered frivolous or malicious.[48] "Frivolous" generally refers to legal actions intended to harass, delay, or embarrass. "Malicious" generally encompasses wrongful actions performed because of wicked or mischievous motives.

NOTES

1. N.C. Gen. Stat. § 106-700 (2021).
2. U.S. Department of Agriculture, *USDA Quick Stats Tool: June 1979 Survey, North Carolina*, distributed by National Agricultural Statistics Service, accessed January 6, 2021, https://quickstats.nass.usda.gov/results/C90690DD-4ADC-3D46-8A70-D832F09BA9D9; "2021 State Agriculture Overview: North Carolina," U.S. Department of Agriculture, National Agricultural Statistics Service, accessed October 21, 2022, https://www.nass.usda.gov/Quick_Stats/Ag_Overview/stateOverview.php?state=NORTH%20CAROLINA.
3. N.C. Gen. Stat. § 7A-38.3 (2021).
4. N.C. Gen. Stat. § 106-701 (2021).
5. 1991 N.C. Sess. Laws 892 (H.B. 978) (amending, in relevant part, N.C. Gen. Stat. § 106-701).
6. N.C. Gen. Stat. § 7A-38.3 (2021).
7. N.C. Gen. Stat. § 106-701 (1979).
8. *Mayes v. Tabor*, 334 S.E.2d 489 (N.C. Ct. App. 1985).
9. N.C. Gen. Stat. § 106-700 (1979).
10. *Durham v. Britt*, 451 S.E.2d 1 (N.C. Ct. App. 1994).
11. 2013 N.C. Sess. Laws 314 (H.B. 614) (amending, in relevant part, N.C. Gen. Stat. § 106-701).
12. N.C. Gen. Stat. § 106-701 (2021).
13. Emery P. Dalesio, "Trial Begins in Suit Blaming Pork Giant for Farm Smells—Case Pits Smithfield Foods against Farm's 10 Neighbors," *Daily Advance* (Elizabeth City, N.C.), April 4, 2018; Chris Berendt, "Murphy-Brown Grower Speaks Out, Perplexed by Litigation," *Sampson Independent* (Clinton, N.C.), May 25, 2014.
14. *In re NC Swine Farm Nuisance Litigation*, No. 5:15-CV-00013-BR, 2017 WL 5178038 (E.D.N.C. Nov. 8, 2017).
15. *In re NC Swine Farm Nuisance Litigation*, 2017 WL 5178038.
16. 2018 N.C. Sess. Laws 113 (S.B. 711) (amending N.C. Gen. Stat. § 106-701). One of the stated reasons for the amendment was that "recently, a federal trial court incorrectly and narrowly interpreted the North Carolina Right to Farm Act in a way that contradicts the intent of the General Assembly and effectively renders the Act toothless in offering meaningful protection to long-established North Carolina farms and forestry operations."
17. 2018 N.C. Sess. Laws 113 (S.B. 711) (amending N.C. Gen. Stat. § 106-701).
18. See, for example, N.C. Gen. Stat. § 105-273 (2021).
19. N.C. Gen. Stat. § 106-701 (2021).

20. N.C. Gen. Stat. § 106-701 (2021).
21. *Rural Empowerment Ass'n for Cmty. Help v. State*, 868 S.E.2d 645 (N.C. Ct. App. 2021). The Law of the Land Clause of the North Carolina Constitution—N.C. Const. art. I, § 19—provides that "no person shall be taken, imprisoned, or disseized of his freehold, liberties, or privileges, or outlawed, or exiled, or in any manner deprived of his life, liberty, or property, but by the law of the land."
22. *Rural Empowerment Ass'n for Cmty. Help*, 868 S.E.2d 645.
23. See *McKiver v. Murphy-Brown LLC*, No. 7:14-CV-180-BR, 2018 WL 6606061 (E.D.N.C. Dec. 17, 2018).
24. 2018 N.C. Sess. Laws 113 (S.B. 711) (amending N.C. Gen. Stat. § 106-701).
25. N.C. Gen. Stat. § 106-702 (2021).
26. N.C. Gen. Stat. § 106-701 (2021).
27. N.C. Gen. Stat. § 143-215.1 (2021).
28. N.C. Gen. Stat. § 143-215.10B (2021).
29. See, for example, *State ex rel. Cobey v. Ballard*, 429 S.E.2d 735 (N.C. Ct. App. 1993) ("The very complex and comprehensive set of regulatory requirements and controls established under the pertinent provisions of Chapter 143 of the General Statutes are clearly distinguishable from the parameters of a private nuisance as that term was understood under common law"); *Biddix v. Henredon Furniture Industrs., Inc.*, 331 S.E.2d 717 (N.C. Ct. App. 1985) ("We conclude that the Clean Water Act does not abrogate the common law civil actions for private nuisance and trespass to land for pollution of waters resulting from violation of a NPDES permit").
30. N.C. Gen. Stat. § 106-701 (2021).
31. N.C. Gen. Stat. § 153A-140 (2021).
32. N.C. Gen. Stat. § 160D-903 (2021).
33. See *Craig v. Cty. of Chatham*, 565 S.E.2d 172, 177 (N.C. 2002). The Swine Farm Siting Act, which governs the placement of swine farms and lagoons, can be found at N.C. Gen. Stat. §§ 106-800 to 106-806 (2021); the state's Animal Waste Management Systems rules can be found at N.C. Gen. Stat. §§ 143-215.10A to 143-215.10M (2021).
34. For a summary of the initial lawsuit, see *McKiver v. Murphy-Brown, LLC*, 980 F.3d 937 (4th Cir. 2020).
35. For a discussion of the award of compensatory damages, see *McKiver*, 980 F.3d 937.
36. Will Doran, "After Smithfield Lost Millions in Lawsuits, N.C. Changed a Law; Was It Constitutional?," *Asheboro (N.C.) Courier-Tribune*, June 22, 2019.
37. 2017 N.C. Sess. Laws 11 (H.B. 467) (adding N.C. Gen. Stat. § 106-702).
38. See *McKiver*, 980 F.3d 937.
39. N.C. Gen. Stat. § 106-702 (2021).
40. *McKiver v. Murphy-Brown, LLC*, 980 F.3d 937, 958 (4th Cir. 2020).
41. *McKiver v. Murphy-Brown, LLC*, No. 7:14-CV-180-BR, 2018 WL 10322917 (E.D.N.C. May 7, 2018).
42. N.C. Gen. Stat. § 1D-25 (2021); see also *McKiver*, 2018 WL 10322917.
43. *McKiver*, 980 F.3d 937.
44. 2018 N.C. Sess. Laws 113 (S.B. 711) (amending N.C. Gen. Stat. § 106-702).
45. N.C. Gen. Stat. § 106-702 (2021).
46. Taft Wireback, "Blust Breaks with GOP over Nuisance Lawsuits," *Greensboro (N.C.) News and Record*, April 11, 2017.
47. Steve Wing, Dana Cole, and Gary Grant, "Environmental Injustice in North Carolina's Hog Industry," *Environmental Health Perspectives* 108, no. 3 (2000): 225–31.
48. N.C. Gen. Stat. § 106-701 (2021).

North Dakota

Proponents advocated North Dakota's right-to-farm law as a tool to protect family farmers and farmland from development.[1] But since the law first passed in 1981, the number of farms in the state has dropped by 28 percent, with 2 percent fewer acres of farmland.[2] So what does this legislation do in practice?

North Dakota's RTF Law at a Glance

North Dakota's law provides no explicit protection for farmland or family farmers. Rather, North Dakota's RTF law centers on protecting certain types of operations from nuisance suits when their activities impact neighboring property, for example through noise or pollution. The types of production that receive protection are expansive, including the commercial production of plants and animals, horticulture, floriculture, viticulture, forestry, dairy, livestock, poultry, bees, and any and all forms of farm products and farm production, as well as the disposal of those products by "marketing or other means."[3] In 1999, North Dakota altered its original law to extend protections to corporations and limited liability companies that complied with the state's Corporate Farming Law, which limits corporate ownership of farmland.[4] Then in 2001, the legislature added language to protect corporations and LLCs regardless of their compliance with the Corporate Farming Law.[5] Also in 2001, livestock auction markets gained RTF protections.

Changes in corporate protection have played a crucial role in different outcomes for farming operations. In a 1986 case, a farmer sued a neighboring corporate landowner, American Crystal Sugar Company, claiming that wastewater lagoons damaged the plaintiff's farmland. While the trial court thought American Crystal's activities qualified as an "agricultural operation," its decision was overturned when the North Dakota Supreme Court ruled

184

Table 2.34 North Dakota's Key RTF Provisions and National Comparison

North Dakota's key RTF provisions		% U.S. states with similar RTF provisions
Operations are immune from lawsuits . . .	if there is a change in locality.	46%
	once in operation for a year.	48%
Operations are not immune from lawsuits . . .	if they are a nuisance from the start.	38%
	if they are negligent.	46%
	if they pollute water.	36%
Other important details	RTF supersedes local ordinances and laws.	62%

that the American Crystal Sugar Company was not protected because it did not meet the requirements of the state's Corporate Farming Law.[6] Since that time, corporations have gained access to RTF protections in North Dakota. In 2005, the state supreme court ruled that Minto Grain, a limited liability corporation, warranted RTF protections when a neighboring family that owned a trucking business claimed nuisances of noise, dust, and fumes.[7] The state supreme court did not believe the legislature originally intended RTF protections for the "preparation and marketing [of agricultural] products by large national corporations"[8] but nonetheless extended protections to Minto Grain, in accordance with recent amendments.

In 2012, North Dakota voters adopted a constitutional amendment sponsored by the North Dakota Farm Bureau, stating, "The right of farmers and ranchers to engage in modern farming and ranching practices shall be forever guaranteed in this state. No law shall be enacted which abridges the right of farmers and ranchers to employ agricultural technology, modern livestock production, and ranching practices."[9] Missouri is the only other state in the nation with a similar constitutional amendment.

Conditions and Activities

A series of conditions clarify the context in which RTF protections apply. If operations meet such conditions, like operating for a year and not being a nuisance at the time it begins, those operations cannot be deemed a nuisance under state or local laws.[10] If conditions around the facility change, the protections for the operation still hold.

Certain activities, though, are not protected by the RTF law. For example, the statute does not protect operations that fail to use proper care (that is, operate negligently) or that pollute any stream water or cause any overflow onto the lands of another.[11] North Dakota's law allows a plaintiff to recover damages when an agricultural operation pollutes stream water but does not stipulate whether this includes groundwater. Air pollution also is not mentioned.

Local Government

North Dakota's RTF law voids any municipal ordinance that declares an operation a nuisance or requires it to stop (when meeting the aforementioned criteria).[12] However, local governments can enforce ordinances when agricultural operations are operating improperly or negligently or are within the corporate limits of a city.[13]

NOTES

1. See Associated Press, "North Dakota's Nuisance Law Could Be Challenged," *Grand Forks (N.D.) Herald*, February 24, 1999; Curt Woodward, "Wrangling in Offensive Odor—State Would Step In for Counties That Don't Have Feedlot Setbacks," *Grand Forks Herald*, March 18, 2005.
2. U.S. Department of Commerce, "Table 1. Farms, Land in Farms, and Land Use: 1982 and Earlier Census Years," in *1982 Census of Agriculture, Volume 1: Geographic Area Series, Part 34: North Dakota State and County Data, Chapter 1: State Data* (Washington, D.C.: U.S. Bureau of the Census, 1984), https://agcensus.library.cornell.edu/wp-content/uploads /1982-North_Dakota-CHAPTER_1_State_Data-121-Table-01.pdf; "2021 State Agriculture Overview: North Dakota," U.S. Department of Agriculture, National Agricultural Statistics Service, accessed October 21, 2022, https://www.nass.usda.gov/Quick_Stats/Ag_Overview /stateOverview.php?state=NORTH%20DAKOTA.
3. N.D. Cent. Code § 42-04-01 (2021).
4. 1999 N.D. Laws 50 (H.B. 1045) (amending, in relevant part, N.D. Cent. Code § 42-04-01).
5. 2001 N.D. Laws 55 (H.B. 1049) (amending, in relevant part, N.D. Cent. Code § 42-04-01).
6. *Knoff v. Am. Crystal Sugar Co.*, 380 N.W.2d 313 (N.D. 1986).
7. *Tibert v. Slominski*, 692 N.W.2d 133 (N.D. 2005).
8. *Tibert*, 692 N.W.2d at 137 (citing *Knoff*, 380 N.W.2d at 316).
9. N.D. Const. art. XI, § 29.
10. N.D. Cent. Code § 42-04-02 (2021).
11. N.D. Cent. Code § 42-04-03 (2021).
12. N.D. Cent. Code § 42-04-04 (2021).
13. N.D. Cent. Code § 42-04-04 (2021).

Ohio

Ohio legislators proposed a right-to-farm law as a tool to preserve agricultural land.[1] But since the law first passed in 1982, the number of farms in the state has dropped by 11 percent, with 12 percent fewer acres of farmland.[2] So what does this legislation do in practice?

Ohio's RTF Law at a Glance

Ohio's RTF law, first passed as the "Agricultural District Program," was among only six in the nation that tailored protection to agricultural districts. County auditors and sometimes councils stipulated what land was enrolled in such districts.[3] Among other things, such districts were required to be at least ten acres or more.[4] However, amendments contained within 2,000 pages of the state's 2019 budget bill and passed that July no longer require operations to take place within an agricultural district.[5] The law now protects agricultural activities on any land exclusively used for agricultural production.[6] Types of production protected include commercial aquaculture, animal husbandry, and commercial crops as well as processing, drying, storage, and marketing. A 2012 amendment also added biomass/biodiesel production as protected activities.[7]

Conditions and Activities

For agricultural activities to be protected through the RTF law, the statute stipulates that they should predate the activities or interests of the person or entity filing the lawsuit. Despite this, Ohio Fresh Eggs, a limited liability corporation with over 2.5 million birds, was able to successfully claim in court that it was there first through general agricultural land use.[8] Initially, a farmer who predated the egg facility filed a complaint with the

Ohio Environmental Protection Agency over air pollution. However, the Ohio Environmental Protection Agency ruled the facility was exempt. The farmer appealed, and Ohio's Environmental Review Appeals Commission ruled that the facility did violate the state's pollution laws. Ohio Fresh Eggs followed with its own appeal. The court then determined that the corporation's activities met the definition of agricultural production as defined in the state's RTF and air pollution control laws.[9] The court also considered whether there was a change in the type of agricultural use of the land, as the farmer had lived on his property since 1967 and the egg operation began in 1996 (as Buckeye Egg Farm Limited Partnership).[10] The court ruled that the LLC operated on land designated for agricultural purposes since at least the 1930s, thus meeting one of the five conditions necessary for exemption under the air pollution control act and overturning the Environmental Review Appeals Commission's decision.[11] In a separate case, a court ruled that even if an agricultural operation bought its land after a plaintiff, it still had the "there first" defense if the type of activity had not changed.[12]

To receive RTF protections, the state also requires that agricultural activities not be in conflict with federal, state, and local laws and be conducted in accordance with common agricultural practices.[13] Common practices and activities include cultivating crops and changing rotation; raising livestock and changing the species of livestock; operating under a livestock contract; storage and application of fertilizer, manure, pesticides, and other chemicals commonly used in agriculture; change in corporate structure or ownership of the operation; the expansion, contraction, or change in operations; and any agricultural practice accepted by local custom.[14] Agricultural activities conducted outside municipal boundaries may not be subject to public nuisance suits or other local or state regulatory violations if they are done in accordance with "generally accepted agricultural practices" and do not have a "substantial, adverse effect on the public health, safety, or welfare."[15] The meanings of "generally accepted agricultural practices" and "substantial, adverse effect" are not defined.

Formerly, Ohio had a unique provision that did not allow one farmer to use the RTF law when suing another farmer. The sweeping 2019 amendments, though, now allow agricultural operators to use the RTF defense, even if sued by a farmer. Farmers who are aggrieved or adversely affected by an agricultural operation's violation of the state's environmental protection laws may also file complaints that sometimes lead to lawsuits.[16]

Table 2.35 Ohio's Key RTF Provisions and National Comparison

Ohio's key RTF provisions		% U.S. states with similar RTF provisions
Operations are immune from lawsuits . . .	if they are there first.	46%
	if there is an ownership change.	26%
	if boundaries or size of operation change	34%
Operations are not immune from lawsuits . . .	if they do not comply with federal laws.	62%
	if they do not comply with state laws.	68%
	if they do not comply with other laws.	50%
Other important details	RTF supersedes local ordinances and laws.	62%
	RTF protects processing.	48%

Local Government

The RTF law allows citizens to bring an action to address a nuisance in the name of the state or a municipal entity respective to the county they live in.[17] In such cases, citizens must post a bond of no less than $500. The particular amount is determined and approved by the court. If the court decides the suit was wrongfully brought, dismissed, or not fully prosecuted, the agricultural operation can claim damages in the amount of the bond. Operations typically cannot claim more than this original bond amount, even if they later claim to have incurred greater expenses in their defense.[18]

Townships have some power to prohibit the use of land or construction of buildings for agricultural purposes when that land is less than five acres in size. However, they have no authority to regulate activities on parcels larger than five acres.[19] For instance, a proposed dairy operation containing over 2,000 cows claimed in court that a township could not require a land use permit for its operation. The court agreed, ruling that the township could not regulate the operation, as it was on agricultural land.[20]

NOTES

1. See legislative preamble to 1982 Ohio Laws (S.B. 78).
2. U.S. Department of Commerce, "Table 1. Farms, Land in Farms, and Land Use: 1982 and Earlier Census Years," in *1982 Census of Agriculture, Volume 1: Geographic Area Series, Part 35: Ohio State and County Data, Chapter 1: State Data* (Washington, D.C.: U.S. Bureau of the Census, 1984), https://agcensus.library.cornell.edu/wp-content/uploads/1982 -Ohio-CHAPTER_1_State_Data-121-Table-01.pdf; "2021 State Agriculture Overview: Ohio," U.S. Department of Agriculture, National Agricultural Statistics Service, accessed

October 21, 2022, https://www.nass.usda.gov/Quick_Stats/Ag_Overview/stateOverview.php?state=OHIO.

3. Barbara Galloway, "Park Farms Vote Delayed in Canton Council Law," *Akron (Ohio) Beacon Journal*, June 8, 1993.

4. Ohio Rev. Code § 929.02 (2021).

5. 2019 Ohio Laws 10 (H.B. 166) (amending, in relevant part, Ohio Rev. Code § 929.04). See also Peggy Hall Kirck, "Budget Bill Alters Ohio's Right to Farm Law," *Morning AgClips*, July 29, 2019, https://www.morningagclips.com/budget-bill-alters-ohios-right-to-farm-law/.

6. It also protects agricultural activities conducted by an entity pursuant to a lease agreement or enrolled in Ohio's property tax reduction program. For more details, see Ohio's current agricultural use valuation program at Ohio Rev. Code § 5713.30 (2021).

7. 2011 Ohio Laws (H.B. 276) (amending, in relevant part, Ohio Rev. Code § 5713.30[A]). See also Ohio Rev. Code §§ 929.01, 929.04 (2021).

8. *Bear v. Jones*, No. 06AP-1271, 2007 WL 2505511 (Ohio Ct. App. Sept. 6, 2007).

9. *Bear*, 2007 WL 2505511, at 6 (citing Ohio Rev. Code § 3704.01(B), which provides that "air contaminant" does not include "emissions from agricultural production activities," as defined in Ohio Rev. Code § 929.01).

10. See *Concerned Citizens of Cent. Ohio v. Schregardus*, 148 Ohio App. 3d 31, 33 (2002) (stating, "The facts underlying this matter are undisputed. In March 1996, the director of OEPA approved an initial livestock waste management plan for Buckeye Egg's Marseilles egg production facility. The plan provided for construction of fourteen laying hen barns to house a total of approximately 2.5 million chickens"). See also *Bear*, 2007 WL 2505511 (citing *Schregardus*, 148 Ohio App. 3d 31).

11. *Bear*, 2007 WL 2505511. Ironically, before this case was decided the U.S. Department of Justice sued the company for failing to comply with the federal Clean Air Act and obtain necessary federal pollution control permits. See "Ohio's Largest Egg Producer Agrees to Dramatic Air Pollution Reductions from Three Giant Facilities," U.S. Department of Justice and U.S. Environmental Protection Agency, News Release, February 23, 2004, available at https://archive.epa.gov/epapages/newsroom_archive/newsreleases/508199b8068c24a58 5256e43007e1230.html. Since states have to implement federal Clean Air Act regulations that are at least as stringent as federal law, it is unclear why the operation received an agricultural exemption from OEPA.

12. *Eulrich v. Weaver Bros., Inc.*, 165 Ohio App. 3d 313 (2005).

13. Ohio Rev. Code § 929.04 (2021).

14. Ohio Rev. Code § 929.04 (2021).

15. Ohio Rev. Code § 3767.13(D) (2021).

16. See, e.g., Ohio's air pollution control law, Ohio Rev. Code § 3704.06(E) (2021); the state's environmental protection regulations under Ohio Rev. Code § 3745.08 (2021); and the state's solid and hazardous waste regulations under Ohio Rev. Code § 3734.101(E) (2021).

17. Ohio Rev. Code § 3767.03 (2021).

18. Ohio Rev. Code § 3767.03 (2021). See also *Shuttleworth v. Knapke*, No. 02CA1582, 2003 WL 588598 (Ohio Ct. App. Feb. 28, 2003) (noting that "these provisions [in Ohio Rev. Code § 3767.03] limit the amount of the awards to the amount of the bond, and limit a defendant's recourse on those awards to a proceeding against the bond the plaintiff posted").

19. Ohio Rev. Code § 519.21 (2021).

20. *Meerland Dairy L.L.C. v. Ross Twp.*, No. 07CA0083, 2008 WL 1991886 (Ohio Ct. App. May 9, 2008).

Oklahoma

Controversy has surrounded the right-to-farm law in Oklahoma since major amendments in the early 1990s.[1] Some argue that the law protects family farms, while others counter that it paves the way for corporate agriculture.[2] Since the law first passed in 1980, the number of farms in the state has increased by 7 percent, with about the same amount of land in farms.[3] So what does the state's RTF statute do in practice?

Oklahoma's RTF Law at a Glance

Oklahoma's RTF law, first passed in 1980, does not explicitly protect family farms or farmland from development. Rather, Oklahoma's RTF law, like those present in the other forty-nine states, centers on protecting certain agricultural activities on farmland and ranchland from nuisance suits when they impact neighboring property, for example through noise or pollution.[4] In 2000, an amendment added the production of livestock or agricultural commodities and forestry activities to the definition of "farmland," including associated buildings and structures.[5] Activities protected from nuisance suits range from growing horticultural and agricultural crops to new technology, pens, barns, fences, and other so-called improvements designed for the sheltering, restriction, or feeding of animal or aquatic life, for storage of produce or feed, or for storage or maintenance of implements.[6]

Conditions and Activities

Initially, operations had to predate neighboring nonagricultural activities to claim protection from nuisance.[7] In 2009, however, the RTF law was amended to substantially expand protections for operations, even if they were not there first.[8] A facility now has to be in operation only for two years to claim RTF protection.[9] Amendments in 2017 added further protections, stipulating that the two-year clock does not restart even if the physical facilities of the farm or ranch subsequently change; a new technology is adopted; the operation ceases farming or production (for up to three years); or the farm or ranch participates in a government-sponsored agricultural program.[10]

Operations that use "good agricultural practices" are protected as long as they comply with federal, state, and local laws.[11] Some state and federal environmental rules and regulations exempt agricultural operations from standards required of other industries.[12] Air pollution, like odor, is not regulated in Oklahoma.[13] The RTF statute does not define the meaning of "good agricultural practices," leaving it often to court rulings. In a 2003 case, codefendant Cargill Inc. argued that its growers applied poultry litter "consistent with good agricultural practices" because they did not have a "substantial adverse affect [sic] on the public health and safety."[14] Oklahoma's statute stipulates that agricultural activities are protected, so long as they do not substantially impact public health or safety.[15] The court nonetheless ruled that Cargill could not use the RTF defense based on another criterion of the law. Since the poultry defendant's application of poultry litter did not predate the use of the lakes as a municipal water supply, it could not use the RTF defense of its practices.[16] The case was later settled out of court. Since the law changed to require only two years in operation to be considered "prior," the court's justification for its ruling in this case may no longer hold.

Local Government

Oklahoma's RTF law does not specifically curtail government authority. However, the Oklahoma Department of Agriculture, Food, and Forestry does not allow municipalities, counties, or other political subdivisions to enact or enforce ordinances or regulations more restrictive than its own as pertains to the care and handling of livestock.[17] Still, local government can enact or enforce ordinances and regulations that pertain to land use or human health and safety.[18] In counties with populations in excess of 550,000 people, local governments may declare what shall constitute a nuisance and provide for the prevention, removal, and abatement of nuisances for those properties acquired by the county through resale and for any property located within an unincorporated area of the county.[19]

Table 2.36 Oklahoma's Key RTF Provisions and National Comparison

Oklahoma's key RTF provisions		% U.S. states with similar RTF provisions
Operations are immune from lawsuits . . .	if boundaries or size of operations change.	34%
	if they use a new technology.	30%
	if there is a cessation or interruption in farming.	26%
	if they are there first.	44%
	once in operation for two years.	6%
Operations are not immune from lawsuits . . .	if they do not comply with state laws.	68%
	if they do not comply with county laws.	42%
	if they do not comply with federal laws.	62%
Other important details	Attorney fees are awarded to prevailing defendant.	34%

Other Important Details

Defendants recover costs and fees when nuisance suits are deemed frivolous.[20] This and similar language may have a chilling effect on the filing of nuisance suits in favor of industrial operators.[21] In 2019, a controversial amendment was passed along party lines, limiting the awards available to successful plaintiffs.[22] Noneconomic damages cannot exceed three times the amount of compensatory damages or $250,000, whichever amount is greater.[23]

The RTF law in Oklahoma also works in dialogue with the Oklahoma Concentrated Animal Feeding Operations Act and the Oklahoma Registered Poultry Feeding Operations Act.[24] In 2007, a court used the Oklahoma Concentrated Animal Feeding Operations Act to affirm a lower court's ruling that feedlot operators had to abate their nuisance because the neighbors had lived there twelve years prior to when the cattle operation began.[25]

NOTES

1. David Zizzo, "Downwind of Corporate Push Law Change Opens Gate to Pig Plantations," *Daily Oklahoman* (Oklahoma City), May 9, 1993.
2. "Group to Protest Right-to-Farm Act Monday at Capitol," *Tulsa (Okla.) World*, April 1, 1995.
3. U.S. Department of Agriculture, *USDA Quick Stats Tool: June 1980 Survey, Oklahoma*, distributed by National Agricultural Statistics Service, accessed October 4, 2020, https://quickstats.nass.usda.gov/results/CB0A30DA-3321-38BF-B0F7-5F295320F814; "2021 State

Agriculture Overview: Oklahoma," U.S. Department of Agriculture, National Agricultural Statistics Service, accessed October 21, 2022, https://www.nass.usda.gov/Quick_Stats /Ag_Overview/stateOverview.php?state=OKLAHOMA.

4. Okla. Stat. tit. 50, § 1.1 (2021).

5. 2000 Okla. Sess. Laws 300 (H.B. 2306) (amending, in relevant part, Okla. Stat. tit. 50, § 1.1).

6. Okla. Stat. tit. 50, § 1.1 (2021).

7. Okla. Stat. tit. 50, § 1.1 (1980).

8. 2009 Okla. Sess. Laws 147 (H.B. 1482) (amending, in relevant part, Okla. Stat. tit. 50, § 1.1).

9. Okla. Stat. tit. 50, § 1.1 (2021).

10. 2017 Okla. Sess. Laws 276 (H.B. 1388) (amending, in relevant part, Okla. Stat. tit. 50, § 1.1).

11. Okla. Stat. tit. 50, § 1.1 (2021).

12. Danielle Diamond, Loka Ashwood, Allen Franco, Aimee Imlay, Lindsay Kuehn, and Crystal Boutwell, "Farm Fiction: Agricultural Exceptionalism, Environmental Injustice and U.S. Right-to-Farm Law," *Environmental Law Reporter* 52 (Sept. 2022): 10727–48.

13. David Zizzo, "Hold Your Nose, but Not Your Breath: No Easy Answers for Smelly Hog Farms' Neighbors," *Daily Oklahoman*, January 12, 1998.

14. *City of Tulsa v. Tyson Foods, Inc.*, 258 F. Supp. 2d 1263 (N.D. Okla. 2003).

15. Okla. Stat. tit. 50, § 1.1 (2021).

16. *Tyson Foods, Inc.*, 258 F. Supp. 2d 1263.

17. Okla. Stat. tit. 2, § 2-4c (2021).

18. Okla. Stat. tit. 2, § 2-4c (2021).

19. Okla. Stat. tit. 50, § 20 (2021).

20. Okla. Stat. tit. 50, § 1.1 (2021).

21. Cordon M. Smart, "The 'Right to Commit Nuisance' in North Carolina: A Historical Analysis of the Right-to-Farm Act," *North Carolina Law Review* 94, no. 6 (2016): 2097–154. For more on the chilling effect of such statutes, see the section "Geopolitical Extraction" in the introduction.

22. 2019 Okla. Sess. Laws 21 (H.B. 2373) (amending, in relevant part, Okla. Stat. tit. 50, § 1.1). See also Jack Money, "Committee Sends Ag Nuisance Bill to Senate," *Oklahoman* (Oklahoma City), March 20, 2019.

23. Okla. Stat. tit. 50, § 1.1 (2021).

24. Okla. Stat. tit. 50, § 1.1 (2021). The Oklahoma Concentrated Animal Feeding Operations Act can be found at Okla. Stat. tit. 2, §§ 20-40 through 20-64; the Oklahoma Registered Poultry Feeding Operations Act can be found at Okla. Stat. tit. 2, §§ 10-9 through 10-9.12.

25. *Woodlake Estates, Inc. v. Sternberger*, 173 P.3d 98 (Okla. Civ. App. 2007).

Oregon

The Oregon legislators who passed and amended the state's right-to-farm law promoted it as a piece of legislation that protected agricultural lands from urban and suburban sprawl.[1] Since Oregon's law was enacted in 1981, the number of farm operations has grown by 2 percent while the amount of acreage in farmland has dropped by 13 percent.[2] So what does this legislation do in practice?

Oregon's RTF Law at a Glance

Oregon's RTF law originally protected farming practices from nuisance suits that pertained to the enjoyment and use of property, similar to other RTF laws nationally.[3] Generally, protected farming practices could occur in any facility or building, or on any land or watercourse, zoned for the commercial production of crops and nursery stock or for the production of livestock, poultry, vermiculture, and their products.[4] However, the Oregon Department of Agriculture and the Oregon Farm Bureau successfully lobbied in 1993 for dramatic changes to the state's RTF law.[5] Among other things, these changes extended RTF protections to forestry practices, including site preparation, timber harvest, slash disposal, road construction, and thinning, as well as disease and insect control, on any land that is zoned for the growing and harvesting of forest tree species.[6]

Most importantly, the amendments added trespass alongside nuisance, effectively shielding agricultural and forestry operations from lawsuits based on the invasion of neighboring property without permission.[7] Further, the 1993 amendments and a later amendment in 1995 added the use of pesticides (including fungicides, herbicides, insecticides, and nematicides) to the definition of protected farming and forestry practices.[8] The inclusion of pesticides as a protected farming and forestry practice has prevented some landowners from recovering compensation for damage resulting from pesticide drift. In 2011, seven landowners, including organic farmers, sued the state, arguing that by allowing pesticide drift the RTF law was unconstitutional because it deprived them of their right to sue for compensation.[9] A state judge dismissed the suit in 2011, to the praise of the Oregon Farm Bureau.

Advocates claimed that the sweeping changes in the 1993 amendments would safeguard farmers from "new arrivals who find that the country isn't quite as pristine as they prefer."[10] The legislature expressly stated that "persons who locate on or near an area zoned for farm or forest use must accept the conditions commonly associated with living in that particular setting."[11] In reality, Oregon's RTF law does not provide protections tailored to long-standing farms. Rather, the law broadly protects farming and forestry practices in areas zoned for farm or forestry uses against claims relating to vibration, odors, smoke, dust, pesticide drift, and irrigation.[12] Such practices receive RTF protections regardless of the amount of acreage, the farm size (for example, small), or the type of organization (for example, family). Further, farm operations are protected regardless of whether they predate other dwellers or rural residents.

Conditions and Activities

To receive RTF protections in areas zoned for farming and forestry, practices must meet a series of criteria.[13] "Farming and forestry practices" refers to modes of operation that (1) are or may be used on farms or forestland of a similar nature; (2) use generally accepted, reasonable, and prudent methods, including for making a profit; and (3) comply with applicable laws. The law also uniquely protects future changes, stating it protects methods that may become generally accepted, reasonable, and prudent ways to operate on a farm.[14] Further, the RTF law protects farming and forestry practices regardless of whether they change or are interrupted.[15] This legal language can serve to protect the consolidation, expansion, and further intensification of agriculture.

When first enacted, Oregon's RTF law did not protect farming practices that were negligent, meaning those that failed to take proper care.[16] However, amendments in 1993 removed that stipulation and added other exceptions.[17] Now, operations lose their RTF protections if someone dies or incurs serious physical injury, but the statute is not clear about the context of the death or injury.[18] In addition, if a farming or forestry practice damages commercial agricultural products, the practice will not be protected by the RTF law.[19] In 2015, an Oregon court interpreted this to mean that "the Right to Farm Act does not give free license to use any farming practices. While farming practices may not be limited by a suburbanite's sensitivities, they may be limited if they cause damage to another farm's crops."[20]

Under some circumstances, Oregon's RTF law protections can extend to farming and forestry practices that are not located in areas zoned for such uses. If a farming or forestry practice is what the law calls a "preexisting nonconforming use"—meaning a use that once complied with local zoning but no longer does due to a change in zoning laws—the practice can be protected from claims of nuisance or trespass.[21] To receive these protections, not only must the practice meet the same requirements that exist for a protected practice in areas zoned for farming or forestry, but the practice must also have existed before any conflicting nonfarm uses.[22] In addition, the practice cannot have significantly increased in size or intensity after the later of either November 4, 1993, or the date on which an urban growth boundary is changed to include the area where the farming practice occurs.[23]

A 1995 amendment made it clear that Oregon's agencies could choose, but were not required, to investigate complaints pertaining to forestry and agriculture.[24] Oregon's RTF law now expressly provides that the Oregon Departments of Environmental Quality, Agriculture, State Lands, and Forestry do not need to investigate any complaint if they "believe that the complaint is based on practices protected" by the state's RTF law.[25]

Local Government

Oregon's RTF law tailors its protections to areas zoned for farming or forestry at the county level or where a farming or forestry practice is a preexisting nonconforming use.[26] The RTF law renders invalid any local ordinance or regulation—currently in effect or subsequently adopted—that makes a farm or forestry practice a nuisance or trespass or that attempts to stop such a practice because it is a nuisance or trespass.[27] This rule applies only to a farm or forestry practice that is otherwise protected under the RTF law.

In a 2004 case, the Oregon Court of Appeals considered as much when a farmer with a herd of sixty goats and guard dogs was cited for violating a county ordinance that prohibited dogs from becoming public nuisances through prolonged noise, in this case barking. The court reversed the violation, concluding that the state's RTF law prohibited the county from enforcing its ordinance against the farmer because using guard dogs was a protected farming practice. The court also noted that the RTF law "promotes a policy of maintaining exclusive use farm land for farming, even at the expense of the neighbors' enjoyment of their property."[28]

Conversely, a farm that used Roundup Ready alfalfa grown from genetically engineered seeds brought an action against its county, arguing that a proposed county ordinance banning the use of genetically engineered seeds conflicted with the state's RTF law and should not be enforced.[29] The court, however, concluded in 2015 that the ordinance sought to protect farmers growing non–genetically engineered crops from significant economic harm caused by genetic drift. Accordingly, the court held that because the ordinance was protecting against a farming practice (the use of genetically engineered seeds) that caused damage to other commercial agricultural products, the ordinance fell within an exception to the RTF law and was therefore valid.[30]

Other Oregon laws also seek to protect farm and forestry practices from nonagricultural and nonforestry uses. Under one such law, in order for a nonagricultural or nonforestry use to be allowed in an area zoned for exclusive farm use, the use must pass a farm impact test confirming that it will not force a significant change to, or significantly increase the costs of, accepted farm or forestry practices on neighboring lands.[31]

The meaning of "significant" came into focus in a series of court cases involving a landfill company that sought to expand its solid waste landfill into an exclusive farm use zone because it was running out of capacity.[32] The county had approved the landfill's expansion, but a coalition of citizens and farmers, including a winery association, sued to stop the expansion. The court considered whether the landfill expansion would violate Oregon's law, which prohibits uses that create a significant change in accepted farm practices or significantly increase the cost of those practices on surrounding agricultural lands. Ultimately, the Supreme Court of Oregon concluded that "a 'significant' change or increase in cost is one that will have an important influence or effect on [a particular accepted farm practice]."[33] The court therefore remanded the case back down to the county's land use board of appeals to determine whether the landfill company could prove that the expansion would neither force a significant change in the neighboring accepted farm practices nor significantly increase the cost of those practices. One legal commentator opined that the court's decision made it "very difficult" moving forward for counties to approve nonfarm and nonforestry uses in exclusive farm use zones "if the adjacent farm operator is able to

Table 2.37 Oregon's Key RTF Provisions and National Comparison

Oregon's key RTF provisions		% U.S. states with similar RTF provisions
Operations are immune from lawsuits . . .	if there is a cessation or interruption in farming.	26%
	if they are there first.	44%
Operations are not immune from lawsuits . . .	if they do not comply with county laws.	42%
	if they do not comply with federal laws.	62%
	if they do not comply with other laws.	50%
	if they do not comply with state laws.	68%
	if they do not comply with environmental laws.	26%
Other important details	RTF supersedes local ordinances and laws.	62%
	Attorney fees are awarded to prevailing party.	14%

marshal evidence of significant cost increases or changes in accepted farm practices."[34]

Attorney Fees

Oregon's RTF law stipulates that courts must award reasonable attorney fees and costs to "either party" that prevails in any action where a farming or forestry practice is alleged to cause a nuisance or trespass.[35] Importantly, the Oregon Supreme Court ruled that a party does not have to *prove* that a farming or forestry practice exists within the scope of the state's RTF law.[36] Instead, a prevailing party can be awarded attorney fees and costs even if it simply *alleges* a farming or forestry practice is a nuisance or trespass. These costs and fees must be awarded at the trial level, as well as if the case goes on to an appeal.

NOTES

1. "A Right-to-Farm," *The Oregonian* (Portland), April 22, 1993; Jim Kadera, "Oregon Agricultural Interests Expand Right-to-Farm Concept," *The Oregonian* (Portland), February 24, 1993. See also 1993 Or. Laws 792 (H.B. 3661) (adding what is now Or. Rev. Stat. § 30.933).
2. U.S. Department of Agriculture, *USDA Quick Stats Tool: June 1981 Survey, Oregon*, distributed by National Agricultural Statistics Service, accessed January 6, 2021, https://quickstats .nass.usda.gov/results/DBC85231-9E97-30A4-BB0E-37029E2AE5CB; "2021 State Agriculture Overview: Oregon," U.S. Department of Agriculture, National Agricultural Statistics

Service, accessed October 21, 2022, https://www.nass.usda.gov/Quick_Stats/Ag_Overview/stateOverview.php?state=OREGON.

3. Or. Rev. Stat. §§ 30.930, 30.935 (1981).

4. Or. Rev. Stat. §§ 30.930, 30.933, 30.936 (2021).

5. See generally 1993 Or. Laws 792 (H.B. 3661); and Kadera, "Oregon Agricultural Interests Expand Right-to-Farm Concept."

6. 1993 Or. Laws 792 (H.B. 3661) (amending, in relevant part, what is now Or. Rev. Stat. §§ 30.936, 30.937, and amending Or. Rev. Stat. § 30.930).

7. 1993 Or. Laws 792 (H.B. 3661) (adding, in relevant part, what is now Or. Rev. Stat. §§ 30.934, 30.936, 30.937, and amending Or. Rev. Stat. § 30.935).

8. 1993 Or. Laws 792 (H.B. 3661) (adding, in relevant part, what is now Or. Rev. Stat. §§ 30.932, 30.939); 1995 Or. Laws 703 (S.B. 766) (amending Or. Rev. Stat. §§ 30.930, 30.932). For the relevant definition of "pesticide," see Or. Rev. Stat. § 634.006 (2021).

9. Mateusz Perkowski, "Right to Farm Law Challenge Fails, May Resurface Again. Judge Dismisses Lawsuit Taking Issues with Ag Protections," *Capital Press* (Salem, Ore.), September 29, 2011.

10. "A Right-to-Farm," *The Oregonian*, April 22, 1993.

11. 1993 Or. Laws 792 (H.B. 3661) (amending, in relevant part, what is now Or. Rev. Stat. § 30.933).

12. Or. Rev. Stat. §§ 30.930, 30.932, 30.936 (2021).

13. Or. Rev. Stat. §§ 30.930, 30.936 (2021).

14. Or. Rev. Stat. § 30.930 (2021).

15. Or. Rev. Stat. § 30.936 (2021).

16. Or. Rev. Stat. § 30.935 (1981).

17. 1993 Or. Laws 792 (H.B. 3661) (amending in relevant part, Or. Rev. Stat. § 30.935).

18. Or. Rev. Stat. § 30.936 (2021).

19. Or. Rev. Stat. § 30.936 (2021).

20. *Schultz Family Farms LLC v. Jackson Cty.*, No. 1:14-cv-01975, 2015 WL 3448069 (D. Or. May 29, 2015).

21. Or. Rev. Stat. § 30.937 (2021).

22. Or. Rev. Stat. § 30.937 (2021).

23. Or. Rev. Stat. § 30.937 (2021).

24. 1995 Or. Laws 703 (S.B. 766) (creating, in relevant part, what is now Or. Rev. Stat. § 30.943).

25. Or. Rev. Stat. § 30.943 (2021).

26. Or. Rev. Stat. §§ 30.936, 30.937 (2021). The RTF law's protections apply even when nonfarm or nonforestry uses are allowed in an area zoned for agriculture. Or. Rev. Stat. § 30.947 (2021).

27. Or. Rev. Stat. §§ 30.934, 30.935 (2021).

28. *Hood River Cty. v. Mazzara*, 89 P.3d 1195 (Or. Ct. App. 2004).

29. *Schultz Family Farms LLC v. Jackson Cty.*, No. 1:14-cv-01975, 2015 WL 3448069 (D. Or. May 29, 2015).

30. The exception the court was referring to is found at Or. Rev. Stat. §§ 30.936, 30.937 (2021).

31. Or. Rev. Stat. § 215.296 (2021).

32. *Stop the Dump Coal. v. Yamhill Cty.*, 435 P.3d 698 (Or. 2019).

33. *Stop the Dump Coal.*, 435 P.3d 698.

34. Edward Sullivan and Carrie Richter, "Op-Ed: Oregon Gets Serious about Preserving Farmland for Farming," *Daily Journal of Commerce* (Portland), April 9, 2019.

35. Or. Rev. Stat. § 30.938 (2021).

36. *Hale v. Klemp*, 184 P.3d 1185 (Or. Ct. App. 2008).

Pennsylvania

When Pennsylvania legislators passed the state's first right-to-farm law in 1982, they justified it as a tool to conserve, protect, and develop agricultural land for agricultural production.[1] Since that time, the state has lost 5 percent of its farm operations and 12 percent of its acres in farmland.[2] So what does this and closely related RTF legislation do in practice?

Pennsylvania's RTF Law at a Glance

Pennsylvania's RTF and related laws provide no explicit protection for farmland, although they are sometimes confused as doing so.[3] Like those present in the other forty-nine states, Pennsylvania's RTF law centers on protecting certain types of operations from nuisance suits when they impact neighboring property, for example through noise or pollution. Pennsylvania's RTF and related laws play out in three parts: the so-titled RTF Law, the Agricultural Communities and Rural Environment Act, and the Nutrient Management Act.

Pennsylvania specifically offers protection from nuisance suits for what it calls "normal agricultural operations," which include the activities, practices, equipment, and procedures used by farmers in the production, harvesting, and preparation for market of agricultural and aquacultural crops, as well as livestock and poultry products.[4] To receive RTF protections, normal agricultural operations must be at least ten contiguous acres in area or, if they are smaller, their yearly gross income must be at least $10,000. Protected agricultural commodities include the processed or manufactured products from farms.

In practice, courts have interpreted "normal agricultural operations" broadly. For example, courts treat the application of biosolids as a normal agricultural operation, affording recycling contractor Synagro Central, LLC, status as an agricultural operation and shielding it from nuisance suits.[5]

Conditions and Activities

Pennsylvania's RTF law protects normal agricultural operations from nuisance lawsuits once they have been operating for at least one year.[6] Even if an operation changes substantially after it has been in operation for a year, the facility can still maintain RTF protections so long as it has an approved nutrient plan. Operations also are allowed to expand or alter their physical facilities and still maintain protection from nuisance suits. However, if the physical facilities of an agricultural operation undergo an important change or alteration that impacts the underlying conditions or circumstances driving the nuisance claims, nuisance suits may be possible.[7]

Often, however, courts protect operations from nuisance suits, even when they change the size of the operation, because of the unique combination of legislative protections offered through the RTF statute, the Agricultural Communities and Rural Environment Act, and the Nutrient Management Act. For example, in a 1999 case, a homeowner sued a neighboring poultry operation with 122,000 hens for excessive flies, odors, excessive noise all hours of the day and night, and finding "eggshells, feathers and dead chickens on his real estate." Even though the homeowner predated the poultry facility, the court used the RTF law to determine that the nuisance and negligence suits were time-barred, since the operation had been up and running for more than a year.[8]

In a 2016 case, residents sued two corporate operators alongside Bowes Farm for spreading food processing waste from a slaughterhouse proximate to their homes. On appeal, the court determined that spreading and storing waste were protected agricultural practices, even though the construction of a storage tank was a substantial change and it was not included in the nutrient management plan. Still, the court concluded that even if the agricultural operation violates federal, state, or local law, it is not necessarily "unlawful." Rather, the important point was that an operation be in "substantial compliance" with federal, state, or local law. Even though the statutes themselves say that agricultural operations lose protection if they violate any federal, state, or local law, the ruling introduced the language of "substantial" to compliance.[9]

Pennsylvania's RTF law also stipulates that normal agricultural operations will lose their protection from nuisance suits if they pollute streams or waters. However, in a 2018 case, the court granted an agricultural operation nuisance suit protection while acknowledging it had polluted water. While evidence showed increased bacteria in runoff water from a concentrated animal feeding operation with a 1.8-million-gallon storage pit for hog urine and feces, the court ruled the CAFO maintained RTF protections for three reasons. First, it had operated at least one year prior to the filing of the nuisance complaints. Second, application of manure to fields qualified as a normal agricultural activity. And third, even though the suit was filed within one year of manure being applied to fields, the facility had a nutrient management plan. The nutrient management plan, alongside the RTF law, thus protected the CAFO from nuisance suits.[10]

Local Government

Pennsylvania's RTF law exempts agricultural operations conducted "in accordance with normal agricultural operations" from nuisance ordinances unless they have a direct adverse effect on public health and safety. This agricultural exemption applies even if that nuisance violates the intent of any federal, state, or local statute or government regulation.[11] Municipalities are also required to "encourage the continuity, development, and viability of agricultural operations within [their] jurisdiction."[12]

The state further limited local government with the passage of the Agricultural Communities and Rural Environment Act, even though the Pennsylvania State Association of Township Supervisors vocally opposed it and others charged it was "legislative/special-interest collusion."[13] The Agricultural Communities and Rural Environment Act followed a highly controversial amendment—supported by the state Farm Bureau but opposed by the Farmers Union—that sought to strip municipalities of their capacity to pass ordinances in 2002.[14] While the controversial Senate Bill 1413 died in an appropriations committee, the Agricultural Communities and Rural Environment Act did not, which was strongly supported by then governor Ed Rendell and the Pennsylvania Farm Bureau.[15]

With its later passage in 2005, the Agricultural Communities and Rural Environment Act similarly removed local governments' capacity to restrict agricultural operations based on their ownership structure or activities.[16] The act applies to any existing ordinance, adoption, or construction, as well as to nutrient or odor management.[17] However, local governments may have the authority to prohibit operations if the state specifically stipulates as much.[18] If any ordinance is believed to be in violation of the act, an owner or operator of a normal agricultural operation may request that the attorney general review it. The secretary and the dean of the College of Agricultural Sciences at the Pennsylvania State University could be called on for expert consultation regarding the "nature of normal agricultural operations."[19] Based on their review, the attorney general could then choose to bring action against a local government.

Pennsylvania requires that local governments defer to the Nutrient Management Act when it comes to the storage, handling, or land application of animal manure. In effect, local governments cannot regulate waste and odor through any ordinances. While local governments cannot provide more oversight, the state allows ordinances that are consistent with the Nutrient Management Act.[20] In one case, neighbors sued operators of a swine CAFO that spread liquid manure. The court separated the agricultural operation's culpability from its farming process. Even though manure was spread in the fields well after the established date of the operation, the court ruled the RTF law barred nuisance action because the operation (but not the farm process) predated the neighbors. The court stated, "Plaintiffs brought their actions against the owners and operators of the farm, not the farming process."[21] In a 2019 case, a township granted a special exception for a swine nursery barn, and objectors appealed the decision. The facility was small enough to skirt nutrient management plan requirements and thus could potentially be liable for nuisances because no plan was in place. The court held that the Nutrient Management Act preempts local regulation of agricultural operations as regards both operations with such plans and those without them. In essence, the Pennsylvania Supreme Court ruled that townships have no authority to manage waste from those activities deemed part of "normal agricultural operation."[22]

Courts often use the Agricultural Communities and Rural Environment Act and the state's RTF law to determine limitations on local governments' authority relative to agricultural operations. In a 2009 case, the court used the RTF law and the Agricultural Communities and Rural Environment Act to determine that a township did not have the authority to differentiate intensive agricultural activities from normal agricultural operations. Initially, the owners and operators of a broiler confinement filed a land use appeal challenging a township's ordinance. The attorney general determined that parts of the ordinance violated the Agricultural Communities and Rural Environment Act and the RTF law, and the court agreed, also suggesting that the Nutrient Management Act already likely regulated such matters. The court consequently dismissed the township's suit against the attorney

Table 2.38 Pennsylvania's Key RTF Provisions and National Comparison

Pennsylvania's key RTF provisions		% U.S. states with similar RTF provisions
Operations are immune from lawsuits . . .	if they use a new technology.	30%
	once in operation for a year.	48%
	if the boundaries or size of operation change.	34%
Operations are not immune from lawsuits . . .	if they pollute water.	36%
	if they do not comply with county laws.	42%
	if they do not comply with federal laws.	62%
	if they do not comply with other laws.	50%
	if they do not comply with state laws.	68%
	if they are negligent.[†]	46%
Other important details	RTF supersedes local ordinances and laws.	62%
	RTF protects processing.	48%

[†] Only applies to agritourism.

general. Separately, a court in a 2012 appeals case used both laws to determine that a sound-emitting device used to repel deer from a tree farm did not qualify as part of a "normal agricultural operation." Consequently, the township's ordinance could bar the device.[23]

NOTES

1. 1982 Pa. Laws 133 (H.B. 1823) (enacting what is now 3 Pa. Stat. § 951).
2. U.S. Department of Commerce, "Table 1. Farms, Land in Farms, and Land Use: 1982 and Earlier Census Years," in *1982 Census of Agriculture, Volume 1: Geographic Area Series, Part 38: Pennsylvania State and County Data, Chapter 1: State Data* (Washington, D.C.: U.S. Bureau of the Census, 1984), https://agcensus.library.cornell.edu/wp-content/uploads/1982-Pennsylvania-CHAPTER_1_State_Data-121-Table-01.pdf; "2021 State Agriculture Overview: Pennsylvania," U.S. Department of Agriculture, National Agricultural Statistics Service, accessed October 21, 2022, https://www.nass.usda.gov/Quick_Stats/Ag_Overview/stateOverview.php?state=PENNSYLVANIA.
3. See Mary Klaus, "Past Farm Legislation Scorned as Piecemeal," *Harrisburg (Pa.) Patriot-News*, September 15, 1987.
4. 3 Pa. Stat. § 952 (2021).
5. *Gilbert v. Synagro Central, LLC*, 131 A.3d 1 (Pa. 2015).
6. 3 Pa. Stat. § 954(a) (2021).
7. *Branton v. Nicholas Meat, LLC*, 159 A.3d 540 (Pa. Super. Ct. 2017).
8. *Horne v. Haladay*, 728 A.2d 954 (Pa. Super. Ct. 1999).
9. 3 Pa. Stat. § 954(b) (2021).
10. *Burlingame v. Dagostin*, 183 A.3d 462 (Pa. Super. Ct. 2018).
11. 3 Pa. Stat. § 956(b) (2021).

12. 3 Pa. Stat. § 953(a) (2021).
13. Lori Devoe, "Paupack Reviews ACRE Proposal," *Reading (Pa.) News Eagle*, June 21, 2005; "Quick Deal: Without Hearings, Factory Farms Gain Advantage over Municipalities," *Harrisburg Patriot-News*, July 12, 2005.
14. Sandi Brown, "Big-Ag Foes Oppose Bill," *Daily News* (Lebanon, Pa.), May 13, 2002; Jim Hook, "Controversial Factory-Farm Bill Goes to House," *Public Opinion* (Chambersburg, Pa.), May 1, 2002; M. Bradford Grabowski, "Farmers Split over New Regulations Bill," *Uniontown (Pa.) Herald-Standard*, November 20, 2002.
15. Aileen Humphreys, "Rendell: ACRE Could Be Adopted in '05," *Lancaster (Pa.) Intelligencer Journal*, November 17, 2004.
16. 2005 Pa. Laws 38 (H.B. 1646) (enacting, in relevant part, what is now 3 Pa. Con. Stat. § 312).
17. 3 Pa. Con. Stat. § 313(a)–(c) (2021).
18. 3 Pa. Con. Stat. § 312(1)(i)–(ii) (2021).
19. 3 Pa. Con. Stat. § 314(a)–(d) (2021).
20. 3 Pa. Con. Stat. § 519(a)–(d) (2021).
21. *Burlingame v. Dagostin*, 183 A.3d 462 (Pa. Super. Ct. 2018).
22. *Berner v. Montour Township*, 217 A.3d 238 (Pa. 2019).
23. *Com., Office of Atty. Gen. ex rel. Corbett v. Richmond Tp.*, 2 A.3d 678 (Pa. Commw. Ct. 2010); *Boswell v. Skippack Township*, No. 389 M.D. 2006, 2012 WL 8670346 (Pa. Commw. Ct. June 27, 2012).

Rhode Island

Legislators justified Rhode Island's right-to-farm law as a tool to protect agricultural operations "affected by the random encroachment of urban land."[1] Since the law was enacted in 1982, the number of farm operations in the state has grown by 51 percent while the amount of land in farms has dropped by 4 percent.[2] So what does the state's RTF law do in practice?

Rhode Island's RTF Law at a Glance

Rhode Island's RTF law does not provide protection for farmland or prevent suburban sprawl. Rather, Rhode Island's law, similar to RTF laws present in the other forty-nine states, protects certain types of agricultural operations from nuisance suits when they impact neighboring property through things such as noise or pollution. For example, in 1986, pig farmer Louis Vinagro advocated the law, what he described as the "freedom of farming act." He saw it as protecting his "Mount St. Smellin," where he housed over a thousand hogs and composted their manure with waste from a nearby landfill.[3]

Originally, Rhode Island's RTF law extended nuisance suit protections to agricultural operations defined as those encompassing commercial enterprises with a primary purpose of horticulture, viticulture, floriculture, forestry, dairy farming, aquaculture, or the raising of livestock, fur-bearing animals, poultry, or bees.[4] A 2004 amendment, however, expanded the definition of agricultural operations. Now, the director of the Department of Environmental Management in consultation with the chief of its Division of Agriculture can determine additional protected agricultural operations, uses, or activities.[5] The 2004 amendment also declared mixed uses of farms and farmlands to be "valuable and viable means of contributing to the preservation of agriculture."[6] A later 2014 amendment then described mixed uses as inclusive of hayrides, crop mazes, classes, tours, and other special events.[7]

In 2018, a court considered whether a nonagricultural mixed use of farmland was a protected agricultural operation under the RTF law. The Rhode Island Supreme Court interpreted the inclusion of mixed uses in the RTF law as a statement of policy rather than an expansion of the legal definition of agricultural operations.[8] The court thus held that hosting weddings for a fee was not a protected agricultural operation, as defined under the state's RTF law. Because it was a nonagricultural activity, the operation remained subject to the town's regulations and ordinances.

Conditions and Activities

Rhode Island's RTF law stands out from those in other states because it protects agricultural operations only from public or private nuisance lawsuits that specifically aim to enjoin, or stop, certain nuisance activities.[9] Unlike those in many other states, Rhode Island's RTF law consequently does not protect any agricultural operation from nuisance suits that aim to recover monetary damages related to the use and enjoyment of one's land or to harm in the form of a loss in property values. Likewise, lawsuits that aim to recover damages—like monetary compensation for impacts on health or awards that seek to punish an operation—can also proceed.

In addition, the RTF law's protections apply to agricultural operations only under certain circumstances. First, the law protects operations from nuisance claims due to odor from livestock, manure, fertilizer, or feed so long as the operations were using generally accepted farming procedures.[10] There has been some controversy over the extent to which Rhode Island provides oversight pertaining to manure management.[11] Second, the law protects against nuisance claims relating to noise from livestock or farm equipment used as part of generally accepted farming procedures. Third, it protects against nuisance claims pertaining to dust from plowing or cultivation. And last, it protects operations from nuisance claims involving the lawful use of pesticides, rodenticides, insecticides, herbicides, or fungicides.[12]

The RTF law makes clear that it applies only to protected "agricultural operations" and does not provide any protections to "nonagricultural" activities, uses, or operations, all of which remain subject to restrictions under applicable laws, regulations, and ordinances.[13] For example, a Rhode Island court held that the RTF law cannot be used to shield the (at that time) illegal growing of marijuana plants in a storage facility because such an activity was not a "traditional agricultural land use" as protected under the RTF law.[14] In addition, the RTF law does not apply to any agricultural operation that

208   RHODE ISLAND

is conducted in a negligent or malicious manner, which generally means a manner involving a desire or intent to harm.[15]

Local Government

Rhode Island's RTF law broadly restricts the ability of cities and towns to regulate agricultural operations that keep animals. Specifically, the law prohibits cities and towns from enforcing ordinances against agricultural operations that regulate and control the construction, location, maintenance, or removal of all places for keeping animals.[16] The RTF law also prevents cities and towns from enforcing ordinances against agricultural operations that control the time and manner of removing manure or driving animals "through the highways." For example, even while flies and odors emanating from things like chicken manure make it difficult to go outside, towns have no jurisdiction over the matter.[17]

The RTF law also protects agricultural operations that want to place seasonal directional signs or displays on a state right-of-way.[18] The Department of Transportation is prohibited from making any rules or regulations that prevent such signage so long as the signage complies with local zoning laws and ordinances.

Rhode Island courts have addressed the tensions that can arise between local zoning regulations and agricultural operations. In one 2001 case, a town sought to enforce a zoning ordinance that would prohibit the owners of a turf farm from excavating land in order to create an irrigation pond for their farm. The turf farm's neighbors complained to the town about excessive dust. The court, however, concluded that the town's interpretation of its zoning ordinance directly conflicted with the farmers' ability to continue farming. In the words of the court, because the state's RTF law was "designed to prevent the creation of nuisances, [it] must be interpreted so as to not seriously infringe on ordinary farming operations within the town."[19]

Various other Rhode Island laws interact with the RTF law in unique ways. For example, rules and regulations in place for the licensing and registration of arborists (those who specialize in the care of individual trees) do not apply to any activity that is protected under the RTF law, like forestry.[20] Also, the state's real estate sales disclosure law requires that property sellers disclose if any farms within their municipality may be protected by the RTF law.[21]

Table 2.39 Rhode Island's Key RTF Provisions and National Comparison

Rhode Island's key RTF provisions		% U.S. states with similar RTF provisions
Operations are not immune from lawsuits . . .	if they are negligent.	46%
	if they do not comply with federal laws.	62%
	if they do not comply with state laws.	68%
Other important details	RTF supersedes local ordinances and laws.	62%

Court Costs

Elsewhere in Rhode Island law (but not in the RTF law specifically), plaintiffs can be liable for court costs when an individual brings a nuisance claim against an agricultural operation in order to stop the alleged nuisance activities and a court finds that there was no reasonable basis for the claim.[22]

NOTES

1. R.I. Gen. Laws § 2-23-2 (1982).
2. U.S. Department of Commerce, "Table 1. Farms, Land in Farms, and Land Use: 1982 and Earlier Census Years," in *1982 Census of Agriculture, Volume 1: Geographic Area Series, Part 39: Rhode Island State and County Data, Chapter 1: State Data* (Washington, D.C.: U.S. Bureau of the Census, 1984), https://agcensus.library.cornell.edu/wp-content/uploads/1982-Rhode_Island-CHAPTER_1_State_Data-121-Table-01.pdf; "2021 State Agriculture Overview: Rhode Island," U.S. Department of Agriculture, National Agricultural Statistics Service, accessed October 21, 2022, https://www.nass.usda.gov/Quick_Stats/Ag_Overview/stateOverview.php?state=RHODE%20ISLAND.
3. D. Morgan McVicar, "Johnston Pig Farmer Vows to Use Mega-Stink Bomb in His War with the DEM," *Providence (R.I.) Journal*, August 31, 1986.
4. R.I. Gen. Laws § 2-23-4 (1982).
5. 2004 R.I. Pub. Laws 178 (S.B. 2166) and 2004 R.I. Pub. Laws 53 (H.B. 7383) (amending R.I. Gen. Laws § 2-23-4).
6. 2004 R.I. Pub. Laws 178 (S.B. 2166) and 2004 R.I. Pub. Laws 53 (H.B. 7383) (amending R.I. Gen. Laws § 2-23-4).
7. 2014 R.I. Pub. Laws 360 (S.B. 2319) and 2014 R.I. Pub. Laws 406 (H.B. 7234) (amending R.I. Gen. Laws § 2-23-4).
8. *Gerald P. Zarrella Tr. v. Town of Exeter*, 176 A.3d 467 (R.I. 2018).
9. R.I. Gen. Laws §§ 2-23-5, 10-1-1 (2021). See also *Pucci v. Algiere*, 261 A.2d 1 (R.I. 1970).
10. R.I. Gen. Laws § 2-23-5 (2021).
11. Cynthia Drummond, "DEM Promises Tighter Controls after Flies Swarm," *Chariho Times* (Wakefield, R.I.), July 16, 2020. For an example of laws relating to manure management for CAFOs, see 250 R.I. Code R. § 150-10-1(k) (2021). For an example of laws relating to the composting of animal manure, see 250 R.I. Code R. § 40-20-3 (2021).
12. R.I. Gen. Laws §§ 2-23-5 to 2-23-6 (2021).
13. R.I. Gen. Laws §§ 2-23-4 to 2-23-5 (2021).

14. *Baird Properties, LLC v. Town of Coventry*, No. KC-2015-0313, 2015 WL 5177710 (R.I. Super. Ct. Aug. 31, 2015) (citing the legislative findings in R.I. Gen. Laws § 2-23-2).
15. R.I. Gen. Laws § 2-23-6 (2021).
16. R.I. Gen. Laws §§ 2-23-5, 23-19.2-1 (2021).
17. Chelsea Phua, "Making a Stink—Large Manure Pile Draws Flies, Complaints," *Providence Journal*, August 13, 2004.
18. R.I. Gen. Laws § 2-23-5 (2021).
19. *Town of N. Kingston v. Albert*, 767 A.2d 659 (R.I. 2001).
20. 250 R.I. Code R. § 70-00-1 (2021).
21. R.I. Gen. Laws § 5-20.8-2 (2021).
22. R.I. Gen. Laws § 10-1-6 (2021).

South Carolina

South Carolina legislators proposed the state's right-to-farm law as a tool to "conserve, protect and encourage the development and improvement of its agricultural land for the production of food and other agricultural products."[1] However, since its RTF law first passed in 1980, the state has lost 28 percent of its farms and 25 percent of its acres of farmland.[2] So what does South Carolina's RTF law do in practice?

South Carolina's RTF Law at a Glance

South Carolina's RTF law provides no explicit protection for farmland. Rather South Carolina's RTF law, like those present in the other forty-nine states, centers on protecting certain types of operations from nuisance suits when they impact neighboring property, for example through noise or pollution. When first passed in 1980, the state's RTF law protected agricultural operations, defined as facilities used for commercial production of crops as well as livestock, poultry, and their products.[3] In 1990, South Carolina dramatically expanded its definition of protected operations to include any land, building, structure, machinery, or equipment used for the commercial production or processing of crops, trees, and animals, as well as of livestock, poultry, honeybees, and their products.[4] The law also protects the products of commercial aquaculture.

Conditions and Activities

Originally, South Carolina's RTF law protected agricultural operations from nuisance suits when the conditions around their location changed, as long as they were in operation for over a year and were not a nuisance at the time they began.[5] A 2002 amendment, however, removed the requirement that

212

operations be up and running for at least one year to have protection from nuisance litigation.[6] Now, the law states that an established agricultural operation or facility cannot be deemed a nuisance—either public (interfering with public rights generally) or private (interfering with individual property rights)—due to any changed conditions around them.[7] Moreover, operations can expand and change their technology without affecting their established start date.[8]

The RTF law does not protect an agricultural operation or facility from being deemed a nuisance when the nuisance results from the negligent (failing to take proper care), improper, or illegal operation of the facility or operation.[9] In addition, the RTF law does not prevent someone from recovering damages for any injuries or harm sustained due to the pollution of or changed conditions of stream water or the overflow of water onto their lands.[10]

Local Government

A 2006 amendment to the state's RTF law drastically reduced the ability of counties to regulate agricultural operations in a manner different from that outlined by state law.[11] Prior to the amendment, county ordinances became null and void if they made any agricultural operation or facility a nuisance. However, counties could still enact moratoriums that banned new construction entirely on industrial agricultural operations.[12] Now, however, local laws and ordinances are also null and void if they are not identical to state laws and regulations, including the licensing regulations of the state's Department of Health and Environmental Control.[13] The legislature's intention with the 2006 amendment was to prohibit counties from regulating agricultural operations and facilities any more than state-level law did.[14]

However, new swine operations, new slaughterhouse operations, and any agricultural operations located within the corporate limits of a city may still be subject to local regulations and ordinances.[15] Counties also can determine whether an agricultural use is a permitted use for county zoning purposes. If an agricultural operation is a permitted use, the regulations of that operation must be identical to those of state law, or they will be null and void.[16]

In one case, a town sued the state Department of Health and Environmental Control for permitting the construction of eight caged layer houses.[17] Specifically, the town argued that the vapors and fumes from the egg-washing facility and spray-field would impact residents and deny them the full enjoyment of their properties. The town also argued that the department failed to properly follow its own guidelines, adopt regulations, or recognize that the layer houses created a nuisance. The court used various aspects of the state's RTF law to rule in favor of the poultry operation. First, the court noted that the layer houses were "state-of-the-art" and minimized dust and odor in a way that was compatible with the surrounding agricultural uses of land. The court also found that the poultry operation served the legislative aim of encouraging the development of agricultural facilities. Finally, the court interpreted the RTF law to limit findings of nuisance against agricultural operations to those situations where the nuisance is actual rather than potential. Because the court found that the layer operation presented "only a possibility for inappropriate discharge of dust and odor," it determined that it was proper for the state to grant the permits.

Setback Law

In related law, South Carolina establishes setback distances for the permitting of agricultural animal facilities.[18] The setbacks are minimum requirements, and if those minimum requirements are met, the RTF law says that the Department of Health and Environmental Control "may not require additional setback distances."[19] However, a separate regulation allows the department to increase the minimum setback distances "on a case-by-case" basis.[20]

These setbacks have been subject to litigation in court. In one case, David Coggins Broilers, Heath Coggins Broilers, and Jim Young, all broiler operators, received state-issued agricultural permits to construct and operate poultry facilities.[21] The proposed facilities would hold anywhere from 162,000 to 237,600 broilers, producing an estimated 988 to 1,449 tons of manure per year.

After receiving the state permits, neighboring landowners—but not residents—filed suit against the poultry operators and the state, objecting to the permits over concerns that the poultry houses would create offensive odors, harm their health and quality of life, and create a nuisance. In addition, the neighbors argued that the facilities needed federal National Pollution Discharge Elimination System permits because their manure runoff would likely enter into the water.

Ultimately, the administrative law judge approved the permits to construct and operate, concluding that the poultry operations were not required to get National Pollution Discharge Elimination System permits. In addition,

Table 2.40 South Carolina's Key RTF Provisions and National Comparison

South Carolina's key RTF provisions		% U.S. states with similar RTF provisions
Operations are immune from lawsuits . . .	if they use a new technology.	30%
	if boundaries or size of operations change.	34%
	if there is a change in locality.	46%
Operations are not immune from lawsuits . . .	if they are negligent.	46%
	if they pollute water.	36%
	if they do not comply with county laws.	42%
	if they do not comply with state laws.	68%
Other important details	RTF supersedes local ordinances and laws.	62%
	RTF protects processing.	48%

although the judge acknowledged that the Department of Health and Environmental Control may increase setback distances on a case-by-case basis, the judge found that the operations had met South Carolina's minimum setback requirements without any need for additional setbacks to address potential odor or air quality issues. The judge did, however, require that the permits be conditioned upon the poultry operators obtaining a stormwater permit—a permit that would require consideration of whether setbacks should be increased in order to ensure compliance with stormwater runoff requirements.

NOTES

1. S.C. Code § 46-45-10 (1980).
2. U.S. Department of Agriculture, *USDA Quick Stats Tool: June 1980 Survey, South Carolina*, distributed by National Agricultural Statistics Service, accessed January 6, 2021, https://quickstats.nass.usda.gov/results/93F3D0C3-51B4-3995-9D63-FB8EBCB67F0B; "2021 State Agriculture Overview: South Carolina," U.S. Department of Agriculture, National Agricultural Statistics Service, accessed October 21, 2022, https://www.nass.usda.gov/Quick_Stats/Ag_Overview/stateOverview.php?state=SOUTH%20CAROLINA.
3. S.C. Code § 46-45-20 (1980).
4. 1990 S.C. Acts 442 (H.B. 4463) (amending S.C. Code § 46-45-20).
5. S.C. Code § 46-45-30 (1980).
6. 2001 S.C. Acts 340 (H.B. 4944) (adding S.C. Code § 46-45-70).
7. S.C. Code § 46-45-70 (2021).
8. S.C. Code § 46-45-40 (2021).
9. S.C. Code § 46-45-70 (2021).
10. S.C. Code § 46-45-50 (2021).
11. See 2006 S.C. Acts 290 (S.B. 1205) (amending S.C. Code § 46-45-60).
12. While moratoriums could be considered and were not banned explicitly in the RTF law,

their capacity to be upheld in court at that time is unclear. See Tucker Lyon, "Poultry Farm Moratorium: Emotions Run High as Orangeburg County Council Votes 5–2 for Moratorium," *Times and Democrat* (Orangeburg, S.C.), August 2, 2005.

13. S.C. Code § 46-45-60 (2021).

14. 2006 S.C. Acts 290 (S.B. 1205) (amending S.C. Code § 46-45-10).

15. S.C. Code §§ 46-45-10, 46-45-60 (2021). Under this law, a "new swine operation" is any porcine production operation that was not in existence on June 30, 2006, and a "new slaughterhouse operation" is an operation that was established after May 30, 2006, and that slaughters more than 200 million pounds of commercial farm animals. S.C. Code § 46-45-20 (2021).

16. S.C. Code § 46-45-60 (2021).

17. *Town of Silverstreet v. S.C. Dep't Health and Envtl. Control*, No. 97-ALJ-07-0358-CC, 1998 WL 1473642 (S.C. Dept. Hlth. Env. Oct. 8, 1998). Four months later, another court made a similar ruling, relying on the rationale from *Town of Silverstreet* to conclude that the *possibility* that an industrial scale poultry operation could become a nuisance was not a sufficient reason to deny the operation its permits. See *Raymond and Linda Lewis, Representatives for the Group CCFCE (Concerned Citizens for Cleaner Environment) v. S.C. Dep't Health and Envtl. Control*, No. 98-ALJ-07-0372-CC, 1998 WL 723921 (S.C. Admin. Law Ct. Sept. 29, 1998). Please note that since these are administrative cases, we did not include them in our national analysis of case law. See the appendix for more details.

18. S.C. Code § 46-45-80 (2021); S.C. Code Regs. 61-43 (2021).

19. S.C. Code § 46-45-80 (2021).

20. S.C. Code Regs. § 61-43 (2021).

21. *Blackmon v. S.C. Dep't Health and Envtl. Control*, No. 17-ALJ-07-0041-CC, 2017 WL 6275969 (S.C. Admin. Law Ct. Nov. 30, 2017).

South Dakota

Proponents of the right-to-farm law in South Dakota have argued it protects the state's agricultural legacy and resources.[1] Since the first RTF law was passed in 1991, the number of farms in the state has dropped by 14 percent, with 4 percent fewer acres of farmland.[2] So what does this legislation do in practice?

South Dakota's RTF Law at a Glance

South Dakota's RTF law does not explicitly protect farmers or farmland. Rather, South Dakota's RTF law, similar to other such statutes nationally, centers on protecting commercial operations from nuisance lawsuits over matters like noise and pollution.[3] Protections are not tied to farmers and ranchers as people or to land as acreage. Rather, commercial operations are defined as "any facility used in the production or processing for commercial purposes of crops, timber, livestock, swine, poultry, livestock products, swine products or poultry products."[4]

Conditions and Activities

South Dakota's RTF law affords commercial agriculture operations broad protections. Once an operation is protected, that status can be assignable, alienable, and inheritable—meaning the protections run with the operation.[5] A facility can claim protected status if the locality around it changes once it has been in operation for a year, as long as it was not a nuisance at the time it began production.[6] Similarly, an operation does not lose its protected status if it temporarily stops production or diminishes in size. The law allows operations to expand in acres or animal units without losing RTF protections if all county, municipal, state, and federal ordinances, laws, and regulations

Table 2.41 South Dakota's Key RTF Provisions and National Comparison

South Dakota's key RTF provisions		% U.S. states with similar RTF provisions
Operations are immune from lawsuits . . .	if boundaries or size of operations change.	34%
	if there is a change in locality.	46%
	if there is a cessation or interruption in farming.	26%
	once in operation for a year.	48%
Operations are not immune from lawsuits . . .	if they are a nuisance from the start.	38%
	if they do not comply with county laws.	42%
	if they do not comply with environmental laws.	26%
	if they do not comply with federal laws.	62%
	if they do not comply with other laws.	50%
	if they do not comply with state laws.	68%
	if they pollute water.	36%
	if they are negligent.	46%
Other important details	Attorney fees are awarded to prevailing defendant.	34%
	RTF protects processing.	48%

are met. Initially, for poultry or livestock operations to expand and still be protected through the RTF law, they had to prove that they could handle their additional waste in accordance with Department of Agriculture rules.[7] However, in 1994, an amendment removed this stipulation.[8] In addition, an operation that expands in acreage or livestock units will lose RTF protections if that expansion can be considered negligent or unreasonable or results in a violation of any county, municipal, state, or federal law.[9]

South Dakota's statute does not protect operations from water-based lawsuits. Any agricultural operation, regardless of protected status, can be held liable for the damage it causes to another's quality or quantity of water, including overflow.[10]

Local Government

A South Dakota court found that townships do not have the authority to regulate the construction of commercial feedlots to abate a nuisance or other potential impacts.[11] The RTF law was not directly at issue in the case. But the court noted that while the RTF law required compliance with county, municipal, state, and federal laws, "noticeably missing is any requirement that the agricultural operation comply with township codes, laws or regulations."[12] South Dakota's law does not protect operations located within incorporated municipalities that predate January 1, 1991 (the date the state's RTF law came into effect).[13]

Other Important Aspects

South Dakota has a unique provision that stipulates an agricultural operation can recover related court costs if it already existed within one mile of the plaintiff before a nuisance lawsuit was brought and there were no reasonable grounds for the lawsuit.[14] An agricultural operation can also recover the money it spent defending itself if a court determines that the lawsuit was frivolous.[15] This shifts the litigation risks away from agricultural operations (typically the defendant) and onto the plaintiff by potentially requiring the plaintiff to pay attorney fees, expert witness fees, and other costs related to preparing for and participating in the lawsuit.[16]

NOTES

1. Dickey Wagner, "Measures Have Different Implications for Agriculture," *Aberdeen (S.D.) American News*, October 23, 2012. Also see state policy to protect agricultural operations from nuisance suits, S.D. Codified Laws § 21-10-25.1 (2021).
2. U.S. Department of Commerce, "Table 1. Historical Highlights: 1992 and Earlier Census Years," in *1992 Census of Agriculture, Volume 1: Geographic Area Series, Part 41: South Dakota State and County Data, Chapter 1: State Data* (Washington, D.C.: U.S. Bureau of the Census, 1992), https://agcensus.library.cornell.edu/wp-content/uploads/1992-South_Dakota-CHAPTER_1_State_Data-1569-Table-01.pdf; "2021 State Agriculture Overview: South Dakota," U.S. Department of Agriculture, National Agricultural Statistics Service, accessed October 21, 2022, https://www.nass.usda.gov/Quick_Stats/Ag_Overview/stateOverview.php?state=SOUTH%20DAKOTA.
3. S.D. Codified Laws §§ 21-10-15.1, 21-10-25.3 (2021).
4. S.D. Codified Laws § 21-10-25.3 (2021).
5. S.D. Codified Laws § 21-10-25.2 (2021).
6. S.D. Codified Laws § 21-10-25.2 (2021).
7. See, e.g., S.D. Codified Laws § 21-10-25.2 (1991).
8. 1994 S.D. Sess. Laws 162 (S.B. 180) (amending S.D. Codified Laws § 21-10-25.2).
9. S.D. Codified Laws § 21-10-25.2 (2021).
10. S.D. Codified Laws § 21-10-25.4 (2021).
11. *Welsh v. Centerville Twp.*, 595 N.W.2d 622 (S.D. 1999).
12. *Welsh*, 595 N.W.2d 622.
13. S.D. Codified Laws § 21-10-25.5 (2021).
14. S.D. Codified Laws § 21-10-25 (2021).

15. S.D. Codified Laws § 21-10-25.6 (2021).

16. Cordon M. Smart, "The 'Right to Commit Nuisance' in North Carolina: A Historical Analysis of the Right-to-Farm Act," *North Carolina Law Review* 94, no. 6 (2016): 2097–154; Loka Ashwood, Danielle Diamond, and Fiona Walker, "Property Rights and Rural Justice: A Study of U.S. Right-to-Farm Laws," *Journal of Rural Studies* 67 (April 2019): 120–29.

Tennessee

In 1982, Tennessee legislators proposed a right-to-farm statute as a tool to prevent farmland from being "permanently lost."[1] But since that time, the number of farms has dropped by 23 percent and the acres of farmland by 13 percent.[2] So what does this legislation do in practice?

Tennessee's RTF Law at a Glance

Tennessee's RTF law provides no specific protection for family farms or means to stop suburban sprawl. Rather, Tennessee's RTF law, like those present in the other forty-nine states, protects certain types of farm operations from nuisance suits when their activities impact neighboring property, for example through noise or pollution. Under the law, protected farms and farm operations include farmland, buildings, machinery, and activities that involve commercial agriculture production, including farm products and nursery stock such as forages, seeds, hemp, trees, vegetables, fruits, livestock, dairy, poultry, apiaries, and other products that involve the use of food, feed, fiber, or fur.[3] Tennessee's law protects farms that apply chemical fertilizers, insecticides, pesticides, and herbicides, as well as farming activities that involve noise, odors, dust, or fumes, including ground and aerial seeding and spraying.

What constitutes a farm operation under Tennessee's RTF law has broadened over time. For example, the Tennessee Supreme Court ruled in 2013, after a series of appeals, that outdoor music concerts, even if used for marketing farm products, were not connected to production. Therefore, the RTF law did not shield the farm.[4] The Tennessee General Assembly then passed an amendment in 2014 that extended RTF protections to the "marketing of farm products" as well as broadened the definition of "agriculture" to include "entertainment activities carried out in conjunction with, but secondary to, commercial production of farm products."[5]

Conditions and Activities

Under Tennessee's initial RTF law, two circumstances created a presumption that farm operations were not nuisances. Either the farm operation had to predate any change in land use or occupancy within one mile of the farm (meaning the farm had to be there first), or the farm operation had to use generally accepted agricultural and management practices created by the Tennessee Department of Agriculture.[6] After a series of amendments and later withdrawals of amendments, one key change resulted. Now, all farm operations are presumed not to be nuisances unless the suing party can prove that they (1) do not conform to generally accepted agricultural practices, based on expert testimony; or (2) do not comply with applicable statutes or rules, including those of the Department of Agriculture and Department of Environment and Conservation.[7]

Since 1979, a related statute has provided additional protections against nuisance lawsuits for feedlots, dairy farms, and poultry production operations, as long as they comply with certain rules of the Tennessee Department of Environment and Conservation.[8] These protections provide what is called an "absolute defense" against nuisance lawsuits, meaning the activities used by the operations are immune from liability if the operations can prove they are complying with the department's rules.[9] These extra protections apply only when the farming operation predates the suing party, in terms of either ownership or use. In addition, "normal" noises, odors, and the operation's appearance cannot be the basis for a nuisance lawsuit if the plaintiffs gained ownership of their land after the operation began.

Poultry farm operators tried to use this defense when sued by a neighboring couple for offensive odors, a cloud of gas, and increased rainwater runoff.[10] When the couple first contracted to purchase their property in 1991, the poultry farm consisted of three small and unused chicken houses. Six months later, the poultry operation expanded to include five new, and much larger, chicken houses. When the neighboring couple sued for nuisance, the poultry operators claimed they met the statutory requirements because their ownership predated that of their neighbors. The trial court disagreed and declared that the neighbors had a sufficient ownership interest in the land before the five new poultry houses were built, meaning the special

Table 2.42 Tennessee's Key RTF Provisions and National Comparison

Tennessee's key RTF provisions		% U.S. states with similar RTF provisions
Operations are immune from lawsuits . . .	when they are there first.[†]	44%
Operations are not immune from lawsuits . . .	if they do not comply with state laws.	68%
	if they do not comply with environmental laws.	26%
	if they do not comply with federal laws.	62%
	if they do not comply with other laws.	50%
	if they do not comply with county laws.	42%

[†] Applies to feedlots, dairy farms, and poultry production houses.

protections for feedlots, dairy farms, and poultry production operations did not apply.

Local Government

While feedlots, dairy farms, and poultry production houses are required to follow local zoning requirements to receive protection, counties have no authority to enact them in agricultural areas.[11] Specifically, county zoning powers "should not be used to inhibit normal agricultural activities,"[12] which prevents counties from regulating structures and land used for agricultural purposes.[13] A Tennessee appellate court interpreted this to include events, such as farm weddings, on land used for commercial production of farm products.[14]

However, counties do have other ways—besides zoning—to regulate agricultural operations. For example, the Tennessee Air Quality Act uses a nuisance-based standard, where it defines air pollution as the presence of air contaminants that could injure human, plant, or animal life or that unreasonably interfere with the enjoyment of life and property.[15] A county air pollution control board can use methods of enforcement against agricultural operations that are allowed by the Tennessee Air Quality Act, such as imposing a fine, requiring actions to reduce the nuisance, or even requiring that the operation stop altogether.[16]

TENNESSEE 223

NOTES

1. See *Shore v. Maple Lane Farms, LLC*, 411 S.W.3d 405 (Tenn. 2013).
2. U.S. Department of Commerce, "Table 1. Farms, Land in Farms, and Land Use: 1982 and Earlier Census Years," in *1982 Census of Agriculture, Volume 1: Geographic Area Series, Part 42: Tennessee State and County Data, Chapter 1: State Data* (Washington, D.C.: U.S. Bureau of the Census, 1984), https://agcensus.library.cornell.edu/wp-content/uploads/1982-Tennessee-CHAPTER_1_State_Data-121-Table-01.pdf; "2021 State Agriculture Overview: Tennessee," U.S. Department of Agriculture, National Agricultural Statistics Service, accessed October 21, 2022, https://www.nass.usda.gov/Quick_Stats/Ag_Overview/stateOverview.php?state=TENNESSEE.
3. Tenn. Code § 43-26-102 (2021).
4. *Shore*, 411 S.W.3d 405.
5. See 2014 Tenn. Pub. Acts 581 (S.B. 1614) (amending the definition of "farm operation" in Tenn. Code § 43-26-102 and the definition of "agriculture" in Tenn. Code § 43-1-113); see also "Greenback Woman Files New Maple Lane Farms Suit," *Maryville (Tenn.) Daily Times*, March 31, 2015.
6. Tenn. Code § 43-26-103 (1982).
7. Tenn. Code § 43-26-103 (2021). For the relevant amendments, see 2002 Tenn. Pub. Acts 604 (S.B. 2135); 2016 Tenn. Pub. Acts 728 (H.B. 1941).
8. Tenn. Code § 44-18-102 (2021).
9. Tenn. Code § 44-18-102 (2021).
10. *Cissom v. Miller*, No. E1999-02767-COA-R3-CV, 2001 WL 456062 (Tenn. Ct. App. Apr. 30, 2001).
11. See Tenn. Att'y Gen. Op. No. 18-30 (July 6, 2018). See also Tenn. Code § 5-1-122 (2021).
12. Tenn. Code § 5-1-122 (2021).
13. Tenn. Att'y Gen. Op. No. 18-30 (July 6, 2018). See also *Shore*, 411 S.W.3d 405.
14. *Jefferson Cty. v. Wilmouth Family Properties, LLC*, No. E2019-02283-COA-R3-CV, WL 321219 (Tenn. Ct. App. Feb. 1, 2021).
15. Tenn. Code § 68-201-102 (2021).
16. *Gen. Portland, Inc. v. Chattanooga-Hamilton Cty. Air Pollution Control Bd.*, 560 S.W.2d 910 (Tenn. Ct. App. 1976). The current Tennessee Air Quality Act can be found at Tenn. Code § 68-201-101 et seq. (for the powers of municipalities and counties under this act, see Tenn. Code § 68-201-115).

Texas

Legislators proposed a right-to-farm law in Texas as a tool to reduce the state's loss of agricultural resources.[1] Since the law was first passed in 1981, the number of operators in the state has grown by 27 percent, while the number of acres in farmland has dropped by 8 percent.[2] So what does the state's RTF law do in practice?

Texas's RTF Law at a Glance

Texas's RTF law provides no explicit protection for farmland. Rather, Texas's RTF law, like those present in the other forty-nine states, centers on protecting certain types of operations from nuisance suits when they impact a neighboring property, such as through noise or pollution. Texas defines nuisance as actions that cause (1) physical harm to a property; (2) physical harm to a person on their property by assaulting their senses or other personal injury; or (3) emotional harm to persons from the deprivation of the enjoyment of their property through fear, apprehension, or loss of peace of mind.[3]

Agricultural operations are protected from lawsuits in regard to such nuisances if they are engaged in soil cultivation, crop production, floriculture, viticulture, horticulture, silviculture, wildlife management, or raising or keeping livestock or poultry, or if the agricultural land has been set aside in compliance with governmental conservation programs.[4] However, in one case, property owners sued their neighbors who were raising chickens for cockfighting for noise and odor complaints. The owners of the fighting cocks claimed protection under Texas's RTF law. The court disagreed and ruled that their operation did not qualify as "poultry" since the chickens were not intended for food.[5]

Texas courts have extended RTF protections to certain trespasses alongside nuisance, although trespass is not directly referenced in the statute.

"Trespass" means the entry of a person onto another's land or causing or permitting a thing to cross the boundary of the premises.[6] For example, neighboring landowners sued a dairy farm for trespass due to the intrusions of manure onto their property following rainstorms. However, the court barred their action by drawing on the state's RTF law.

Conditions and Activities

An agricultural operation is protected from nuisance suits if it has lawfully existed for one year.[7] The one-year clock begins on the date operations commence. However, if the operation expands the size of its facilities, the one-year clock will restart from the date in which the expanded facility commences operation.[8] In addition, an operation may expand the boundaries of its occupied land without restarting the one-year clock, so long as it does not also substantially change the nature of the operation.[9]

The one-year time clock and allowance for change has afforded agricultural operations broad immunity and limited neighbors' ability to sue.[10] One court ruling stipulated that operations had to "substantially" change for their clock to restart, adding another layer of nuisance suit protection.[11] The same court also ruled that it does not matter when the complaining party discovers the nuisance but rather when the material circumstances of production began. Another court ruled that even if the operation changes but the nuisance claim does not (like flies, dust, or smell), the operation nonetheless is considered by the law to be unchanged.[12] The court also ruled that the agricultural operation was not required to prove when its farm first began, just when it began spreading manure and plowing it into the soil. In a third case, a married couple who lived across the highway from a grain storage facility alleged that the dust from the operation blew onto their property. The court ruled that the storage facility was substantially unchanged for at least one year and thus received RTF protection from the nuisance lawsuit.[13]

Texas's statute also protects agricultural "improvements" if the improvement is not prohibited by law at the time of construction or otherwise restricts the flow of water, light, or air onto other land.[14] The law defines "agricultural improvement" as including "pens, barns, fences, and other improvements designed for the sheltering, restriction, or feeding of animal or aquatic life, for storage of produce or feed, or for storage or maintenance of implements."[15]

Texas's RTF law requires that agricultural operations adhere to federal, state, and local laws in order to receive protection from nuisance suits.[16] Sixty property owners tried to use this criterion in their lawsuit against a cattle feedlot for nuisance, including flies, dust, and smell. They argued in part that the cattle feedlot was not operating lawfully, but the court ruled that the neighbors had not provided a clear enough argument to support their claim.[17] In a more recent case, a court awarded plaintiffs $6 million in damages in 2019 and 2020 from nuisances related to sixteen poultry barns. When the nuisances were not abated, the court ordered Sanderson Farms to stop its farming activities. The Texas Commission on Environmental Quality had previously found Sanderson Farms in violation of nuisance statutes due to odors, noise, emissions, and runoff.[18]

RTF and Local Governance

Texas's statute requires facilities to comply with local governmental regulations that existed at the time the operation began.[19] Additionally, local governments can regulate any agricultural operation that risks the health and safety of residents.[20] In accordance, political subdivisions such as cities and counties have some power to enact laws that pertain to agricultural operations. Additionally, if a city expands to include an existing operation, that existing operation is required to comply with regulations that impact health and safety.[21]

However, the power of local government remains limited. A 2009 bill introduced to Texas's agricultural code bars the application of the state's animal cruelty statutes to agriculture livestock. Because of this, local governments are prohibited from imposing their own animal cruelty regulations on livestock operations.[22]

Additionally, public hearings once required to permit such animal operations no longer exist in Texas.[23]

Attorney Fees

Any person who brings a lawsuit against an operation that qualifies for RTF protection is liable for all legal costs and expenses incurred by the agricultural operation in defending itself.[24] This and similar language may have a chilling effect on the filing of nuisance suits in favor of industrial operators.[25] In one case, owners of a horse ranch sued a dairy farm for allegedly discharging "90,000 gallons of thick, brown, sludgy toxic, dairy lagoon effluent" onto their property, killing their horses and damaging their

Table 2.43 Texas's Key RTF Provisions and National Comparison

Texas's key RTF provisions		% U.S. states with similar RTF provisions
Operations are immune from lawsuits . . .	once in operation for a year.	48%
	if boundaries or size of operation change.	34%
Operations are not immune from lawsuits . . .	if they do not comply with environmental laws.	26%
	if they do not comply with federal laws.	62%
	if they do not comply with other laws.	50%
	if they do not comply with state laws.	68%
	if they do not comply with county laws.	42%
Other important details	Attorney fees are awarded to prevailing defendant.	34%
	RTF supersedes local ordinances and laws.	62%

land. The dairy operators filed a cross-claim for attorney fees. One of the ranch owners, representing herself, had to pay the dairy operators $100,000 in attorney fees, and her claims for prosecution were also dismissed. The court stated, "This case illustrates the dangers of proceeding pro se," or self-representation in the court of law.[26]

NOTES

1. Tex. Agric. Code § 251.002 (1981).
2. U.S. Department of Agriculture, *USDA Quick Stats Tool: June 1981 Survey, Texas*, distributed by National Agricultural Statistics Service, accessed December 1, 2020, https://quickstats .nass.usda.gov/results/162F2390-1ADF-354B-B8F3-A459D4125A48; "2021 State Agriculture Overview: Texas," U.S. Department of Agriculture, National Agricultural Statistics Service, accessed October 21, 2022, https://www.nass.usda.gov/Quick_Stats/Ag_Overview /stateOverview.php?state=TEXAS.
3. *Ehler v. LVDVD, L.C.*, 319 S.W.3d 817 (Tex. App. 2010).
4. Tex. Agric. Code § 251.002 (2021).
5. *Hendrickson v. Swyers*, 9 S.3d 298 (Tex. App. 1999).
6. *Ehler*, 319 S.W.3d 817.
7. Tex. Agric. Code § 251.004(a) (2021).
8. Tex. Agric. Code § 251.003 (2021).
9. Tex. Agric. Code § 251.004(a) (2021).
10. William Patrick, "Sanderson Loses $6 Million Smell Suit," *Palestine (Tex.) Herald-Press*, November 12, 2019.
11. *Holubec v. Brandenberger*, 111 S.W.3d 32 (Tex. 2003).
12. *Barrera v. Hondo Creek Cattle Co.*, 132 S.W.3d 544 (Tex. App. 2004).

13. *Cal-co Grain Company, Inc. v. Whatley*, No. 13-05-120-CV, 2006 WL 2439973 (Tex. App. Aug. 24, 2006).
14. Tex. Agric. Code § 251.006(a)–(b) (2021).
15. Tex. Agric. Code § 251.006(c)(2) (2021).
16. Tex. Agric. Code § 251.004 (2021).
17. *Barrera*, 132 S.W.3d 544.
18. Shelli Parker, "Sanderson Farms Fails to Comply with 'Smell Suit' Orders," *Athens (Tex.) Daily Review*, October 16, 2020.
19. Tex. Agric. Code § 251.005(b)(1) (2021).
20. Tex. Agric. Code § 251.004(a) (2021).
21. Tex. Agric. Code § 251.005(c) (2021).
22. Tex. Agric. Code § 251.005(3) (2021), referencing Tex. Penal Code § 42.09(f) (2021).
23. Steven H. Lee, "Farming Factory Giant, Corporate Hog Farms Are Gaining a Foothold in the Panhandle, but Small Operators Are Raising a Stink," *Dallas Morning News*, July 30, 1995; Steven H. Lee, "Hog Farms Find Home in Texas but Some Neighbors Raise Health Concerns," *Dallas Morning News*, October 3, 1999.
24. Tex. Agric. Code § 251.004(b) (2021).
25. Cordon M. Smart, "The 'Right to Commit Nuisance' in North Carolina: A Historical Analysis of the Right-to-Farm Act," *North Carolina Law Review* 94, no. 6 (2016): 2097–154. For more on the chilling effect of such statutes, see the section "Geopolitical Extraction" in the introduction.
26. *Paselk v. Rabun*, 293 S.W.3d 600 (Tex. App. 2009).

Utah

Legislators introduced a right-to-farm law in Utah as a tool to preserve agricultural land.[1] Since legislators passed additional RTF-related statutes between 1994 and 1995,[2] the number of farm operations has increased by 19 percent, while the state's farmland has dropped by over 6 percent.[3] So what does this legislation do in practice?

Utah's RTF Laws at a Glance

Utah's RTF statutes provide nuisance protections for agricultural and, notably, industrial and mining areas.[4] Similar to those in the other forty-nine states, Utah's RTF-related laws protect certain types of agricultural operations within these areas from nuisance suits when they impact neighboring property, for example through noise or other pollution. Utah has enacted and amended a variety of different codes—criminal, judicial, agricultural, and county—to give agricultural operations exclusive privileges in the context of nuisance suits.[5] Agricultural operations are broadly defined to include activities involved in the commercial production of crops, orchards, livestock, poultry, aquaculture, livestock products, or poultry products, as well as the facilities used to produce those things.[6] The statutes provide different details for the operations and activities protected in mining and industrial areas.

Conditions and Activities

In 2019, amendments created three conditions that those who seek to sue agricultural operations must meet: (1) the plaintiff must be the legal possessor of the property that is alleged to be affected by the nuisance; (2) the alleged land or buildings affected must exist less than one-half mile away from the source of the nuisance; or (3) the plaintiff must file the lawsuit less than one year after the establishment of the agricultural operation or any fundamental change to that operation.[7] That same year, amendments also created a series of substantial exceptions to fundamental changes.[8] Importantly, a "fundamental change" does not include a change in ownership or size, the use of new technologies, a change in the type of agricultural product being produced, an interruption in farming that lasts three years or less, or participation in a government-sponsored agricultural program.[9] The law presumes that an operation is using sound agricultural practices if it is following federal, state, and local laws and regulations, which include zoning ordinances.[10]

The 2019 amendments also introduced a sweepingly broad summary of nuisances that agricultural operations were not liable for, including "anything that is injurious to health, indecent, offensive to the senses, or an obstruction to the free use of property, so as to interfere with the comfortable enjoyment of life or property."[11] This defense becomes a complete defense for agricultural operations that are located in an agricultural protection area, which are designated by county commissioners.[12] "Complete defense" means that even if a plaintiff makes a variety of charges against an agricultural operation, all of them can be dismissed at the same time and not be considered separately.

Local Governance

Agricultural protection areas, as designated by county commissioners, provide agricultural entities restriction-free operation for up to twenty years.[13] However, even operations outside of such protected areas are shielded from nuisance suits. The 2019 amendments exempt agricultural operations from any ordinance of a political subdivision that would make them a nuisance as long as they are conducted in a "normal and ordinary course" of agricultural operations or use sound agricultural practices.[14] Sound agricultural practices are considered to be those that conform with federal, state, and local laws and regulations. However, some state and federal environmental rules and regulations exempt agricultural operations from standards required of other industries.[15] If the activity or operation impacts public health or safety, these protections do not apply.[16]

Table 2.44 Utah's Key RTF Provisions and National Comparison

Utah's key RTF provisions		% U.S. states with similar RTF provisions
Operations are immune from lawsuits ...	if boundaries or size of operations change.	34%
	if they use a new technology.	30%
	if they produce a different product.	26%
	if there is an ownership change.	26%
	if there is a cessation or interruption in farming.	26%
	once in operation for a year.	48%
Operations are not immune from lawsuits ...	if they do not comply with federal laws.	62%
	if they do not comply with state laws.	68%
	if they do not comply with county laws.	42%
	if they do not comply with other laws.	50%
Other important details	RTF protects processing.	48%
	RTF protects mining operations.	4%
	RTF supersedes local ordinances and laws in agricultural zones.	12%
	RTF supersedes local ordinances and laws.	62%

Other Important Aspects

In any nuisance lawsuit against an agricultural operation, the court must award costs and attorney fees to the agricultural operation if it is not found to be a nuisance or if the nuisance claim was either frivolous or malicious.[17] If, however, an agricultural operation asserts a defense against a nuisance claim that is both frivolous and malicious and the court finds the operation did commit a nuisance, the court must award costs and attorney fees to the plaintiff.

In addition, Utah's RTF laws require that the owner of any new subdivision located within 300 feet of an agriculture protection area provide notice on the plat provided to the county recorder "that the property is located in the vicinity of an established agriculture protection area in which normal agricultural uses and activities have been afforded the highest priority use status."[18] The notice must also state that the use and enjoyment of the property is conditioned upon the user's acceptance of any annoyance or inconvenience that may result from the agricultural uses and activities within the protected area.

NOTES

1. Senator Leonard Blackham introduced S.B. 227 as a bill "for preserving agricultural land for the ability to be self-reliant." See Brent Israelsen, "Proposal Would Protect Prime Farming Zones," *Deseret News* (Salt Lake City), February 18, 1994.

2. For the relevant legislation, see 1994 Utah Laws 58 (S.B. 227) (enacting, in relevant part, Utah Code §§ 17-41-402, 17-41-403, and 17-41-404); and 1995 Utah Laws 73 (S.B. 149) (repealing and reenacting what was then Utah Code § 78-38-7).

3. U.S. Department of Agriculture, *USDA Quick Stats Tool: June 1994 Survey, Utah*, distributed by National Agricultural Statistics Service, accessed October 16, 2020, https://quickstats.nass.usda.gov/results/E3CFFC02-6E39-3D56-AAC8-7F591A7442D6; "2021 State Agriculture Overview: Utah," U.S. Department of Agriculture, National Agricultural Statistics Service, accessed October 21, 2022, https://www.nass.usda.gov/Quick_Stats/Ag_Overview/stateOverview.php?state=UTAH.

4. See, e.g., Utah Code § 17-41-403 (2021): "(1) A political subdivision shall ensure that any of the political subdivision's laws or ordinances that define or prohibit a public nuisance exclude from the definition or prohibition: (a) for an agriculture protection area, any agricultural activity or operation within an agriculture protection area conducted using sound agricultural practices unless that activity or operation bears a direct relationship to public health or safety; (b) for an industrial protection area, any industrial use of the land within the industrial protection area that is consistent with sound practices applicable to the industrial use, unless that use bears a direct relationship to public health or safety."

5. See supra note 2. See also, e.g., 2019 Utah Laws 81 (S.B. 93) (enacting the Agricultural Operations Nuisances Act, Utah Code § 4-44-101 et seq.); 2019 Utah Laws 81 (S.B. 93) (amending, in relevant part, Utah Code §§ 17-41-403, 76-10-803); and "Legislature Passes Record Number of Bills," *Deseret News*, March 2, 1995.

6. Utah Code § 4-44-102 (2021).

7. 2019 Utah Laws 81 (S.B. 93) (amending, in relevant part, Utah Code § 4-44-201(1)).

8. 2019 Utah Laws 81 (S.B. 93) (amending, in relevant part, Utah Code § 4-44-102(2)).

9. 2019 Utah Laws 81 (S.B. 93) (amending, in relevant part, Utah Code § 4-44-102(2)).

10. 2019 Utah Laws 81 (S.B. 93) (amending, in relevant part, Utah Code § 4-44-202).

11. 2019 Utah Laws 81 (S.B. 93) (amending, in relevant part, Utah Code § 4-44-102(3)).

12. 2019 Utah Laws 81 (S.B. 93) (amending, in relevant part, Utah Code § 17-41-403, which references Utah Code § 4-44-201).

13. Jeff Vice, "Protection Status Hatched for Egg Farm," *Deseret News*, March 6, 1996.

14. 2019 Utah Laws 81 (S.B. 93) (amending, in relevant part, Utah Code § 4-44-202(3)).

15. Cordon M. Smart, "The 'Right to Commit Nuisance' in North Carolina: A Historical Analysis of the Right-to-Farm Act," *North Carolina Law Review* 94, no. 6 (2016): 2097–154; Danielle Diamond, Loka Ashwood, Allen Franco, Aimee Imlay, Lindsay Kuehn, and Crystal Boutwell, "Farm Fiction: Agricultural Exceptionalism, Environmental Injustice and U.S. Right-to-Farm Law," *Environmental Law Reporter* 52 (Sept. 2022): 10727–48.

16. Utah Code § 17-41-403(1)(a) (2021).

17. Utah Code § 4-44-201(3) (2021).

18. Utah Code § 17-41-403(4)(a) (2021).

Vermont

Vermont legislators justified the state's right-to-farm law by calling agricultural lands "unique and irreplaceable resources" that are dependent upon the "preservation of agriculture."[1] Since the law was enacted in 1982, the state has lost 24 percent of its farmland while the number of farm operations has grown by 8 percent.[2] So what does this legislation do in practice?

Vermont's RTF Law at a Glance

Vermont's RTF law provides no explicit protection of farmland or farms by size (for example, small) or organization (for example, family). Instead, Vermont's RTF law—similar to those in the other forty-nine states—protects agricultural activities from nuisance suits when they impact neighboring property, for example through noise or pollution. Since the passage of controversial amendments in 2003, Vermont's RTF law defines "protected agricultural activities" broadly, including the cultivation and use of land for producing food, fiber, and horticultural and orchard crops, as well as the raising, feeding, and management of animals and bees.[3] Tilling, planting, irrigating, and harvesting crops are also protected activities, along with the operation of greenhouses. In addition, Vermont's RTF law protects the on-site production of fuel or power from agricultural products, as well as composting activities, ditching and subsurface drainage of farm fields, the handling of livestock wastes and by-products, and the storage and application of fertilizers and pesticides.

Conditions and Activities

Since its enactment, Vermont's RTF law has protected agricultural activities by creating a rebuttable presumption that they are not nuisances so long as

234

they exist prior to surrounding nonagricultural activities.[4] In practice, the law presumes agricultural activities are not nuisances unless the party claiming otherwise provides counterevidence. In its original form, Vermont's RTF law provided a rebuttable presumption against nuisance suits only for agricultural activities that were consistent with good agricultural practices and that were established prior to any surrounding nonagricultural activities.[5]

However, a landmark ruling prompted the reconsideration of the law by the legislature. The 2003 case concerned owners of an orchard, which originally consisted of a farmhouse and farm buildings.[6] The owners subsequently sold off the farmhouse while maintaining their orchard. The orchard owners later began waxing and packing the apples on-site for shipment, markedly increasing truck traffic and noise. The owners of the farmhouse filed a nuisance suit against the orchard owners. The Vermont Supreme Court held that the RTF law did not protect the orchard owners because the new agricultural activities did not predate the purchase of the farmhouse by the plaintiffs. Further, the court noted that the facts of this case did not involve urban encroachment into an agricultural area, one of the stated justifications for Vermont's RTF law.

After the ruling, the then chairwoman of Vermont's Agriculture Committee said the ruling "virtually strips the law of any protections for farmers."[7] A Farm Bureau county representative said amending the law was crucial for farms "to survive into the future."[8] Initially, proposed amendments included specifically defining the "secondary effects" of farming that were protected, like odor, dust, pests, fumes, the glare of artificial light, and traffic.[9] However, the bill met major opposition by constitutional scholars and small farmers.[10] One legal professor warned, "What you are about to do is change two centuries of common law."[11] An early version of the bill also included a provision advocated by the anti–genetically engineered seed movement that would have made seed makers liable for crop damage caused by genetically engineered seeds. However, the measure was cut from the bill.[12]

Notably, the legislature changed the RTF law's stated purpose from preventing urban encroachment to helping the "agricultural industry to survive" by preventing nuisance lawsuits over new technologies, diversification of products, and an increase in farm sizes.[13] Specific statutory protections reflecting this changed intent are not in the body of the law, however, but rather are part of the legislative findings and purpose. Vermont's amendments also created four conditions necessary for agricultural activities to receive immunity from nuisance liability: (1) the activity must follow federal, state, and local laws and regulations; (2) the activity must be consistent with

Table 2.45 Vermont's Key RTF Provisions and National Comparison

Vermont's key RTF provisions		% U.S. states with similar RTF provisions
Operations are immune from lawsuits . . .	if they are there first.	44%
Operations are not immune from lawsuits . . .	if they do not comply with county laws.	42%
	if they do not comply with federal laws.	62%
	if they do not comply with other laws.	50%
	if they do not comply with state laws.	68%
	if they do not comply with environmental laws.	26%

good agricultural practices; (3) the activity must have been in existence prior to surrounding nonagricultural activities; and (4) the activity must not change significantly after a surrounding nonagricultural activity begins.[14] However, if those suing can show that the agricultural activity has a substantial adverse effect on health, safety, or welfare or that it creates a noxious and significant interference with the use and enjoyment of neighboring property, they can file a nuisance suit.[15] Nonetheless, this puts the burden of proof on the plaintiffs.[16]

At the same time that it proposed amendments to the state's RTF law, the legislature also considered a "Large Farms" bill.[17] Working in dialogue with the RTF law, the legislature enacted in 2003 a Nonpoint Sources Pollution Reduction Program for the handling and disposal of animal wastes, stating that "meeting these standards shall not be borne by farmers only, but rather by all members of society, who are in fact the beneficiaries."[18] The law set up permitting and grievance procedures for small, medium, and large animal feeding operations—a lot or facility where animals are maintained forty-five days or more during the year.

Vermont legislators continue to consider further amendments advocated by the Farm Bureau to protect larger farms from so-called litigious neighbors.[19]

Local Government

Vermont's RTF law does not prevent state or local boards of health from stopping nuisances that impact public health.[20] However, the state separately limits the power of counties and municipalities to regulate agriculture. Municipalities cannot regulate "required agricultural practices" and "accepted silvicultural practices" defined by the secretary of the Agency of Agriculture, Food and Markets and by the commissioner of the Department of Forests, Parks and Recreation.[21]

NOTES

1. Vt. Stat. tit. 12, § 5752 (2021); *Trickett v. Ochs*, 838 A.2d 66 (Vt. 2003).
2. U.S. Department of Commerce, "Table 4. Farms, Land in Farms, and Land Use, by Size of Farm: 1982 and 1978," in *1982 Census of Agriculture, Volume 1: Geographic Area Series, Part 45: Vermont State and County Data, Chapter 1: State Data* (Washington, D.C.: U.S. Bureau of the Census, 1984), https://agcensus.library.cornell.edu/wp-content/uploads/1982 -Vermont-CHAPTER_1_State_Data-121-Table-04.pdf; "2021 State Agriculture Overview: Vermont," U.S. Department of Agriculture, National Agricultural Statistics Service, accessed October 21, 2022, https://www.nass.usda.gov/Quick_Stats/Ag_Overview/stateOverview .php?state=VERMONT.
3. Vt. Stat. tit. 12, § 5752 (2021).
4. Vt. Stat. tit. 12, § 5753(a)(1) (2021).
5. Vt. Stat. tit. 12, § 5753 (1982); amended by 2003 Vt. Acts & Resolves 149, § 12 (H. 778, effective June 3, 2004).
6. *Trickett*, 838 A.2d 66.
7. Lisa Rathke, "Legislators Will Seek to Restore Farm Protections," *Rutland (Vt.) Herald*, January 1, 2004.
8. Rathke, "Legislators Will Seek to Restore Farm Protections."
9. James Jardine, "GE Seed Labeling, Farm Bills Given Preliminary Approval," *Caledonian-Record* (St. Johnsbury, Vt.), April 8, 2004.
10. "Farm Feud," *Barre (Vt.) Times Argus*, May 5, 2004.
11. Darren M. Allen, "State House Politicians Debate Farm Issues Again," *Rutland Herald*, May 5, 2004.
12. Lisa Rathke, "Right-to-Farm Bill Advances to Senate for Debate," *Barre (Vt.) Times Argus*, May 6, 2004.
13. 2003 Vt. Acts & Resolves 149 (H. 778) (amending, in relevant part, Vt. Stat. tit. 12, § 5751).
14. 2003 Vt. Acts & Resolves 149 (H. 778) (amending, in relevant part, Vt. Stat. tit. 12, § 5753(a) (1)).
15. Vt. Stat. tit. 12, § 5753(a)(2) (2021).
16. Rathke, "Right-to-Farm Bill Advances to Senate for Debate."
17. Jardine, "GE Seed Labeling, Farm Bills Given Preliminary Approval."
18. 2003 Vt. Acts & Resolves 149, §§ 2, 14 (H. 778) (adding, in relevant part, Vt. Stat. tit. 6, § 4801).
19. Guy Page, "Daily Chronicle: Farm, Forest Lawmakers May Protect Farmers from Nuisance Lawsuits, Livestock from Inhumane Conditions," *True North Reports* (Burlington, Vt.), December 3, 2019.
20. Vt. Stat. tit. 12, § 5753(b) (2021).
21. Vt. Stat. tit. 24, § 4413(d)(1)(A)–(B) (2021).

Virginia

Virginia's right-to-farm law has pitted farmer against farmer, with advocates understanding it as crucial to farming while opponents say it protects industries that "are not really farming."[1] Since the enactment of the original RTF law in 1981, Virginia has lost 29 percent of its farm operations and 21 percent of its acres of farmland.[2] So what does the RTF law do in practice?

Virginia's RTF Law at a Glance

Virginia's RTF law provides no explicit protection for farmland or farms based on size (for example, family farm). Rather, Virginia's RTF law, like those present in the other forty-nine states, centers on protecting agricultural operations from nuisance suits when they impact neighboring property, for example through noise or pollution. Virginia's RTF law protects agricultural operations from public nuisance suits (those brought by the government on behalf of the general public) and private nuisance suits (those brought by people, like neighbors).[3] Protected agricultural operations include those devoted to the "bona fide" production of crops, animals, or fowl.[4] This includes the production of fruits, vegetables, meat, dairy, poultry, tobacco, and nuts, and nursery, floriculture, and silviculture products. A Virginia court ruled in 2016 that aquaculture operations were not protected under the state's RTF law.[5]

Importantly, a 2018 amendment substantially expanded Virginia's RTF protections. Now any party that has a business relationship with the agricultural operation receives protection from nuisance suits.[6] Associated businesses could include, for example, poultry or swine integrators, investment groups, or waste handling companies.

Conditions and Activities

To receive RTF protections, agricultural operations must be in "substantial compliance" with best management practices and any applicable laws or regulations.[7] "Substantial compliance" means that agricultural operations adhere to best management practices to such a degree that they do not cause "significant risk to human health or safety." In effect, this means that as long as agricultural operations meet existing laws and regulations, they are shielded from nuisance suits, even if they impact human health or safety. Potential litigants have to prove a "significant" impact; otherwise the law presumes that the operation is compliant.

Certain activities, however, are not protected by Virginia's RTF law. For example, the statute does not protect against claims that an agricultural operation failed to use proper care (that is, operated negligently) or against other claims such as trespass.[8] For example, neighbors sued Sussex Surry LLC and Synagro Central Inc. for damages related to negligence, private nuisance, and trespass. The companies sprayed and spread by-products of wastewater treatment plant processing that the plaintiffs alleged caused them severe health problems. The judge ruled that the companies qualified as agricultural operations that were likely entitled to RTF protection. However, the judge left it to the jury to determine whether the companies acted negligently or were improperly managed.[9]

Since passage of amendments in 2018, the law also stipulates that lawsuits cannot be brought by those who already knew about the operation when their "occupancy" began.[10] Further, only persons with an ownership interest in the property that is impacted by the alleged nuisance can file suit.[11] In practice, this can leave out family members, renters, and others without clear title to their property but who may be impacted by operations.

The RTF law does not afford protections to an agricultural operation that pollutes any stream water or causes any overflow onto the lands of another.[12]

Local Government

Virginia's RTF law voids local ordinances that would make any agricultural operation a nuisance or require that nuisance to stop.[13] In a 1985 case, the court ruled that vacant lots with overgrown weeds are allowed, so long as they are used for general farming and not managed negligently or improperly.[14]

Table 2.46 Virginia's Key RTF Provisions and National Comparison

Virginia's key RTF provisions		% U.S. states with similar RTF provisions
Operations are immune from lawsuits . . .	when they are there first.	44%
Operations are not immune from lawsuits . . .	if the operation is negligent	46%
	if they do not comply with county laws.	42%
	if they do not comply with environmental laws.	26%
	if they do not comply with federal laws.	62%
	if they do not comply with other laws.	50%
	if they do not comply with state laws.	68%
	if they pollute water.	36%
Other important details	RTF supersedes local ordinances and laws.	62%

Since a controversial amendment in 1994, local government's power became even further constrained. Localities can no longer require a special exception or use permit for agriculture or silviculture activities in areas zoned agricultural.[15] A critic said the amendment "gives guarantees of protection without any responsibility and obligation."[16] In one case, a county tried to impose a zoning ordinance on a log yard, but the court ruled it could not, as the RTF law protected operations in Agricultural Residential zoning districts.[17] In another case, a court ruled that the RTF law superseded a 1987 zoning ordinance that required a special exemption permit for a nursery's expansion.[18]

More generally, the law bars localities from regulating any of the following activities of an agricultural operation, unless they substantially impact the health, safety, or general welfare of the public: agritourism; sales of agricultural or silvicultural products; preparation, processing, or sales of food products; and other activities and events customary at Virginia agricultural operations.[19]

Limits on Damages

Virginia's RTF law limits the damages—meaning monetary settlements—that those who sue agricultural operations can receive in private nuisance suits.[20] Compensatory damages for permanent nuisances cannot be more than the amount by which an agricultural operation reduces the fair market value of the person's property. Damages for temporary nuisances are limited to the diminution in fair market value of the person's property.

If a person brings multiple private nuisance suits against different operations, that person can only receive compensation equal to the fair market value of their property. This is true even if the person bringing the lawsuit includes additional defendants, such as those who have a business relationship with the agricultural operation.

While these limitations on settlements are similar to those in neighboring West Virginia, they do not go as far. Crucially, Virginia allows people to recover compensation (up to any amount) for physical or mental injuries caused by an alleged nuisance, so long as it is shown by objective and documented medical evidence that the nuisance endangered life or health.[21]

NOTES

1. Pat Murphey, "Right to Farm Bill Argued," *Harrisonburg (Va.) Daily News-Record*, January 23, 1995; M. W. Goodwin, "Urban vs. Rural Issue Simmers in Dinwiddie," *Richmond (Va.) Times-Dispatch*, 1994.
2. U.S. Department of Agriculture, *USDA Quick Stats Tool: June 1981 Survey, Virginia*, distributed by National Agricultural Statistics Service, accessed January 6, 2021, https://quickstats .nass.usda.gov/results/7ADB5C51-B175-3DFB-A96D-8F3EA4F4CFEA; "2021 State Agriculture Overview: Virginia," U.S. Department of Agriculture, National Agricultural Statistics Service, accessed October 21, 2022, https://www.nass.usda.gov/Quick_Stats/Ag_Overview /stateOverview.php?state=VIRGINIA.
3. Va. Code § 3.2-302(A) (2021).
4. Va. Code § 3.2-300 (2021).
5. *Cty. of York v. Bavuso*, No. 160104, 2016 WL 6304568 (Va. Oct. 27, 2016).
6. Va. Code § 3.2-302 (2021) (amended by 2018 Va. Acts 147 (H.B. 987)).
7. Va. Code § 3.2-302(A) (2021).
8. Va. Code § 3.2-302(A) (2021).
9. *Wyatt v. Sussex Surry, LLC*, No. CL06-6900, 2007 WL 5969399 (Va. Cir. Ct. Nov. 2, 2007).
10. Va. Code § 3.2-302(A) (2021) (amended by 2018 Va. Acts 147 (H.B. 987)); Kelly Clark, "Agriculture Lawsuit Bill Heads to House Floor," *Harrisonburg (Va.) Daily News-Record*, February 2, 2018.
11. Va. Code § 3.2-302(C) (2021).
12. Va. Code § 3.2-302(B) (2021).
13. Va. Code § 3.2-302(E) (2021).
14. *French v. Town of Mt. Jackson*, No. 2606, 1985 WL 306829 (Va. Cir. Ct. July 2, 1985).
15. Va. Code § 3.2-301 (2021) (amended by 1994 Va. Acts 779 (S.B. 513)).
16. Murphey, "Right to Farm Bill Argued."
17. *Buckley v. Loudoun Cty. Bd. of Zoning Appeals*, No. 20141, 2002 WL 31943390 (Va. Cir. Ct. June 4, 2002).
18. *Layng v. Gwinn*, No. C162042, 2000 WL 1052936 (Va. Cir. Ct. Feb. 24, 2000).
19. Va. Code § 15.2-2288.6(1)–(4) (2021).
20. Va. Code § 3.2-302(C) (2021).
21. Va. Code § 3.2-302(C) (2021).

Washington

· ·

Washington's legislators justified the state's right-to-farm law as preventing "urbanizing areas" from forcing the "premature removal of lands from agricultural uses and timber production."[1] But since first enacting its RTF law in 1979, the state nonetheless has 4 percent fewer farming operations and 11 percent fewer acres of farmland.[2] So what does this law do in practice?

Washington's RTF Law at a Glance

Washington's RTF law does not provide agriculture any explicit statutory protection from urban sprawl, but courts have used the legislature's stated purpose to determine the law's meaning. Like similar RTF laws nationally, Washington's law centers on protecting agricultural activities and forest practices from nuisance suits when they impact neighboring property, for example through noise or pollution. Specifically, the state defines nuisances as "whatever is injurious to health or indecent or offensive to the senses, or an obstruction to the free use of property, so as to essentially interfere with the comfortable enjoyment of life and property."[3]

In one case, the Buchanan family farm sued a concentrated animal feeding operation and a meat processing plant on adjacent properties—Simplot Feeders Limited Partnership (Simplot) and Iowa Beef Processing Inc. (IBP)—owned by IBP and Tyson Fresh Meats Inc. The Buchanan family had farmed their 320-acre farm since 1961, when the neighboring property was a rangeland. Since that time, IBP began operating a meat processing and rendering plant, while Simplot developed a CAFO that held over 40,000 cattle.[4] The Buchanans sued Simplot and IBP in federal court for nuisance, trespass, and negligence. In terms of trespass, they complained of flies and manure dust that damaged their crops. Under nuisance, they complained about foul and obnoxious odors.

However, the corporate operators attempted to use the RTF law to dismiss the charges against its CAFO and plant. They argued their operations qualified as protected agricultural activities broadly, which Washington's RTF law defines as inclusive of any conditions or activities that occur within a farm in connection with commercial production of farm products. Specifically, the law defines "protected agricultural activities" sweepingly, including most everything that occurs on a farm in connection with the commercial production of farm products. Activities protected from nuisance suits include odors; dust; fumes; use of roads, drains, and canals; keeping of bees for production or apiculture; the employment and use of labor; the use of drains and waterways; and the "prevention of trespass." Protected activities also include the use of new practices and equipment consistent with technological development within the agricultural industry.[5] The law explicitly protects the "conversion from one agricultural activity to another" as well as "new practices and equipment consistent with technological development within the agricultural industry."[6] Protected farms include land, buildings, freshwater ponds, and freshwater culturing and growing facilities, as well as machinery used in commercial production of farm products. Farm products are defined similarly broadly, encompassing dairy, forages, poultry, livestock, vegetables, trees, fish, and related products, as well as food, feed, fiber, and fur.[7]

While the processing plant and CAFO technically fit within the definition of agricultural activities, the state's supreme court gave more weight to the legislative intent behind the state's RTF law.[8] In 1998, the court held that the Washington State Legislature did not protect all agricultural uses but rather those in urbanizing areas. Further, the court suggested that the law is designed to protect agricultural uses that were there first. The court offered that the RTF act "must be applied cautiously and narrowly." Nonetheless, as recently as 2019, over two decades after the first nuisance suit was filed, Tyson, IBP, and Simplot continue to attempt to dismiss a case brought by the Buchanans, which calls for the nuisance-causing activities to stop and also claims damages.[9]

Washington's broad language in its RTF law provides protection to larger operations, even those that do not necessarily appear at first glance to be a farm. For example, a landfill that operated as an indoor composting facility for a mushroom farm successfully qualified as a "farm."[10] Homeowners near the landfill sued, claiming that hazardous substances and odors being released from the landfill interfered with their use of their land. The court ruled that the operation did indeed qualify as a "farm" and merited RTF protection. The court stated, "Since mushrooms are farm products, the ICF [indoor composting facility], which produces compost for the mushrooms to grow [in], is an 'agricultural activity' because it is an 'activity which occurs . . . in connection with the commercial production of farm products . . . and includes . . . odors.' Mushrooms cannot grow without the compost and, therefore, the compost activities cannot be separated from the mushroom growing."[11]

Conditions and Activities

Washington's protection of farming activities and forestry practices from nuisance suits remains subject to a few conditions. They must be established prior to surrounding nonagricultural and nonforestry activities. The RTF law states that such practices must be "good," which are then presumed to be reasonable and warrant protection.[12] The law treats "good" as conforming with applicable laws and rules.[13] Accordingly, some activities that qualify as forestry practices—like a quarry—can lose RTF protection if they violate water quality laws.[14]

Amendments in 1992 afforded agricultural activities complying with the law unlimited operational hours, regardless of the hours of the day or night or day of the week.[15] As one news article put it, "Farmers could drive their tractors or run their combines in the middle of the night."[16] But the amendments also introduced a much broader definition of "agriculture," which from then forward included the commercial production of farm products—not just crops—opening up protections to all kinds of processing activities.[17] However, RTF protections do not apply if the activity or practice has a substantial adverse effect on public health and safety.[18]

The 1992 amendments also afforded RTF protections to forestry, so long as a forestry operation was established before surrounding nonagricultural activities. Forestry practices protected from nuisance suits now include those conducted on or directly pertaining to forestland, which include growing, harvesting, or processing timber.[19] Members of a residential community sued their uphill neighbor, the Seattle Gymnastics Society, after it clear-cut timber on its property as part of repairing a ski lodge, which led to an avalanche.[20] The gymnastics society attempted to use the RTF defense. The lower court ruled in favor of the downhill landowners, and the gymnastics society appealed.[21] The court of appeals reversed this on grounds that the gymnastics society had been engaged in forestry practices, in general, since long before the residential community members obtained their property,

244 WASHINGTON

such as the growing of trees. On further appeal, the state supreme court ruled that without proof that the uphill neighbor was engaging in an actual forestry activity prior to the development of neighboring residential uses, the clear-cutting of timber could not be protected by the RTF law.[22]

Similarly, a court ruled that an apple orchard's use of propane cannons and cherry guns—while a new and expanded activity—was not exempt from a nuisance action. The homeowners, who were established prior to the surrounding nonagricultural activities, thus could move forward with their nuisance suit.[23]

Local Government

Washington's RTF law can limit a municipality's ability to stop certain agricultural practices if considered nuisances, but not trespass. For example, an appeals court considered whether the discharge of excess irrigation water by an orchard was protected by the RTF law.[24] In the case, water drainage from the orchard "fouled" a well on private property that was developed after the establishment of the orchard. Later, runoff from the orchard exposed a city sanitary water line, and the city as well as the Kiona Irrigation District sought to stop the orchard's irrigation practice through an injunction. The court ruled that the RTF law did not protect the orchard because the discharge of water was off-site trespass and categorically different. However, the court nonetheless ruled the orchard was only partially responsible, and thus the injunction needed to be revisited.[25]

Otherwise, the RTF law does not explicitly address the power of local government. Some Washington counties have passed their own RTF laws that typically expand the exceptions provided to agriculture.[26]

Attorney Fees and Investigation Costs

Washington's law was amended in 2005 to award attorney fees to those engaged in agricultural activities that successfully defend themselves against a nuisance claim.[27] However, this legal language does not work the other way around, which discourages the filing of nuisance suits.[28] A "farmer" who prevails in an action where an agricultural activity was claimed to be a nuisance can recover the full costs and expenses reasonably incurred by the farmer as a result of the lawsuit. In addition, a farmer who prevails in any claim based on an allegation that the agricultural activity on a farm violated laws, rules, or ordinances may recover the full costs and expenses

Table 2.47 Washington's Key RTF Provisions and National Comparison

Washington's key RTF provisions		% U.S. states with similar RTF provisions
Operations are immune from lawsuits . . .	if they use a new technology.	30%
	if they produce a different product.	26%
	if they are there first.	44%
Operations are not immune from lawsuits . . .	if they do not comply with county laws.	42%
	if they do not comply with environmental laws.	26%
	if they do not comply with federal laws.	62%
	if they do not comply with other laws.	50%
	if they do not comply with state laws.	68%
Other important details	Attorney fees are awarded to prevailing defendant.	34%
	RTF protects processing.	48%

reasonably incurred by the farmer.[29] While "farm," "farmland," and "farm products" are defined by the law, "farmer" is not, making it unclear if any entity engaged in agricultural or forestry activities is eligible.

The costs that farmers can recover include (1) actual damages (including lost revenue and the replacement value of crops or livestock damaged or unable to be harvested as a result of the claim); (2) reasonable attorney fees and costs; and (3) exemplary damages if a court finds that the claim was initiated maliciously and without probable cause.[30]

However, defendants cannot recover fees and costs from governmental entities pursuing enforcement.[31] Nonetheless, state and local agencies can recover their investigative costs and expenses if a court finds that the entity filing the complaint did so maliciously or without probable cause.[32] Like the curbing of the filing of nuisance suits, such language also discourages the formal filing of complaints against agricultural or forestry operations.[33]

NOTES

1. Wash. Rev. Code § 7.48.300 (2021).
2. U.S. Department of Agriculture, *USDA Quick Stats Tool: June 1979 Survey, Washington*, distributed by National Agricultural Statistics Service, accessed January 6, 2021, https://quickstats.nass.usda.gov/results/AA1C6DD1-7BD3-3ADE-89F4-DE0F01C7FBBB; "2021 State Agriculture Overview: Washington," U.S. Department of Agriculture, National Agricultural Statistics Service, accessed October 21, 2022, https://www.nass.usda.gov/Quick_Stats/Ag_Overview/stateOverview.php?state=WASHINGTON.

3. Wash. Rev. Code. § 7.48.010 (2021). See also *Buchanan v. Simplot Feeders, Ltd. Partnership*, 134 Wash.2d 673, 687 (Wash. 1998).

4. *Buchanan v. Simplot Feeders Ltd. Partnership*, 952 P.2d 610 (Wash. 1998).

5. Wash. Rev. Code § 7.48.310(1) (2021).

6. Wash. Rev. Code § 7.48.310(1) (2021).

7. Wash. Rev. Code § 7.48.310(2), (4) (2021).

8. *Buchanan*, 952 P.2d 610.

9. *Buchanan v. Simplot Feeders, LLC*, No. 4:19-CV-5209-TOR, 2019 WL 7763826 (E.D. Wash. Oct. 29, 2019).

10. *Vicwood Meridian P'ship v. Skagit Sand and Gravel*, 98 P.3d 1277 (Wash. Ct. App. 2004).

11. *Vicwood Meridian P'ship*, 98 P.3d 1277.

12. Wash. Rev. Code § 7.48.305(1)–(2) (2021).

13. Wash. Rev. Code § 7.48.305(2) (2021).

14. *Gill v. LDI*, 19 F.Supp.2d 1188 (W.D. Wash. 1998).

15. 1992 Wash. Sess. Laws 151 (S.H.B. 2457) (amending, in relevant part, Wash. Rev. Code § 7.48.305).

16. *World* staff writer, "Senate Gives Farmers Even More Rights," *Wenatchee (Wash.) World*, March 4, 1992.

17. *World* staff writer, "Senate Gives Farmers Even More Rights."

18. Wash. Rev. Code § 7.48.305(1) (2021).

19. Wash. Rev. Code § 7.48.310(5) (2021) (as amended by 1992 Wash. Sess. Laws 52 [H.B. 2330] and 2009 Wash. Sess. Laws 200 [S.B. 5562]).

20. *Alpental Cmty. Club, Inc. v. Seattle Gymnastics Soc.*, 111 P.3d 257 (Wash. 2005).

21. *Alpental Cmty. Club, Inc. v. Seattle Gymnastics Soc.*, 86 P.3d 784 (Wash. Ct. App. 2004).

22. *Alpental Cmty. Club*, 111 P.3d 257.

23. *Davis v. Taylor*, 132 P.3d 783 (Wash. Ct. App. 2006).

24. *City of Benton City v. Adrian*, 748 P.2d 679 (Wash. Ct. App. 1988).

25. *Adrian*, 748 P.2d 679.

26. Paul Lavigne Sullivan, "Pierce County Considers Law to Protect Its Farmers—Urban vs. Rural: As Homes Encroach on Land, County Ponders Law to Safeguard Farm Practices," *Tacoma News Tribune*, August 31, 2001; Steven Friederich, "Outgoing Commissioners Will Take Up 'Right to Farm' Law," *Aberdeen (Wash.) Daily World*, December 27, 2012; Steven Friederich, "Right to Farm Discussion Revived," *Aberdeen Daily World*, February 14, 2012.

27. 2005 Wash. Sess. Laws ch. 511 (S.B. 5962) (enacting, in relevant part, what is now Wash. Rev. Code § 7.48.315).

28. Cordon M. Smart, "The 'Right to Commit Nuisance' in North Carolina: A Historical Analysis of the Right-to-Farm Act," *North Carolina Law Review* 94, no. 6 (2016): 2097–154; Kyle Silk-Eglit, "The Fundamentals of the Right to Farm Act," *Wenatchee World*, May 1, 2012.

29. Wash. Rev Code § 7.48.315(1)–(2) (2021).

30. Wash. Rev Code § 7.48.315(3)–(4) (2021).

31. Wash. Rev Code § 7.48.315(5) (2021).

32. Wash. Rev Code § 7.48.320 (2021).

33. For more on the chilling effect of such statutes, see the section "Geopolitical Extraction" in the introduction.

West Virginia

Legislators passed the right-to-farm law in West Virginia, describing it as a tool to protect and preserve "agricultural productive operations" from the "infringement upon agricultural lands and agricultural operations by other uses and occupancies."[1] Since the law first passed in 1982, farm operations in the state have grown by 19 percent while the acreage farmed has dropped by nearly 2 percent.[2] So what does this legislation do in practice?

West Virginia's RTF Law at a Glance

West Virginia's RTF law initially provided sweeping protections for agriculture from any adverse actions generally, the only state in the nation to do so.[3] Typically, RTF laws center on protecting agricultural operations from nuisance suits in particular, when they cause, for example, odors or other pollution. West Virginia, however, did not tailor its RTF protections to nuisance suits until a series of amendments in 2019.[4] Now, agricultural operations—which include any facility used for agriculture—are explicitly protected in the state's RTF law from public nuisance suits (filed on behalf of the people by the government) and private nuisance suits (filed by individuals).[5]

Still, agricultural operations also remain protected from adverse actions broadly. West Virginia sweepingly defines protected elements of agriculture, ranging from food, fiber, and woodland products, to cultivation, stillage, livestock, dairy, forestry, packing, milling, marketing, and any other "legal plant or animal production and all farm practices."[6] The law also broadly defines "protected agricultural lands" to include any amount of land and improvements, as long as the products produced from it total more than $1,000 annually. Prior to the 2019 amendments, agricultural operations

248

had to be at least five acres to gain protection but now have no minimum acreage requirement.[7]

Conditions and Activities

West Virginia's current RTF protections give near-blanket immunity to any kind of agricultural conduct from court actions, including nuisance suits. West Virginia's RTF law places the financial burden and risk on any entity (public or private) seeking compensation for pollution or other nuisances resulting from intensive agricultural operations. This happens through caps on damages, constraining who can sue and when, and the burden of attorney fees, all detailed below.[8]

Under the law, three requirements must be met before a nuisance suit can be filed against an agricultural operation.[9] First, only the majority of legal landowners that have been adversely affected by an agricultural operation can file a nuisance suit. Second, the landowners must live within half a mile of the agricultural operations—a stipulation similar to that in North Carolina, which similarly amended its RTF law a year earlier.[10] Finally, a nuisance suit can be filed against an agricultural operation only if the operation is materially violating a federal, state, or local law. The law does not define what "materially" means.

Crucially, West Virginia's RTF law states that no "conduct of agriculture upon agricultural land" can be deemed adverse to other land uses (except for other agricultural uses).[11] This may mean that only the owners of land used for agriculture can file a nuisance suit against a neighboring agricultural operation.[12] The law, therefore, seems to protect agricultural operations from nuisance suits brought by those engaged in residential, commercial, business, or governmental land uses. There is one exception to this near-blanket immunity, but the meaning of the exception is not entirely clear, and we found no case law that has interpreted the law. Under this exception, a neighboring person complaining about an agricultural operation may be able to file suit if that person was there first and if the agricultural operation could cause that person or his or her property physical damage.[13] Again, however, because the RTF law protects all agricultural conduct—without a specific start date—this exception may be a paper tiger.

In addition to the limits on who can bring a lawsuit against an agricultural operation, West Virginia's RTF law provides various protections against claims of nuisance, specifically for agricultural operations that have been in operation for more than one year.[14] For example, operations cannot be considered a nuisance if they were not one at the time they began and if the nuisance conditions being complained of have existed, without substantial change, since the operations began. In addition, an agricultural operation that has been in existence for more than one year cannot be found to be a nuisance because of any changed conditions in or around the location of the operation. In such cases, the operation will have an absolute defense against a nuisance claim—meaning it cannot be held liable for wrongdoing—so long as the operation provides proof that it has existed for more than one year and was complying with federal and state laws as well as all regulations and permits.

Even while tailoring some protections to operations that have been running for a year, the state's RTF law also protects operations regardless of how long they have been in existence. For example, agricultural operations are protected from nuisance suits so long as they utilize commonly accepted agricultural practices.[15] The law assumes that commonly accepted agricultural practices are those that comply with all applicable federal and state laws. Neither can an agricultural operation be considered a nuisance if it undergoes a "reasonable expansion."[16] A reasonable expansion can include purchasing additional land for the operation, introducing the use of new technology, transferring the operation, applying a Natural Resources Conservation Service program or USDA program to the operation, or any other change that does not affect the operation's compliance with applicable laws and does not have a substantial adverse effect on the environment or create a hazard to public health or safety.

None of West Virginia's protections against nuisance lawsuits apply to situations in which the alleged nuisance is the result of negligence (failing to take proper care) or when the alleged injuries or damages are due to an agricultural operation's violation of federal, state, or local laws.[17]

Local Government

No state or local government can bring a criminal or civil action against agricultural operations that meet state and federal laws, permits, and regulations.[18] In essence, this means the RTF law supersedes local governance. Moreover, since a 2019 amendment to the RTF law, municipal laws cannot be applied to any agricultural operation that is subsequently annexed or otherwise brought within the municipality's corporate boundaries.

Table 2.48 West Virginia's Key RTF Provisions and National Comparison

West Virginia's key RTF provisions		% U.S. states with similar RTF provisions
Operations are immune from lawsuits . . .	if there is a cessation or interruption in farming.	26%
	if boundaries or size of operations change.	34%
	if there is a change in locality.	46%
	if they use a new technology.	30%
	if they produce a different product.	26%
	if there is an ownership change.	26%
	if they are there first.	44%
	once in operation for a year.	48%
Operations are not immune from lawsuits . . .	if they are a nuisance from the start.	38%
	if they are negligent.	46%
	if they do not comply with state laws.	68%
	if they do not comply with federal laws.	62%
Other important details	Attorney fees are awarded to prevailing defendant.	34%
	RTF supersedes local ordinances and laws.	62%

Attorney Fees and Limits on Damages

The 2019 amendments to West Virginia's RTF law added a completely new set of provisions that limit the damages that are available in nuisance lawsuits, as well as the attorney fees and costs that can be imposed.[19]

Most importantly, the law now limits damages to those that pertain to property values.[20] This means a person cannot recover damages related to the loss of use and enjoyment of property or any personal health impacts. The West Virginia amendment came two years after a similar RTF law amendment was passed in neighboring North Carolina, where legislators responded to court settlements against large-scale hog operations by limiting the compensation that neighbors could receive.[21]

West Virginia's current law limits compensation for permanent nuisances (those that cannot be remediated) to the reduction in the fair market value of the plaintiff's property caused by the nuisance.[22] Damages for temporary nuisances (those that can be abated through, for example, changing practices) are limited to the diminution in fair market value of the property.

In no case may a plaintiff's total damages exceed the diminished value of the property that is the subject of the nuisance lawsuit. In addition, if the same plaintiff brings multiple lawsuits against one or more agricultural operations, that plaintiff may not recover more, in total damages, than the fair market value of his or her property. Finally, punitive damages (that punish for bad behavior) are not allowed in any nuisance lawsuit brought against an agricultural operation. These 2019 amendments are particularly egregious for poor and minority rural communities, where property values are low and residents no longer can receive compensation for medical impacts.[23] The amendments may further enable predatory practices, as operations strategically locate where people have the least amount of money to counter them and are entitled to the least amount of monetary compensation.

Finally, any person who brings a nuisance suit against an agricultural operation that has been up and running for more than a year is liable for all costs and expenses incurred by the operation's defense.[24] This includes, but is not limited to, attorney fees, court costs, travel, and other related expenses. This and similar language may have a chilling effect on the filing of nuisance suits in favor of industrial operators.[25]

NOTES

1. W. Va. Code § 19-19-1 (1982).
2. U.S. Department of Commerce, "Table 1. Farms, Land in Farms, and Land Use: 1982 and Earlier Census Years," in *1982 Census of Agriculture, Volume 1: Geographic Area Series, Part 48: West Virginia State and County Data, Chapter 1: State Data* (Washington, D.C.: U.S. Bureau of the Census, 1984), https://agcensus.library.cornell.edu/wp-content/uploads/1982-West_Virginia-CHAPTER_1_State_Data-121-Table-01.pdf; "2021 State Agriculture Overview: West Virginia," U.S. Department of Agriculture, National Agricultural Statistics Service, accessed October 21, 2022, https://www.nass.usda.gov/Quick_Stats/Ag_Overview/stateOverview.php?state=WEST%20VIRGINIA.
3. W. Va. Code § 19-19-4 (1982).
4. Since our research uncovered no news coverage of RTF cases in the state, we do not know if, in practice, protection from adverse actions generally plays out differently than nuisance suit protections more specifically.
5. 2019 W. Va. Acts 7 (S.B. 393) (amending W. Va. Code § 19-19-2; adding W. Va. Code § 19-19-7).
6. W. Va. Code § 19-19-2 (2021).
7. 2019 W. Va. Acts 7 (S.B. 393) (amending W. Va. Code § 19-19-2).
8. Our research uncovered no cases that utilized the right-to-farm defense, and likewise no news coverage of any RTF cases in the state, suggesting the law has stifled legal action.
9. W. Va. Code § 19-19-7 (2021).
10. See 2018 N.C. Sess. Laws 113 (S.B. 711) (amending N.C. Gen. Stat. § 106-701).
11. W. Va. Code § 19-19-4 (2021).
12. W. Va. Code §§ 19-19-4, 19-19-7 (2021).
13. W. Va. Code § 19-19-4 (2021).
14. W. Va. Code § 19-19-7 (2021).
15. W. Va. Code § 19-19-7 (2021).

16. W. Va. Code § 19-19-7 (2021).

17. W. Va. Code § 19-19-7 (2021).

18. W. Va. Code § 19-19-7 (2021).

19. See 2019 W. Va. Acts 7 (S.B. 393) (adding, in relevant part, W. Va. Code § 19-19-8).

20. W. Va. Code § 19-19-8 (2021).

21. See 2017 N.C. Sess. Laws 11 (H.B. 467) (amending N.C. Gen. Stat. § 106-702).

22. W. Va. Code § 19-19-8 (2021).

23. Taft Wireback, "Blust Breaks with GOP over Nuisance Lawsuits," *Greensboro (N.C.) News and Record*, April 11, 2017.

24. W. Va. Code § 19-19-8 (2021).

25. Cordon M. Smart, "The 'Right to Commit Nuisance' in North Carolina: A Historical Analysis of the Right-to-Farm Act," *North Carolina Law Review* 94, no. 6 (2016): 2097–154. For more on the chilling effect of such statutes, see the section "Geopolitical Extraction" in the introduction.

Wisconsin

Legislators advocated the right-to-farm law in Wisconsin as a tool to prevent the loss of farmland and protect family farms.[1] But since first codified in 1982, the number of farms in the state has dropped by 30 percent, with 23 percent fewer acres of farmland.[2] So what does this legislation do in practice?

Wisconsin's RTF Law at a Glance

Wisconsin's law provides no explicit protection for farmland or family farmers. Rather, Wisconsin's RTF law protects income-producing or livelihood-based agricultural activities and uses from nuisance suits over matters that impact neighboring properties, like noise or pollution.[3] Protected areas of agriculture are expansive, including aquaculture, floriculture, crop and forage production, beekeeping, raising livestock, fur farming, forest management, and land enrolled in federal or state agricultural conservation payment programs.[4] Protected agriculture uses include storing and processing agricultural products and processing agricultural wastes.

Conditions and Activities

To receive RTF protections in Wisconsin, agricultural activities and uses should predate those of aggrieved neighbors without having been significantly interrupted.[5] Also, no threats to public health or safety can be present. However, Wisconsin's RTF law interprets uninterrupted agricultural uses and activities broadly. For example, the law does not consider a change in the agricultural use or practice to be significant. Wisconsin's RTF law consequently protects almost any agricultural use or activity, so long as it does not substantially threaten public health or safety.

Under Wisconsin's RTF law, only plaintiffs are required to pay the costs

Table 2.49 Wisconsin's Key RTF Provisions and National Comparison

Wisconsin's key RTF provisions		% U.S. states with similar RTF provisions
Operations are immune from lawsuits . . .	if they are there first.	44%
Other important details	Attorney fees are awarded to prevailing defendant.	34%
	RTF protects processing.	48%

of litigation if they lose, but not defendants.[6] This shifts the litigation risks away from agricultural operations and onto plaintiffs by requiring them to pay attorney fees, expert witness fees, and other costs related to preparing for and participating in lawsuits. For example, in a 2000 lawsuit, a crop and cattle farmer claimed his neighbor's commercial cranberry farm flooded his property, creating a nuisance that curtailed his capacity to farm.[7] The circuit court ruled in favor of the cranberry farm, and on appeal, the court further ruled there was insufficient evidence to prove the cranberry farm caused the flooding. The appellate court therefore ordered the cattle and grain farmer to pay the reasonable attorney fees of the prevailing defendant—the commercial cranberry farm.

Local Government

Wisconsin's RTF law encourages local governments to use zoning to prevent nuisance conflicts.[8] But in practice, state statutes limit their authority to do so. For example, the Wisconsin Livestock Facility Siting Law prevents political subdivisions from enacting or enforcing zoning ordinances that prohibit livestock facilities in agricultural districts.[9] An exception is made if reasonable scientific findings demonstrate that the ordinance protects public health or safety.

Limits on Damages

Even if an agricultural operation is sued and found to be a nuisance, the RTF law substantially limits what Wisconsin courts can award or what activities they can restrict, unless public health or safety is threatened.[10] Courts must consult public agencies with expertise in agricultural matters to ensure the suitability of actions required to address the nuisance. Also, the agricultural operation must be granted "a reasonable time" of no less than one year to comply with any order. Further, courts cannot impose any actions to address the nuisance that would negatively impact the economic viability of the operation.

NOTES

1. Wis. Stat. § 823.08 (1982).
2. U.S. Department of Commerce, "Table 1. Farms, Land in Farms, and Land Use: 1982 and Earlier Census Years," in *1982 Census of Agriculture, Volume 1: Geographic Area Series, Part 49: Wisconsin State and County Data, Chapter 1: State Data* (Washington, D.C.: U.S. Bureau of the Census, 1984), https://agcensus.library.cornell.edu/wp-content/uploads/1982 -Wisconsin-CHAPTER_1_State_Data-121-Table-01.pdf; "2021 State Agriculture Overview: Wisconsin," U.S. Department of Agriculture, National Agricultural Statistics Service, accessed October 21, 2022, https://www.nass.usda.gov/Quick_Stats/Ag_Overview/stateOver view.php?state=WISCONSIN.
3. Wis. Stat. §§ 91.01(2)(a), 823.08(2) (2021). See also Michael Buelow, "Senate Approves 'Right to Farm': Bill Would Protect Farmers from Lawsuits, Say Sponsors," *St. Paul (Minn.) Pioneer Press*, January 10, 1996; and Associated Press, "Bill to Save Farmers from Frivolous Suits Approved 96–1," *St. Paul Pioneer Press*, October 13, 1995.
4. Wis. Stat. § 91.01 (2021).
5. Wis. Stat. § 823.08 (2021).
6. Wis. Stat. § 823.08 (2021).
7. *Zink v. Khawaja*, 608 N. W.2d 394 (Wis. Ct. App. 2000).
8. Wis. Stat. § 823.08 (2021).
9. Wis. Stat. § 93.90 (2021).
10. Wis. Stat. § 823.08 (2021).

Wyoming

Wyoming's right-to-farm law, called the Right to Farm and Ranch Act, has been on the books since 1991. In 2015, the legislature retrospectively declared the purpose of the law as forever guaranteeing the right to farm and ranch in the state.[1] Since the RTF law passed in 1991, the number of Wyoming farm operations has increased by 35 percent while the farmland acreage has dropped by 16 percent.[2] So what does this and related legislation purport to do?

Wyoming's RTF Law at a Glance

Wyoming's RTF law provides no explicit protection for family ranches, farms, or land. Like those present in the other forty-nine states, the law centers on protecting certain types of operations from nuisance suits when they impact neighboring property, for example through noise or pollution.[3] It does so by protecting commercial farm and ranch operations from public and private nuisance claims.[4] As originally enacted, the law defined protected farms and ranches as "land, buildings, livestock and machinery used in the commercial production and sale of farm and ranch products."[5] A 1999 amendment expanded this definition to include farm and ranch operations, defined as "the science and art of production of plants and animals useful to man [except wildlife], including but not limited to, the preparation of these products for man's use and their disposal by marketing or otherwise, and includes horticulture, floriculture, viticulture, silviculture, dairy, livestock, poultry, bee and any and all forms of farm and ranch products and farm and ranch production."[6]

257

Table 2.50 Wyoming's Key RTF Provisions and National Comparison

Wyoming's key RTF provisions		% U.S. states with similar RTF provisions
Operations are immune from lawsuits . . .	if they are there first.	44%
Operations are not immune from lawsuits . . .	if they are a nuisance from the start.	38%
	if they do not comply with other laws.	50%
	if they do not comply with state laws.	68%

Conditions and Activities

In order for a farm or ranch operation to be protected under the RTF law, two conditions must be met.[7] First, the operation must conform to generally accepted agricultural management practices. Second, the operation must have existed before any change in the land use adjacent to the farm or ranch occurred, and prior to that change the farm or ranch must not have been a nuisance.[8] The phrase "generally accepted agricultural management practices" is not defined in the statute.[9]

Nearly fifteen years before Wyoming enacted its RTF law, a different law was enacted to provide an absolute defense against claims of nuisance for certain feedlot operations, so long as they can prove compliance with the applicable rules of the Wyoming Department of Environmental Quality.[10] An absolute defense means that the feedlot would be immune from nuisance liability. This defense applies only to feedlots established before the person or persons bringing the nuisance lawsuit gained ownership of their land and only if the conditions alleged to have caused the nuisance are subject to local regulations or related to the activities of the Wyoming Department of Environmental Quality.[11] A feedlot, for purposes of this law, is an area where livestock are confined, primarily for the purposes of feeding and growth prior to slaughter.[12]

Local Government

Neither Wyoming's RTF law nor its feedlot law contains any provisions that specifically address either law's impact on municipalities. However, the state's county code was amended in 2008 to explicitly reference the RTF law.[13] It now stipulates that counties cannot "impair or modify any rights afforded to farm or ranch operations" under the state's RTF law.[14] Attempts to try to give counties more power to determine nuisances have failed to pass in the legislature.[15]

NOTES

1. 2015 Wyo. Sess. Laws 175 (S. File 9) (creating Wyo. Stat. § 11-44-104).
2. U.S. Department of Agriculture, *USDA Quick Stats Tool: June 1991 Survey, Wyoming*, distributed by National Agricultural Statistics Service, accessed October 22, 2020, https://quickstats.nass.usda.gov/results/DBF6BBF3-86D7-3287-B660-8AD753FB2B02; "2021 State Agriculture Overview: Wyoming," U.S. Department of Agriculture, National Agricultural Statistics Service, accessed October 21, 2022, https://www.nass.usda.gov/Quick_Stats/Ag_Overview/stateOverview.php?state=WYOMING.
3. See Wyo. Stat. §§ 11-44-101 to 11-44-104 (2021).
4. Wyo. Stat. § 11-44-102 (2021).
5. 1991 Wyo. Sess. Laws 58 (S. File 7) (creating Wyo. Stat. §§ 11-44-101 to 11-44-103).
6. 1999 Wyo. Sess. Laws 60 (H.B. 12) (amending Wyo. Stat. § 11-44-102).
7. Wyo. Stat. § 11-44-103 (2021).
8. Wyo. Stat. §§ 11-44-103 to 11-44-104 (2021).
9. In a separate section of Wyoming's RTF act, a definition of "generally accepted" practices is referenced. See Wyo. Stat. § 11-44-104 (2021) (referencing Wyo. Stat. § 11-29-115). However, that section of the RTF act does not appear to apply to the requirement that farm and ranch operations follow generally accepted agricultural management practices.
10. 1977 Wyo. Sess. Laws 59 (creating what is now Wyo. Stat. §§ 11-39-101 to 11-39-104).
11. Wyo. Stat. § 11-39-102 (2021).
12. Wyo. Stat. § 11-39-101, "Feedlot" (2021).
13. 2008 Wyo. Sess. 81 (S. File 27) (amending Wyo. Stat. § 18-2-101).
14. Wyo. Stat. § 18-2-101 (2021).
15. Jennifer Frazer, "Senate Votes against Nuisance Legislation," *Wyoming Tribune-Eagle* (Cheyenne), January 17, 2007.

Cultivating Democracy in Agriculture

Since the late 1970s, when RTF laws were first adopted, the number of U.S. farms producing poultry, dairy, hog, beef, hay, soy, corn, and wheat have dropped by between 27 percent and 87 percent (see table 1.4). Over a similar period, RTF litigation has increased, with CAFOs and business firms winning most of the cases that they are party to (figure 1.1). The largest corporate operators win the most in states where they dominate production. They do better the higher they appeal a case, leveraging the power they have at the state level also in federal court. Their power accumulates through interwoven forms of takings: taking of community rights to self-autonomy, taking of property rights from smaller holders, and taking of market power from farmers. Business firms do so by adopting legal forms that diffuse responsibility and culpability.

The disproportionate power of business firms and CAFOs is not inevitable or natural but afforded through governance. Ultimately, if not serving democracy, these structures become a threat to its sustenance.[1] But laws and processes can be undone or redone to create a just and plentiful agriculture. We consider how to end legislatures' favored treatment of multinational agribusiness in order to achieve agricultural, rural, and environmental justice. We focus on three areas ready for transformation: market power and the government, RTF amendments and repeal, and the U.S. and state constitutions.

Market Power and the Government

Accessing different routes to buy, sell, exchange, barter, or give away empowers eaters and growers. The most powerful corporate agribusinesses, however, thrive in contexts with fewer market options for growers and eaters. RTF laws currently benefit CAFOs and business firms the most in states dominated by poultry and hog contract farming (table 1.7). These massive sites of production marginalize farmers' power while enabling global control over food, as the United States is the second largest exporter of chicken and pork globally.[2] Under predatory contract arrangements, those few domestic growers that remain often have little to no choice about whom to buy their supplies from, where to sell their products, or the kind of buildings to use.[3] Best estimates show that WH Group's Smithfield Foods—a firm mostly run and held by shareholders and executives in China—exerts the most control over the market for pork slaughter.[4] Smithfield Foods Inc. and Murphy-Brown LLC, also owned by WH Group, are companies that have used RTF laws to defend themselves in North Carolina, Iowa, and Mississippi. Like Smithfield, similarly powerful companies like JBS, Tyson, and Hormel own and operate in pork, as well as poultry and beef, diffusing their market power across the agri-food network.

Farmers and communities benefit from affirmative vehicles for community wealth generation, like local banks, sale barns, locker houses, grain elevators, mills, community gardens, Community Supported Agriculture farms, agriculture of the middle, and regional processors and retailers.[5] These are examples where distributive and accessible markets create relationships that build the fabric of democratic society. Local, community-based determination and action have facilitated the creation of such businesses that keep capital circulating locally. Yet these social and ecologically embedded forms of agriculture can falter when facing the market and statutory power of corporate agribusiness. Some current efforts to curb concentration include a proposed national moratorium on large agribusinesses, food and beverage manufacturing, and grocery retail mergers.[6] Another route is enforcing the Packers and Stockyards Act, designed in 1921 to take on monopoly power when it can be proved that there is competitive injury. This includes demonstrating that companies are engaged in price-fixing or bid-rigging. These approaches, however, remain of their time—a century ago—when farm markets were more discrete and cross-sectoral global financial investment in agriculture less hegemonic. Other forms of investment ownership, like securities, derivatives, and debt, as well as subsidiaries that reduce risk and private companies with limited disclosures, can enable extractive finance, rather than regenerative and locally circulating wealth. This centralization of profit via global investment works against the distribution of market power through dispersed access to property rights. Limiting or scaling to increase payments to farmers who live where they grow food or raise animals provides a potentially transformative route to help community-based agriculture thrive.

To date, however, the U.S. government continues to provide the bulk of its subsidies to the largest agricultural operations, regardless of whether the ultimate beneficiaries are foreign. In the 1970s, "Get big or get out" was the mantra of U.S. secretary of agriculture Earl Butz. Nearly fifty years later, Secretary Sonny Perdue demonstrated that little had changed when he told U.S. dairy farmers in Wisconsin struggling to keep their operations afloat that "in America, the big get bigger and the small go out."[7] When Perdue spoke in 2019, Wisconsin dairy farms were shuttering at an alarming rate, with some dairy farmers taking their own lives in despair.[8] Since 1978, eight out of every ten dairy farms have gone out of business nationally (see table 1.4). The extent of dairy farm decline nationally is second only to the loss of hog farms. Meanwhile, subsidies continue to be awarded based on the amount of production, and by ignoring size the government effectively awards more funds to the largest operators. The USDA's 2022 Spot Market Hog Pandemic Program provided a payment of $54 per head for up to 10,000 hogs. "Legal entities" were welcome to apply.[9] With no disclosures of beneficiaries, each corporate subsidiary of a mostly foreign-held company like WH Group could apply and receive such funds. A recent Government Accountability Office review of the Coronavirus Food Assistance Program noted that it paid producers $13.8 billion for field crops, $9.8 billion for livestock, $3 billion for dairy, and $4.4 billion for other commodities. The Accountability Office reviewed just ninety of the applications (a total of $87.3 million) for this cumulative $31 billion in assistance. Over half of the producers in its review did not provide enough support for their payments, suggesting their requests were "improper." The office found that "33 producers provided support (e.g., sales receipts) for a lesser amount than they claimed, and nine producers did not clearly establish ownership of commodities they claimed."[10]

More mundane and embedded forms of governmental support also prop up the largest of corporate and absentee operators. The USDA's Environmental Quality Incentives Program funds industrial animal operations' disposal of their extreme amounts of waste. Manure digesters, touted as a way to reduce air pollution by processing waste at large industrial animal facilities, is the centerpiece of the USDA's plan to reduce greenhouse gas emissions. Using public funds—through such programs as the Environmental Quality Incentives Program, the Rural Energy for America Program, and AgStar—the USDA is subsidizing these methane digesters without attention to what or who makes money off them. Such subsidies for digesters help the largest CAFOs and operations at a cost of up to $5 million at any specific site.[11] Foreign-held companies like Smithfield Foods Inc. further benefit from USDA subsidies for grain production, as they lower their feed costs for millions of animals fed in confinement. Business firms can make more raising hogs in the United States than in China.[12] U.S. grain farmers, similar to their fellow animal farmers, likewise have been undercut by subsidies funneled to the largest operators, as six of every ten corn farmers have gone out of business since 1978 (see table 1.4).

Government-supported finance has helped drive consolidation and inequality in lending. In 1997, the Farm Credit System (FCS)—a U.S. government-sponsored enterprise—began extending loans to foreign-owned entities, just before the hog crash of 1998, when prices hit their lowest level for live hundredweight since 1964. The exodus of hog farmers from the sector accelerated in earnest, and in the early years of the twenty-first century, FCS began approaching and encouraging bankrupted or vulnerable farmers to take on loans to build larger hog confinements. Policy changes have pushed lenders associated with the FCS and banks at large to consolidate dramatically, leaving farmers and rural communities with fewer options. Today, the FCS provides the most loans of any banking entity to the largest pork conglomerates, according to a recent study.[13] This is a key financial lifeline for a highly concentrated system. FCS itself, however, does not disclose to whom or what it provides loans according to basic demographic data, like race, ethnicity, or veteran status. Requiring that business firms like corporations, companies, and partnerships disclose their ownership helps counter concentration, absentee investment, and foreign landownership. Disclosures of the ultimate beneficiaries of loans and subsidies empower local people and offer a means to stop umbrella companies or intersectoral investors from repeatedly accessing the public purse through their subsidiaries that by name appear independent but are interconnected. Bipartisan legislation, introduced in 2022, seeks to bar FCS from providing loans to foreign entities and investors.[14] A 2023 rule now requires that Farm Credit institutions disclose basic demographic data on whom it lends to.[15] In addition to tracking foreign entities accessing government-supported loans, this information could be leveraged to ensure that socially disadvantaged farmers and ranchers at large, Indian Nations, and Black farmers specifically have access to these funds.[16]

Elite companies are financially dependent on one another, making the food production system vulnerable in times of crisis, with severe consequences for eaters, animals, and those few actors left in the food production chain.[17] During the COVID-19 pandemic, Smithfield Foods' CEO Ken Sullivan claimed that processing plant workers had to stay on the line or else the country would be on the brink of starvation. Simultaneously, Sullivan told industry representatives there was "plenty of meat" for export.[18] Processing facilities eventually temporarily shuttered as workers contracted and died from COVID-19 at alarming rates, with an estimated $11.2 billion in associated costs.[19] When hogs could not be slaughtered, rather than pay additional feed costs and with no place to take the incoming piglets, millions of hogs were euthanized by various means, including shutting down the ventilator systems in CAFOs.[20] Major pork firms received "disposal assistance" payments for their troubles.[21]

The receipt of the bulk of public subsidies and finance by an ever-shrinking number of actors in food production circulates into electoral influence. Our review of news articles covering the inception, adoption, and amendments of RTF laws on a state-specific level found that local and state American Farm Bureau Federation chapters are formative players in RTF legislation. Today, the national nonprofit organization calls itself "the voice of agriculture" made up of "farm and ranch families working together."[22] However, the Farm Bureau gained its initial foothold through the U.S. government. The Federal Office of Extension first issued a Farm Bureau Organization Plan in 1917, creating an alliance with the USDA.[23] Since 1939, the bureaus moved away from their quasi-governmental structure and created insurance companies. Even though Farm Bureau chapters are registered as nonprofits, some—like the Iowa Farm Bureau—receive most of their operating budget from "FBL Financial, a for-profit publicly traded company listed on the New York Stock Exchange."[24] Taken together, the Farm Bureau "commands a multi-billion dollar revenue-generating enterprise of insurance companies and for-profit farmer cooperatives and a stock portfolio that includes the major agribusiness companies Archer Daniels Midland, ConAgra, Monsanto (now Bayer), Phillip Morris, and Dow Dupont."[25]

Farm Bureau chapters, while long present in news coverage of RTF laws, are recently taking on a more direct role in RTF litigation.[26] The earliest court reference to the Farm Bureau in our data set took place in 1971, when the court cited a case where the Massachusetts Farm Bureau supported curtailing zoning laws to enable the expansion of a corporate dairy farm.[27] Since then, the presence of Farm Bureaus in RTF litigation has become more pronounced. In 2021, state Farm Bureau chapters played a role in three cases, the most of any year in our data set.[28] In one case, the Mississippi Farm Bureau Federation wrote a brief in support of the Oxbow Group LLC and other parties to the lawsuit who were using propane cannons—which issue a sonic blast that frightens away wildlife—on their cropland.[29] The other two cases played out in North Carolina. In a Murphy-Brown, LLC case, a court cited a case concerning North Carolina's Farm Bureau Mutual Insurance company.[30] In the third case, the North Carolina Bureau Federation Inc. teamed up with the State of North Carolina to stop rural empowerment groups trying to contest the constitutionality of the state's RTF law.[31]

Contradictorily, the Farm Bureau continues to support RTF legislation and litigation that is the least beneficial to the sole proprietor farmers that are the backbone of its public image. Some farmers and communities have made strides in pointing out the contradiction in message and action by the Farm Bureau. Farmer Matt Howe in Illinois issued a letter of resignation to the Fulton County Farm Bureau Board of Directors after it lent its support to the construction of a 20,000-head swine facility next to his home: "I simply cannot continue to offer my time and resources to an organization which supports the installation of these CAFOs without regard to the effect on residences and family farms to which so many people have devoted their time and constant attention, for some generations."[32] Howe and the community group he worked with, Neighbors Opposing a Polluted Environment (NOPE), went on to successfully prevent the construction of the CAFO in their community. The Farm Bureau has yet to change its position on CAFOs.

Changing or Repealing RTF Laws

RTF laws have capitalized upon very real divisions and loss. Farmers have indeed gone out of business in droves, and rural areas are often extracted from for urban and global consumption. And in capitalizing on this crisis, RTF laws have deepened it. Considering agriculture to be the exception to the rules has made it even more sharply decentered from the communities it can sustain and create. A different path forward calls for considering farming rights relative to the homes of those who live within the space of agriculture, as its fruits also fill the tables of those in cities. An agriculture of home, building upon Indigenous teachings where land gives people common strength and lifeways, offers potential to connect the health of animals to the health of communities.[33] Thinking of agriculture as where people live rather than as a site of extraction reinvigorates agrarian ideals of distribution and sustenance.[34] Facilitating an agriculture that does not divide can come from distributing power through homemaking.

One potential route is to simply abolish RTF laws, as their outcomes on the aggregate have polarized home and agriculture. The extension of RTF

RTF PROVISIONS THAT SERVE CAFOS AND BUSINESS FIRMS

—Immunity once they are up and running for a year.

—Immunity if they use a new technology.

—Immunity if the product or activities change.

—Immunity if operations are interrupted or stop.

—Immunity if ownership changes.

—Immunity if they use accepted or prevailing agricultural practices.

—Court costs awarded only to defendant.

—Standing limited to legal possessors of real property.

—Standing limited to residents who live within half a mile of alleged nuisance.

—Protection extended to operations generally defined as processing.

—RTF supersedes local governance.

—Burden of litigation fees on plaintiff.

These existing statutory elements of RTF laws found in some states serve absentee business firms and CAFO interests the most, curtailing democracy in agriculture.

---

laws to processing in nearly half of all states demonstrates how RTF laws have veered far from their supposed purpose (for example, Michigan's Agricultural Processing Act or Utah's protection of industrial areas and mines alongside agriculture). Like court rulings in Alabama and Mississippi pertaining to timber, these statutory provisions and court interpretations make clear that their purpose is dispossessing the less powerful to enable the more powerful to accumulate further wealth and control by insulating them from nuisance lawsuits. In these situations, the agricultural orientation of the laws blurs substantially and supports the overall repeal of RTF laws. Perhaps most important of all, RTF laws protect agricultural operations generally but not specifically for the small and medium-size farms that are most beneficial for communities and sustainability. No RTF law in the nation, for example, tailors its protection to family farms. This disadvantages the types of farms most crucial for a democratic and distributed system of agriculture.

There are also, however, more targeted and statute-specific routes that may be more conducive to change-making, depending on the state. For example, states that do not allow RTF laws to supersede local governance have fewer CAFOs and business firms winning in court. In the Northeast, CAFO and business firm cases win proportionately fewer total RTF cases. This is also the region where, on the aggregate, states leave local governments, like townships, municipalities, villages, and towns, with the ability to determine land use decisions (see table 1.5). The transfer of wealth and power from local communities—for example, in the Lincoln Township case in Missouri—can even be a transfer of wealth and power abroad. Democracy on a fundamental level is about giving people who live in a place power over governing it. Reforming laws to return autonomy to communities is an important route to consider moving forward.

CAFOs and business firms win most RTF cases in court by drawing on the statutory provision that they are immune from lawsuits once they are up and running for a year. Similar to removing local governance at large, this provision discounts longevity, environment, and place—all crucial dimensions of home in agriculture. In contrast, some states instead have a "there first" provision, where the so-defined agricultural operation has to be in existence before those surrounding it to have immunity. However, the stated purpose in most RTF law preambles typically is that of expanding and preserving agriculture. The "there first" provision is dependent upon the way in which protected agricultural operations are defined and contextualized in preambles. For example, West Virginia treats all forms of agriculture as "there first," meaning that a pasture once used for free-range chickens is assumed to be the same as a 100,000-head broiler feeding operation. Likewise, the suite of accompanying provisions—immunity when there is a new technology, when the product changes, when operations stop or are interrupted, or when ownership changes—can be repealed or carefully reworded to empower the farms and people that were there first. Land reform efforts could also be incorporated into RTF laws, making explicit the protection of land from industrial and suburban sprawl or provisions to keep land rights and access proximate to those who live in a local community.

Like the definition of "agricultural operations," "agricultural practices" are unclearly defined across the nation and unattuned to specifics of place. Firms and CAFOs that utilize the RTF defense typically do so because their practices have a negative impact on the social ecology of those around them. For RTF laws to play an inspirational rather than a detrimental role in agriculture, protected practices can be rooted in the local social ecology. While a minority of states, like Missouri and Louisiana, defer to their flagship universities for some standards, even these aggregate understandings at a state level overlook much nuance. Statutes can be reformed to enable people embedded in communities to determine what (if any) is an acceptable agricultural practice that deserves immunity from nuisance, trespass, and negligence suits.

RTF AMENDMENTS CONDUCIVE TO AN AGRICULTURE OF HOME

—Operation must be "there first."

—There are no unique limits on compensatory or punitive damages.

—Local laws and ordinances supersede RTF laws.

—Operations are protected in accordance with longevity in place and living in proximity to farming operation.

—Public divulgence of ownership structure includes firm parentage, as applicable.

—Operations with unclear ultimate beneficiaries do not receive protection.

—CAFOs do not receive protection.

—Business firms do not receive protection.

—"Accepted" agricultural practices are defined as those determined by the local government.

Some RTF statutes have less of a detrimental impact on farmers, residents, and homeowners, like the "there first" provision. This list also includes new criteria not yet found in RTF laws that may help strengthen democracy by empowering communities and local farmers.

RTF laws also increasingly place litigation risks and burdens on plaintiffs, deterring them from filing nuisance suits against the largest of agricultural operations in the first place. Compensatory and punitive damage caps limit or eliminate types of monetary compensation that people can receive when operations cause staggering impacts to their well-being and their homes. With fewer financial repercussions for their actions, entities like Smithfield's Murphy-Brown LLC have less motive not to engage in the same behavior in another space at another time. The less the cost of a taking, the more insignificant it is for business firms' bottom line. Likewise, stipulating that only plaintiffs bear the burden of court and attorney fees when they lose benefits the largest of operators, which generally win as defendants but not as plaintiffs (see table 1.2). Repealing these statutes may help provide plaintiffs more equal opportunity to access and utilize the court.

The Constitution

At a basic level, state and federal constitutions seem an immediate and generative route for challenging RTF laws based on property rights. An originalist approach to the constitutional protection of property, however, has not stood up against RTF laws in court.[35] Of the thirty-eight RTF cases in our data set that made an explicit constitutional reference, Iowa was initially the only one with a successful state-level constitutional challenge to a RTF law.[36] That case was overturned by the Iowa Supreme Court in 2022, after membership in the court had changed.[37] To date, the U.S. Supreme Court has yet to review an RTF case. Taken together, this suggests two key points: that the constitutional protection of property as currently conceived does not equally protect all owners (but instead favors large ones), and that some constitutional amendments may help to give footing to dimensions of property less protected by courts, namely home and environment.

Constitutions offer the potential to counteract two dangerous situations for democracy: when the majority crushes the minority through legislation and when a despot rules the executive branch. Property, to the chagrin of some and the delight of others, receives constitutional protections, suggesting a level of untouchable reverence. The Fifth Amendment of the U.S. Constitution states that no person shall "be deprived of life, liberty, or property, without due process of law; nor shall private property be taken for public use, without just compensation." The Fourteenth Amendment further requires that property be afforded "due process of law" and "equal protection." Likewise, every state constitution includes some defense of property rights. Then, nuisance lawsuits grant individuals the right to defend their property from others, based on the idea that so long as one is not injuring or hampering another's use and enjoyment of their property, holders can utilize their property as they like.[38] In effect, such a framing put early limits on what extent profit-seeking forms of property ownership could hijack social goods like clean air, clean water, peace, and serenity.[39]

Yet constitutional challenges to RTF laws centered on property rights typically fail because courts now treat the economy as a public good, regardless of whether that economy produces a public benefit. Even though for centuries U.S. courts have provided a remedy for injuries concerning property, RTF laws legally remove those remedies from those who suffer at the hands of industrial agriculture. In Iowa, the issue of remedy was the very reason why the RTF law was initially deemed partially unconstitutional, as the Iowa Supreme Court ruled that property owners stripped of their rights were warranted compensation. That ruling was reversed in 2022 when the court concluded that the legislature could use RTF laws to remove remedies for property owners.[40] As in Iowa, courts nationally tend to affirm that the state legislatures can modify or amend common law as well as state statutes through legislation. Courts also have ruled that unless every facet

270 CULTIVATING DEMOCRACY IN AGRICULTURE

of a property right is taken—for example, not just enjoyment but also the capacity to make money—plaintiffs cannot establish that their property has actually been taken. As a result, legislatures and lobbying interests are free to pass legislation that strips individuals of their most democratic dimensions of property rights, where people have the freedom to health, safety, and community through residence or ownership. Dehumanized through the metrics of industrial production, communities cannot prosper on the scraps of their property rights left behind.

While RTF preambles often state that agriculture is in the public interest and agricultural operations receive generous public subsidies, these enterprises are still able to claim "private" status in court. For those trying to protect their homes by asserting their own property rights, they face a double-edged sword: agriculture is public because of its relationship to food but also retains private status through investors' profit. Operations protected by RTF laws then avoid the stipulation that just compensation be provided for "public use" takings. Even in the less likely cases that a CAFO or firm loses, states increasingly limit how much can be awarded. North Carolina, for example, limits compensation to the fair market value of the property for permanent nuisances and to the rental value for temporary nuisances.[41] No punitive damages are allowed at all, unless the operation has "been subject to a criminal conviction or a civil enforcement action taken."[42] Unlike most other industries—which can be punished for egregious conduct through punitive damages—the law prevents courts from punishing agricultural operations for engaging in grossly negligent practices or deterring them from doing so because courts are already prohibited from imposing a fine that recognizes the reality of their destructive conduct.

Plaintiffs also have tried to make the constitutional argument that RTF laws violate the Equal Protection Clause of the Fourteenth Amendment. Plaintiffs assert that RTF laws exemplify crony capitalism by discriminating against residential landowners in favor of politically powerful industries. These arguments have not gained traction either. Courts tend to respond that RTF laws purport to apply generally to agriculture, not to a specific industry, like swine. Our findings, however, identify specific industries benefiting more from RTF laws: CAFOs win the most in hog- and poultry-dominated states, while sole proprietor farmers are the least likely to win in court (see table 1.7). The reality is that the largest of operators and owners, on the aggregate, receive favorable treatment. The defense of property, unless closely tied to a distributive ideal good for the many, ceases to serve democracy of the people. RTF laws have weaponized the most dangerous

CULTIVATING DEMOCRACY IN AGRICULTURE 271

facets of property born in colonialism, codified in enslavement, disallowed by gender, and differentiated according to rural space.[43] Notions that industrial production and extraction must overshadow people's and communities' autonomy now reigns.

Unlike RTF laws, anti-corporate farming laws routinely have been held to be unconstitutional based upon their disparate treatment of large corporate entities. Courts in four midwestern states—South Dakota, North Dakota, Iowa, and Nebraska—have found anti-corporate farming laws unconstitutional, in whole or in part, since the start of the twenty-first century. Anti-corporate farming laws generally attempt to limit business entities' ownership in land by limiting nonfamily corporate or other entity investment.[44] Ten states have anti-corporate farming laws, and nine of them are in the Midwest, the same region where firms are winning the most using RTF laws. Indiana—the state where firms and CAFOs win the most with RTF laws—has an anti-corporate farming law, but it affords its protections only to land. Market power stipulates land's power, and if transnational corporations dominate markets, they also exert disproportionate power over land use. Further, Indiana provides exceptions to its anti-corporate farming law for confined feeding operations and the raising or producing of eggs or poultry.[45] The law also allows foreign business entities to own up to 320 acres used for crop farming and up to 10 acres for timber production. It is not clear if Indiana's statute limits acreage ownership to independent LLCs or traces them back to shared financial holding companies. In our data set, anti-corporate statutory or constitutional provision references in RTF statutes or case law are not drawn on to constrain corporate power. Rather, anti-corporate statutes are used to extend protections to specific business firms by citing exceptions and definitions.

For the decisions of the courts to match the rights and needs of the governed, constitutional amendments may provide another, more effective legal means to counter RTF legislation. Cementing the power of local government statutorily and constitutionally can create a rights-based framework that has proved generative for returning wealth to communities with a long history of extraction and expropriation.[46] One set of rights, like property, cannot be expected to achieve every moral good or, in contrast, responsibility for every moral harm. Likewise, environmental rights may not always provide for the right to home. However, considered as a suite of rights, constitutional amendments may offer a tool for people to gain standing to achieve the democratic outcomes necessary for the preservation of life, the equal protection of laws, and the people's pursuit of happiness.

Two constitutional amendments—one about food and the other the environment—offer insights into the possibilities, but also potentially adverse outcomes, of constitutional amendments. In 1971, for example, Pennsylvania citizens adopted an environmental rights amendment, Article I, Section 27, which states, "The people have a right to clean air, [to] pure water, and to the preservation of the natural, scenic, historic and esthetic values of the environment. Pennsylvania's public natural resources are the common property of all the people, including generations yet to come. As trustee of these resources, the Commonwealth shall conserve and maintain them for the benefit of all the people." This amendment later came to bear on a 2012 Pennsylvania Supreme Court case pertaining to Act 12, a bill passed by the legislature with the oil and gas industry's support. Like laws governing industrial agricultural operations, the bill sought to cement the hydraulic fracturing industry's ability to site at will, without local consent. If it had been enforced, Act 12—like RTF laws—would have preempted local government from barring fracking and imposed a gag order on physicians who connected local exposure and pollution to health issues.[47] The Pennsylvania Supreme Court, however, used the environmental rights amendment as the basis of its ruling that Act 12 violated the constitution, as it stipulated that water and air belonged to the public trust and the people of Pennsylvania.

Without an explicit distributive orientation through words like "collective," "the people," and "access," amendments can become vulnerable to co-optation. Maine's 2021 right-to-food constitutional amendment uses language similar to that found in RTF laws. Advocated by the Food and Agriculture Organization of the United Nations since 2011, such amendments seek to treat access to food as a human right.[48] However, the language used to encode such a right can be problematic. The words "acquisition," "production," and "harvesting" confuse the importance of social ecology. Unlike Pennsylvania's, Maine's amendment lacks community embeddedness by not using "common," as in "public good," but instead "individuals," which can in practice include corporations: "All individuals have a natural, inherent and unalienable right to food, including the right to save and exchange seeds and the right to grow, raise, harvest, produce and consume the food of their own choosing for their own nourishment, sustenance, bodily health and well-being, as long as an individual does not commit trespassing, theft, poaching or other abuses of private property rights, public lands or natural resources in the harvesting, production or acquisition of food."[49] Maine's amendment potentially allows for industrial interests to acquire the goods and means of production, without attention to how the food is grown, local

Table 3.1 Existing and Potential Rights-Based Constitutional Amendments

	Right-to-farm	Right-to-home	Right-to-food	Right-to-health	Right-to-environment
Safeguard from speculative investment		•		•	
Reduce unsustainable debt		•		•	
Promote highest attainable standard of physical and mental health		•		•	•
Promote people's rights to clean air, clean water, and preservation of environment (Pennsylvania)		•			•
Promote rights of farmers and ranchers to engage in farming and ranching practices (Missouri)	•		•		
Promote individuals' right to consume, grow, harvest, produce, and save seeds (Maine)			•		

Note: Different rights-based amendments have the potential to help support an agriculture of home and offset the most deleterious impacts of RTF laws.

governance, home, environment, or health. The right-to-food framework can then potentially reify the problematic orientation of the right to farm. Some other alternative rights-based amendments for consideration include home and health (see table 3.1).

Agricultural, Rural, and Environmental Justice

Alexis de Tocqueville wrote in his 1835 account of American democracy, "Governments in general have only two methods of overcoming the resistance of the governed: their own physical force and the moral force supplied to them by the decisions of the courts."[50] A gulf is open and widening between the outcomes of the court, the devastating loss of farmers in the United States, and the democratic impulse that remains for those determined to protect their homes.[51]

Access to a clean environment, food, farming, a peaceful home, and the means for good health are matters at the center of democracy. RTF laws at face value seem to support such ends but in practice have constrained access to them by hastening the exit of local farmers and increasing the power of the largest operators. Overall repeal of RTF laws or specific statutory amendments may help reform these laws to better serve rural communities by centering agriculture on home. Protecting the basis of all life through codifying in the constitution the right to a beautiful, safe, and clean environment may temper the most egregious outcomes of RTF laws, where communities and those living in the countryside have few tools left to protect the places they call home.

The ease with which such legislative-minded reforms can proceed depends on the money and resources available to transnational corporate actors in agriculture that are positioned to benefit the least from such changes. Federal subsidization of the largest corporate actors has materialized in a Farm Bureau motivated mainly by insurance concerns and major shareholders; a government subsidy system most easily accessed by corporate powerholders; secured investors making money from agricultural derivatives least accessible to the public; and monopolies and oligopolies largely unchallenged by laws that have not entirely caught up with just how concentrated market power in agriculture is. Taking on concentrated power gives a chance to people who seek to provide and access food locally, with pride, longevity, and purpose rooted in place.

Markets, laws, and rights become what their government makes them: a more direct and accessible democratic trifecta, or an exclusive and highly consolidated authoritarian trifecta. Locally led and community-based efforts show that direct democratization of agriculture in the face of great, but unjust, power is possible.[52] The task now at hand is building a democratic tapestry for agriculture, where people no longer fear for their future but look forward to the abundance of tomorrow built upon the access of today.

NOTES

1. Alexis de Tocqueville, *Democracy in America* (New York: Anchor Books, 1969). Tocqueville saw the courts as an important check on the legislative and executive branches: "The great object of justice is to substitute the idea of right for that of violence, to put intermediaries between the government and the use of its physical force" (139).
2. Bill Winders and Elizabeth Ransom, "Expanding Production, Consumption, and Trade," in *Global Meat: Social and Environmental Consequences of the Expanding Meat Industry*, ed. Bill Winders and Elizabeth Ransom (Cambridge, Mass.: MIT Press, 2019), 1–24.
3. Predatory practices are enabled by the very limited market space that farmers operate in. Predatory contracts often require that farmers use only those inputs supplied by the contractor, with a specified quality and quantity. Often the contractor controls the production practices and also the type of consumption. For more, see Mary K. Hendrickson, Philip H. Howard, and Douglas H. Constance, "Power, Food and Agriculture: Implications for Farmers, Consumers and Communities," Division of Applied Social Sciences Working Paper,

University of Missouri College of Agriculture, Food and Natural Resources, The Bichler and Nitzan Archives, Toronto, 2017, https://philhowardnet.files.wordpress.com/2017/11/hendrickson-howard-constance-2017-final-working-paper-nov-1.pdf.

4. Hendrickson, Howard, and Constance, "Power, Food and Agriculture."

5. For more on the importance of local banks, see F. Carson Mencken and Charles M. Tolbert, "Community Banks and Loans for Nonmetropolitan Businesses: A Multilevel Analysis from the 2007 Survey of Business Owners," *Rural Sociology* 83, no. 2 (2018): 376–401. For more on community farms, see Monica M. White, "'A Pig and a Garden': Fannie Lou Hamer and the Freedom Farms Cooperative," *Food and Foodways* 25, no. 1 (2017): 20–39. For more on farmers' markets and CSA, see Michael Carolan, "More-Than-Active Food Citizens: A Longitudinal and Comparative Study of Alternative and Conventional Eaters," *Rural Sociology* 82, no. 2 (2017): 197–225. For more on the financialization and corporatization of the food system at large, and retail specifically, see Jennifer Clapp, *Food*, 3rd ed. (Cambridge, Mass.: Polity Press, 2020). For more on agriculture of the middle, see Thomas A. Lyson et al., eds., *Food and the Mid-level Farm: Renewing an Agriculture of the Middle* (Cambridge, Mass.: MIT Press, 2008).

6. Food and Agribusiness Merger Moratorium and Antitrust Review Act of 2022, S. 4245, 117th Cong. (2022), https://www.congress.gov/bill/117th-congress/senate-bill/4245.

7. Michael Bell, Loka Ashwood, Isaac Leslie, and Laura Schlachter, *An Invitation to Environmental Sociology*, 6th ed. (Thousand Oaks, Calif.: Sage Publications, 2021), 151.

8. David Wahlberg, "As Wisconsin Dairy Farmers Struggle, New Effort Aims to Prevent Suicide," *Wisconsin State Journal* (Madison), January 27, 2019, https://madison.com/news/local/health-med-fit/as-wisconsin-farmers-struggle-new-effort-aims-to-prevent-suicide/article_db83a562-0652-5e57-a664-c9fee368fffe.html.

9. U.S. Department of Agriculture, Farm Service Agency, "Spot Market Hog Pandemic Program," Farmers.gov, accessed July 29, 2022, https://www.farmers.gov/archived/smhpp?utm_medium=email&utm_source=govdelivery.

10. Government Accountability Office, "Coronavirus Food Assistance Program: USDA Should Conduct More Rigorous Reviews of Payments to Producers," GAO-22-104397 (September 2022).

11. See Amy Mayer, "For Dairy Farmers, This Technology Turns Methane from Cow Manure into Cash," *Marketplace*, accessed October 28, 2022, https://www.marketplace.org/2021/07/21/for-dairy-farmers-this-technology-turns-methane-from-cow-manure-into-cash/; Mark A. Moser, Richard P. Mattocks, Stacy Gettier, and Kurt Roos, "Benefits, Costs and Operating Experience at Seven New Agricultural Anaerobic Digesters," US Environmental Protection Agency, accessed February 8, 2023, https://19january2017snapshot.epa.gov/sites/production/files/2014-12/documents/lib-ben.pdf; Erin McDuff, "USDA Seeks Applications for Renewable Energy, Energy Efficiency Loan Guarantees and Grants," USDA Rural Development, accessed October 28, 2022, https://www.rd.usda.gov/newsroom/news-release/usda-seeks-applications-renewable-energy-energy-efficiency-loan-guarantees.

12. Phil Howard, "Corporate Concentration in Global Meat Processing: The Role of Feed and Finance Subsidies," in *Global Meat: Social and Environmental Consequences of the Expanding Meat Industry*, ed. Bill Winders and Elizabeth Ransom (Cambridge, Mass.: MIT Press, 2019), 31–54.

13. The government-sponsored Farm Credit System provides the most loans of any entity to the top ten pork powerhouses, according to Uniform Commercial Code filings. For more, see Loka Ashwood, Andy Pilny, John Canfield, Mariyam Jamila, and Ryan Thompson, "From Big Ag to Big Finance: A Market Network Approach to Power in Agriculture," *Agriculture and Human Values* 39, no. 4 (2022): 1421–34.

14. Jacqui Fatka, "Legislators Make Noise on Foreign-Owned Farmland," *Farm Progress*, September 28, 2022, https://www.farmprogress.com/farm-policy/legislators-make-noise-foreign-owned-farmland.

15. "Small Business Lending Data Collection Rulemaking," Consumer Financial Protection Bureau, accessed April 28, 2023, https://www.consumerfinance.gov/1071-rule/.

16. Alma Adams, Sanford Bishop, Rosa DeLaura, and Shontel M. Brown, letter to Gene L. Dorado, comptroller general of the United States, July 20, 2022, in author's possession; Virginia State University–Small Farm Outreach Program, "Challenges and Issues in Accessing and Utilization of Capital by Socially Disadvantaged Farmers and Ranchers," December 30, 2019, https://www.self-help.org/docs/default-source/PDFs/alcorn-final-report-(revised)-(1).pdf?sfvrsn=2. Also see David Beck, "Creating a Farm Credit System Equitable and Sustainable Ag Grant Program," Self-Help Credit Union (website), February 24, 2022, https://www.self-help.org/docs/default-source/PDFs/expanding-farm-credit-39-s-impactv2.pdf.

17. Ashwood et al., "From Big Ag to Big Finance."

18. House Select Subcommittee on the Coronavirus, *"Now to Get Rid of Those Pesky Health Departments!": How the Trump Administration Helped the Meatpacking Industry Block Pandemic Worker Protections*, staff report, May 2022, 10, https://coronavirus.house.gov/sites/democrats.coronavirus.house.gov/files/2022.5.12%20-%20SSCC%20report%20Meatpacking%20FINAL.pdf.

19. Tina L. Saitone, K. Aleks Schaefer, and Daniel P. Scheitrum, "COVID-19 Morbidity and Mortality in US Meatpacking Counties," *Food Policy* 101 (2021): 1–18.

20. Jeremy N. Marchant-Forde and Laura A. Boyle, "COVID-19 Effects on Livestock Production: A One Welfare Issue," *Frontiers in Veterinary Science* 7 (2020), article 585787, https://doi.org/10.3389/fvets.2020.585787.

21. Ashwood et al., "From Big Finance."

22. See "Farm Bureau: The Unified National Voice of Agriculture," Farm Bureau, accessed July 28, 2022, https://www.fb.org/.

23. Garrett Graddy-Lovelace, "U.S. Farm Policy as Fraught Populism: Tracing the Scalar Tensions of Nationalist Agricultural Governance," *Annals of the American Association of Geographers* 109, no. 2 (2019): 395–411. The article summarizes the history of the organization, identifying its birth in the 1914 Smith-Lever Act and the 1917 Farm Bureau Organization Plan issued by the Federal Office of Extension, which cemented the American Farm Bureau Federation.

24. Austin Frerick, "From Friend to Foe: Mission Drift of Farm Bureaus and Commodity Checkoff Programs" (unpublished paper from conference proceedings, Big Ag and Antitrust Conference, Yale Law School, January 21, 2021), 7.

25. Graddy-Lovelace, "U.S. Farm Policy," 398.

26. This includes submitting amicus curie briefs, serving as supporting appellants, and being actual defendants themselves, with courts referencing support cases where the Farm Bureau was party or making simple references to them as supporting parties.

27. *Cumberland Farms of Conn., Inc. v. Zoning Bd. of Appeal*, 359 Mass. 68, 73–74, 267 N.E.2d 906, 910 (1971). This case is the oldest one in our data set, and even though it predates the named enactment of RTF laws, we included it because it is about agricultural nuisance.

28. There were twenty-one cases in total that included the Farm Bureau.

29. *Briggs v. Hughes*, 316 So. 3d 193 (Miss. 2021). The Delta Council, the Mississippi Cattlemen's Association, the Mississippi Poultry Association, the Mississippi Loggers Association, and the Mississippi Forestry Association also served as amici curiae in support of the appellees.

30. *Barden v. Murphy-Brown, LLC*, No. 7:20-CV-85-BR, 2021 WL 965915, at *14–15 (E.D.N.C. Mar. 15, 2021).

31. *Rural Empowerment Ass'n for Cmty. Help v. State*, 868 S.E.2d 645 (N.C. App. 2021).

32. Loka Ashwood, "'No Matter If You're a Democrat or a Republican or Neither': Pragmatic Politics in Opposition to Industrial Animal Production," *Journal of Rural Studies* 82 (2021): 586.

33. Robin Wall Kimmerer, *Braiding Sweetgrass: Indigenous Wisdom, Scientific Knowledge and the Teaching of Plants* (Minneapolis: Milkweed Editions, 2013).

34. For a critique and history of agrarian populism, see Maywa Montenegro de Wit, Antonio Roman-Alcalá, Alex Liebman, and Siena Chrisman, "Agrarian Origins of Authoritarian Populism in the United States: What Can We Learn from 20th-Century Struggles in California and the Midwest?," *Journal of Rural Studies* 82 (2021): 518–30.

35. Christine Meisner Rosen, "'Knowing' Industrial Pollution: Nuisance Law and the Power of Tradition in a Time of Rapid Economic Change, 1840–1864," *Environmental History* 8, no. 4 (2003): 565–97.

36. *Gacke v. Pork Xtra, L.L.C.*, 684 N.W.2d 168 (Iowa 2004).

37. *Garrison v. New Fashion Pork LLP*, 977 N.W.2d 67, 72 (Iowa 2022) (overruling the test relied upon in *Gacke*, 684 N.W.2d at 172, which was used to adjudicate constitutional challenges to Iowa's RTF law).

38. Serena M. Williams, "CAFOs as Neighbors: An Analysis of Kentucky Nuisance Law and Agricultural Operations," *Sustain* 5 (2001): 14–20.

39. Rosen, "'Knowing' Industrial Pollution."

40. The 2021 case *Rural Empowerment Ass'n for Cmty. Help*, 868 S.E.2d 645, provides a particularly telling example of how constitutional challenges have failed in North Carolina and dovetail into federal law. Also see *Garrison v. New Fashion Pork, LLP*, 977 N.W.2d 67 (Iowa 2022).

41. N.C. Gen. Stat. § 106-702(a) (2021).

42. N.C. Gen. Stat. § 106-702(a1) (2021). The North Carolina RTF law does not apply to negligence claims. Section 106-702(d) of the statute states, "This Article does not apply to any cause of action brought against an agricultural or forestry operation for negligence, trespass, personal injury, strict liability, or other cause of action for tort liability other than nuisance, nor does this Article prohibit or limit any request for injunctive relief that is otherwise available." N.C. Gen. Stat. § 106-702(d) (2021).

43. Brenna Bhandar, *Colonial Lives of Property: Law, Land, and Racial Regimes of Ownership* (Durham: Duke University Press, 2018).

44. Rick Welsh, Chantal Line Carpentier, and Bryan Hubbell, "On the Effectiveness of State Anti-corporate Farming Laws in the United States," *Food Policy* 26 (2001): 543–48.

45. Ind. Code § 32-22-3-0.5(a)(4) (2022).

46. Adam Calo, Kirsteen Shields, and Alastair Iles, "Using Property Law to Expand Agroecology: Scotland's Land Reforms Based on Human Rights," *Journal of Peasant Studies*, forthcoming.

47. Eliza Griswold, *Amity and Prosperity: One Family and the Fracturing of America* (New York: Farrar, Straus and Giroux, 2018).

48. Lidija Knuth and Margret Vidar, *Right to Food Studies: Constitutional and Legal Protection of the Right to Food around the World* (Rome: Food and Agriculture Organization of the United Nations, 2011).

49. Me. Const. art. I, § 25.

50. Tocqueville, *Democracy in America*, 139.

51. Government and corporate takings of land violate the landownership ethic, increasing animosity toward and distrust of the state. See Loka Ashwood, *For-Profit Democracy: Why the Government Is Losing the Trust of Rural America* (New Haven: Yale University Press, 2018).

52. For inspiration, see Saru Jayaraman and Kathryn De Master, eds., *Bite Back: People Taking on Corporate Food and Winning* (Oakland: University of California Press, 2020); Loka Ashwood, "'No Matter If You're a Democrat or a Republican or Neither': Pragmatic Politics in Opposition to Industrial Animal Production," *Journal of Rural Studies* 82 (2021): 586–94; and Annette Aurélie Desmarais, *La Vía Campesina: Globalization and the Power of Peasants* (Ann Arbor: Pluto Press, 2007).

ACKNOWLEDGMENTS

This project has been an intellectual journey supported by many scholars and lawyers, including Conner Bailey, Scott Edwards, Lisa Pruitt, Kim Richman, Anthony Schutz, Jessica Shoemaker, and Susan Schneider. Crystal Boutwell provided integral research support that set a high bar for the rest of us to stay organized, motivated, and on task. The North Carolina Environmental Justice Network, the Missouri Rural Crisis Center, and communities we interacted with helped us recognize the significance of right-to-farm legislation. We benefited from early presentations of this research at the Alabama Farm Expo and the annual meetings of the Rural Sociological Society and the American Association of Geographers. Later we benefited from feedback we received when we spoke at the Yale Big Ag and Antitrust Conference and as part of the Rural Reconciliation Project speakers' series at the University of Nebraska–Lincoln.

This research project received support from the U.S. Department of Agriculture, National Institute of Food and Agriculture, Award No. 2018-68006-36699. Farm Aid and the University of Kentucky's Center for Health Equity Transformation Just-in-Time Award provided funds to make the electronic version of our book open access. We thank them for helping us reach a wider audience.

The support staff at UNC and our copy editor did fantastic, and crucial, work. Thank you, Julie Bush, Erin Granville, Elizabeth Orange, and Thomas Bedenbaugh. Our editor, Lucas Church, led the editorial process with unflinching support and dexterity. Without his creativity and generosity, we would not have been able to deliver this book in its form, aimed at integrating direct aid, academic scholarship, and public accessibility. We thank him for it.

APPENDIX

The findings presented in this book utilized a mixed-methods approach spanning five years of interdisciplinary research. The research team included legal experts and social scientists. We used both quantitative and qualitative approaches at the national and state level to study the course of right-to-farm inception to present day. Details on the specific data and methodology are provided below.

Statutes and Case Law

For this project, original and current right-to-farm statutes for all fifty states were gathered using both Westlaw and LexisNexis. In some states where RTF provisions are found in related statutes, these statutes were also gathered from Westlaw and LexisNexis. For our quantitative work, we analyzed all publicly available cases from judicial courts that we could acquire through Westlaw and LexisNexis until the end of 2021. We found these cases through keyword searches pertaining to agricultural nuisance and right to farm. Settlements out of court are not publicly available and thus were not part of our analysis. We analyzed the highest-level court cases, meaning we did not analyze lower-level court outcomes. We made this decision to identify, to the best of our ability, ultimate wins. However, this did leave out lower court rulings, specifically the burden of litigation on certain parties due to appeal.

We excluded cases from administrative courts unless they were appealed to a judicial court. We also included two cases in Illinois that appeared before the Illinois Pollution Control Board, because the state or any person can bring a nuisance case either to court or to the board (in other words, these cases were not simply agency ones). The oldest case in our data set is from 1971 and the most recent 2021—a total of fifty years. Within this initial set of 297 cases, we identified 197 that made dispositive use of RTF laws, meaning cases where the RTF law was used to determine the merits and outcomes of the case, not those that simply referenced RTF law in passing. This book presents findings from those 197 cases.

NVivo utilizes two key methods for analysis: codes and attributes. We utilized NVivo to code, apply attributes to, and run queries on our data set. Our team consisted of five coders: three coders trained in sociology and two practicing lawyers. We continued to refine our codebook until our kappa score, which measures continuity between coders, was above .9. We ended up with codes we utilized to identify trends in the statutes and the case law. All statutes were coded for immunity provisions, definitions, commodities, limitations on damages and relief, legal mechanisms, power of local governance, responsible stewardship, timing of operation, and protection of related hazardous industries. Statutory attributes were used to analyze historical trends in RTF laws. Cross-coding matrices identified the number of states with similar RTF provisions, as displayed in the individual state and national tables.

Case-law codes identified the outcome of the case, the use of specific statutory provisions, the interests at stake, the commodities at hand, and the key statutes utilized. Case law was assigned attributes corresponding to region, party types, court level, hearing type, whether the case was dispositive, and whether the case was a class action suit. Cross-coding matrices using both attributes and codes tracked national and regional trends in court outcomes, as discussed throughout this book.

The state tables draw on the same case-law and statutory data set developed in NVivo, which is current up until 2021. While a few descriptions include crucial 2022 court outcomes, these are not reflected in the quantitative analysis.

Agricultural and Forestry Data

Each state was a "case," in NVivo's terms, which enabled us to do more complicated queries based on attributes and codes. We also created static sets of different outcomes and descriptors—for example, static sets of dispositive cases based on winning party types. We then identified a series of attributes for case law and states.

Our state attributes were drawn from a variety of resources. Data for states ranking in the top five for animal inventory by sector (table 1.5) were collected at the state level for hogs, milk cows, beef cattle, broilers, and layers, utilizing raw inventory numbers. Our animal inventory numbers were derived from the U.S. Department of Agriculture's *2017 Census of Agriculture* (*COA*), which draws animal inventory from numbers reported for specific farms on the National Agricultural Statistics Service (NASS) crop or livestock survey.[1] We used 2017 timber inventory numbers drawn from *Forest Resources of the United States*.[2]

The agricultural data presented in the individual state summaries in part 2 describing the change in operations and land in acres utilized for agriculture were collected from the USDA's NASS. For each state, the total land in acres as well as the number of agricultural operations were collected at two points, corresponding to the year that each state enacted its RTF law and 2021. For state data collected during 2021, USDA survey data from 2021 was used. For earlier years, if a state enacted its RTF law during a USDA *COA* year (i.e., 1978, 1982, 1987, etc.), *COA* data were used. For all other years, we used annual survey data corresponding to the year of RTF statutory enactment for each state.

Farm Operations Data

In table 1.4, we present data drawn from each *COA* between 1978 and 2017 to demonstrate the change in the number of operations over time by sector. *COA* data prior to 1997 are not available through the USDA's NASS, so for the data that were unavailable through the Quick Stats Query Tool, we retrieved the information from various *COA* tables made available through Cornell University's USDA *COA* Historical Archive. For ease in reporting where the data were retrieved, a detailed list by sector is provided below.

For wheat, we retrieved the 1978 data from table 28 in the *1978 COA*, the 1982 data from table 41 in the *1982 COA*, the 1987 data from table 42 in the *1987 COA*, and the 1992 data from table 42 in the *1992 COA*. For the census years 1997 to 2017, we retrieved the data from the Quick Stats tool, reporting the number of operations with area harvested for wheat production. For the years 1978 to 1992, we utilized the number of operations producing wheat for all purposes.

For corn, we retrieved the 1978 data from table 28 in the *1978 COA*, the 1982 data from table 41 in the *1982 COA*, the 1987 data from table 42 in the *1987 COA*, the 1992 data from table 42 in the *1992 COA*, the 1997 data from table 42 in the *1997 COA*, and the 2002 data from table 34 of the *2002 COA*. For the census years 2007 to 2017, we retrieved the data from the Quick Stats tool and reported the number of operations with area harvested for corn production. For the years 1978 to 2002, we utilized the number of operations producing corn for all purposes.

For soy, we retrieved the 1978 data from table 28 in the *1978 COA*, the 1982 data from table 41 in the *1982 COA*, the 1987 data from table 42 in the *1987*

APPENDIX 283

COA, and the 1992 data from table 42 in the *1992 COA*. For the census years 1997 to 2017, we retrieved the data from the Quick Stats tool and reported the number of operations with area harvested for soy production. For the years 1978 to 1992, we utilized the number of operations producing soybeans for all purposes.

For hay, we retrieved the 1978 data from table 28 in the *1978 COA*, the 1982 data from table 41 in the *1982 COA*, the 1987 data from table 42 in the *1987 COA*, the 1992 data from table 42 in the *1992 COA*, and the 1997 data from table 42 in the *1997 COA*. For the census years 2002 to 2017, we retrieved the data from the Quick Stats tool and reported the number of operations with area harvested for hay production. For the years 1978 to 1997, we utilized the number of operations with acres harvested for hay production.

For beef, we retrieved the 1978 data from table 18 in the *1978 COA*, the 1982 data from table 17 in the *1982 COA*, the 1987 data from table 20 in the *1987 COA*, and the 1992 data from table 28 in the *1992 COA*. For the census years 1997 to 2017, we retrieved the data from the Quick Stats tool and reported the number of operations with beef cattle and/or cow inventory. For the years 1978 to 1992, we utilized the number of operations with beef cow inventory.

For hogs and pigs, we retrieved the 1978 data from table 18 in the *1978 COA*, the 1982 data from table 17 in the *1982 COA*, the 1987 data from table 20 in the *1987 COA*, and the 1992 data from table 31 in the *1992 COA*. For the census years 1997 to 2017, we retrieved the data from the Quick Stats tool and reported the number of operations with hogs and pig inventory. For the years 1978 to 1992, we utilized the number of operations with hogs and pig inventory.

For dairy, we retrieved the number of farms reporting dairy product sales for all years, 1978 to 2017. The 1978 data were retrieved from table 10 in the *1978 COA*, the 1982 data from table 11 in the *1982 COA*, the 1987 data from table 47 in the *1987 COA*, the 1992 data from table 2 in the *1992 COA*, the 1997 data from table 2 in the *1997 COA*, the 2002 data from table 2 in the *2002 COA*, the 2007 data from table 2 in the *2007 COA*, the 2012 data from table 2 in the *2012 COA*, and the 2017 data from table 2 in the *2017 COA*.

For poultry, we retrieved the 1978 data from table 18 in the *1978 COA*, the 1982 data from table 17 in the *1982 COA*, the 1987 data from table 20 in the *1987 COA*, and the 1992 data from table 20 in the *1992 COA*. For the census years 1997 to 2017, we retrieved the data from the Quick Stats tool and reported the number of operations with poultry inventory. For the years 1978 to 1992, we utilized the number of operations with poultry inventory.

For fruits, nuts, and berries, we retrieved the number of farms reporting sales of fruits, nuts, and/or berries for all years, 1978 to 2017. The data for 1978 and 1982 were collected from table 11 in the *1982 COA*, the 1987 and 1992 data from table 2 in the *1992 COA*, the 1997 data from table 2 in the *1997 COA*, the 2002 and 2007 data from table 2 in the *2007 COA*, and the 2012 and 2017 data from table 2 in the *2017 COA*. After 2002, this sector includes tree nuts.

For vegetables, sweet corn, and melons, we retrieved the number of farms reporting sales of vegetables, sweet corn, and/or melons for all years, 1978–2017. The data for 1978 and 1982 were collected from table 11 in the *1982 COA*, the 1987 and 1992 data from table 2 in the *1992 COA*, the 1997 data from table 2 in the *1997 COA*, the 2002 and 2007 data from table 2 in the *2007 COA*, and the 2012 and 2017 data from table 2 in the *2017 COA*. After 2002, this sector includes potatoes and sweet potatoes.

Finally, for nursery and greenhouse products (which include mushrooms), we retrieved the number of farms reporting sales of nursery and greenhouse products for all years, 1978 to 2017. The data for 1978 and 1982 were collected from table 11 in the *1982 COA*, the 1987 and 1992 data from table 2 in the *1992 COA*, the 1997 data from table 2 in the *1997 COA*, the 2002 and 2007 data from table 2 in the *2007 COA*, and the 2012 and 2017 data from table 2 in the *2017 COA*. After 2002, this sector includes floriculture and sod.

Race and Poverty Data

Data describing the percentage of racial minorities at the state level were collected from the U.S. Census Bureau's American Community Survey (ACS) 2020 five-year estimates. For all states except Delaware, New Jersey, and Rhode Island, "rural" is defined as individuals and families residing outside of metropolitan areas. For Delaware, New Jersey, and Rhode Island, "rural" is defined using the U.S. Census Bureau definition, where rural encompasses individuals/families residing outside of urban areas.[3] Rural racial minority thresholds in figure 1.4 are drawn from the percentage of a state's rural population by race, where "racial minority" was defined as race or ethnicity other than white alone.

State-level rural poverty data were collected from the U.S. Census Bureau's 2021 ACS one-year estimates. As with the rural racial minority data, for all states except Delaware, Massachusetts, New Jersey, and Rhode Island, "rural" is defined as individuals and families residing outside of metropolitan areas. For Delaware, Massachusetts, New Jersey, and Rhode Island, "rural" is defined using the U.S. Census Bureau definition, where rural en-

APPENDIX 285

compasses individuals/families residing outside of urban areas.[4] The data presented in figure 1.3 is drawn from 2021, where rural poverty is defined as the percentage of people living below the poverty line. We collected county-level poverty data used to describe trends in rural counties in the Midwest presented in part 1 of the book from the 1980 and 2020 Decennial Censuses available from the U.S. Census Bureau.

We created thresholds for the data featured in figures 1.3 and 1.4: low, medium, and high for rural poverty levels; and low (0 to 5 percent), moderately low (5 to 14.99 percent), moderately high (15 to 24.99 percent), and high (above 25 percent) rural racial minority levels. We identified levels of racial minorities in line with established thresholds for environmental injustice. However, all rural racial minority levels are above the low level, so we did not report according to this criterion.[5] For rural poverty levels, we treated the high level in line with the 20 percent used to identify persistent poverty counties and identified medium and low levels in dialogue with this. We identified medium rural poverty as 10 to 19 percent and low as less than 10 percent. We rounded down poverty numbers. Unlike studies that document the locations of CAFOs, we relied on state-level data to analyze trends in court outcomes relative to race and poverty for two reasons. First, most of the publicly available cases did not include locational details about the operation sued. Second, our analysis centers on state-level variation in statutes, making state-level demographic data (like state-level agricultural data) most appropriate to analyze trends.

Regions

We utilized five regions in our analysis: Southeast, West, Southwest, Northeast, and Midwest. The Southeast includes twelve states: Alabama, Arkansas, Florida, Georgia, Kentucky, Louisiana, Mississippi, North Carolina, South Carolina, Tennessee, Virginia, and West Virginia. The West encompasses eleven states: Alaska, California, Colorado, Hawaii, Idaho, Montana, Nevada, Oregon, Utah, Washington, and Wyoming. The Southwest spans four states: Arizona, New Mexico, Oklahoma, and Texas. The Northeast comprises eleven states: Connecticut, Delaware, Maine, Maryland, Massachusetts, New Hampshire, New Jersey, New York, Pennsylvania, Rhode Island, and Vermont. Finally, the Midwest includes twelve states: Illinois, Indiana, Iowa, Kansas, Michigan, Minnesota, Missouri, Nebraska, North Dakota, Ohio, South Dakota, and Wisconsin.

News Articles

We drew on news articles to contextualize the interests at work during the initial adoption of RTF laws and subsequent amendments. We did keyword searches in the Access World News database for "right-to-farm" and "agricultural nuisance." We narrowed these searches to newspapers on a per-state level, which allowed us to access more local news coverage. Articles derived from these searches appear throughout the book.

NOTES

1. U.S. Department of Agriculture, National Agricultural Statistics Service, *2017 Census of Agriculture, Volume 1, Chapter 2, State Data* (Washington, D.C.: U.S. Department of Agriculture, 2019).
2. Sonja N. Oswalt, W. Brad Smith, Patrick D. Miles, and Scott A. Pugh, *Forest Resources of the United States, 2017: A Technical Document Supporting the Forest Service 2020 RPA Assessment* (Washington, D.C.: U.S. Department of Agriculture, Forest Service, 2019). Thank you to Dr. Conner Bailey for directing us to this data.
3. Michael Ratcliffe, Charlynn Burd, Kelly Holder, and Allison Fields, "Defining Rural at the U.S. Census Bureau," *American Community Survey Brief,* December 2016, https://www .census.gov/content/dam/Census/library/publications/2016/acs/acsgeo-1.pdf.
4. Ratcliffe et al., "Defining Rural at the U.S. Census Bureau."
5. See Daniel R. Faber and Eric J. Krieg, "Unequal Exposure to Ecological Hazards: Environmental Injustices in the Commonwealth of Massachusetts," *Environmental Health Perspectives* 110, no. 2 (April 2002): 277–88.